SUNSET OF AMERICA

How The Golden Dream Can Be Saved

Alfred J. Lindsey
Michael A. Deblois

Copyright © 2000 Alfred J. Lindsey/Michael A. Deblois
Library of Congress Catalog Card Number 96-86460
ISBN 0-9575772-0-9

Published by Cedar Street Press
100 Holden Terrace, Macomb, Illinois 61455
Phone 309/837-2160
Fax 309/652-3444

First Edition

Cover Photography by Joan G. Lindsey

Copyright © January, 2000, by Alfred J. Lindsey and Michael A. Deblois. All rights reserved. Printed in the United States of America. No part of this book may be used in any manner whatsoever without written permission of the authors except in the case of brief quotations in critical articles and reviews. Every effort has been taken to locate copyright owners of material reproduced in this book. Omissions brought to our attention will be corrected in subsequent editions.

10 9 8 7 6 5 4 3 2 1

In the Lord I take refuge;
How can you say to my soul,
  "Flee as a bird to your mountain;
For, behold, the wicked bend the bow,
They make ready their arrow
  Upon the string,
To shoot in darkness at
  The upright in heart.
If the foundations are destroyed,
What can the righteous do?"

Psalm 11:1-3

Let us therefore lay aside
the deeds of darkness
and put on the armor
of light.

Romans 13:12

DEDICATION

This book is lovingly dedicated to the memory of my beloved wife Joan Marie Lindsey, now with the Lord; and to my dear parents, Alfred and Dorothy Lindsey, who lovingly raised me in a Christian home; and to Joan G. Lindsey, my lovely wife, whom I love with all my heart and soul.
~Alfred J. Lindsey

It is with sincere love and affection that I dedicate my portion of this book to my help-meet, wife, and loving confidant Sue Deblois; whose encouragement is my comfort, whose love is my heart's passion, and whose co-labor in ministry my continued joy and delight. Also, to two very dear mentors, teachers and friends: Dr. Robert L. Gray, Dr. Wendell K. Babcock Both men I consider to be "Pastors of Pastors." And to the Congregation of the Argyle Bible Church, Colchester, Illinois whose ministry to my family and me has provided joy for the journey.

~Michael A. Deblois

SUNSET OF AMERICA

CAN THE GOLDEN DREAM BE SAVED?

Chapter One
    Sunset of the American Dream 13

Chapter Two
    Night Gathers: Man's Own Religion 37

Chapter Three
    Elite Power Forces: Government and Mass Media 59

Chapter Four
    Other Elite Power Forces 85

Chapter Five
    The Results: Watching a Nation Die 107

Chapter Six
    Four Cardinal Principles of Hope 145

Chapter Seven
    What the Schools Must Do 165

Chapter Eight
    What the Home Must Do 187

Chapter Nine
    What the Church Must Do 215

Chapter Ten
    A Personal Note to the Reader.......................... 249

Epilogue
    The Dawn Can Come Again 253

Index 256

PREFACE

I had the high good fortune to be reared in an era of hope, idealism, patriotism, and Christian values, when America's very creed, it's magnificent agreed-on values, was thought to be the social and political hope of humankind. The word *Christian* was revered, and the religion of Jesus Christ evoked a solemn admiration in the nation. Man's most lofty goals and hopes were personified in the *Bible*, the great American documents, and the creed of the nation. Through the Great Depression, World War II, and the post-war years, hope hung like a halo over the beloved nation.

For a decade, I was a businessman and, for over thirty years, a professor. In a sense, I have been taking the pulse of America and its people for over five decades; and, I tell you, there is a grave crisis in the Christian and moral underpinnings of the nation and its people that calls to doubt the very future of the United States and its golden dream. America, beyond any intelligent doubt, is in deep crisis, the twilight of its greatness.

Man's religion, humanism, increasingly gained authority in the minds and lives of Americans. This religion-philosophy challenged, and now perhaps has exceeded, Christianity and the consensus values of the nation as the molder of reasoning, morality, and behavior. Elite forces, far, far more powerful than the schools, are, in one way or another, educating against the historical underpinnings and into a sensate, narcissistic, hedonistic, nihilistic, amoral, immoral social order.

Though some claim otherwise, it is not too late to call back the dawn, and the purpose of this book is to do just that: to save America and its golden dream.

For nearly six years, I have been writing this book; in the beginning, like many others, I felt there was little hope; but, over time, I began to get a vision of precisely how to save America and its golden dream. This involves an in--depth consideration of the powerful sources educating with such power the social, political, and religious aspects of the nation; the terrible results of this instruction; and, based on this information, the plan to salvage the American Dream.

Answers lie in what the home, school, church, and people must do. This demands a careful analysis of the schools, families, and churches. This having been accomplished, the bold plan to salvage the American Dream is, step-by-step, made clear. The dawn can be called back. The road will be long and demanding, the price, in human terms, very high; yet this dear land, sanctioned of God, paid for by the blood of heroes, ennobled by the great documents and behavior of the nation, the shining light upon the hill, must be saved. We can win! We must! Here is how it can be done.

Alfred J. Lindsey
Macomb, Illinois

In order for the principles of this book to breathe life into our society the church of Jesus Christ alive in the world today must awaken from her slumber. Nothing short of a revival toward the basic fundamentals of true *Bible-based* Christianity focused toward the Great Commission will accomplish that in our land and around the world. Yet the church will continue her repose until that self-same spark of revival first begins in each individual child of God. Our society is searching like never before for solid answers and for a meaningful truth that promotes hope and security for living in a sin-sickened world. With the technology and untold resources at our disposal, there is no excuse for the body of Christ in failing to provide hope for a hurting world, doing so in a manner that is attractive to the seeker, and practical for those who desire to "taste and see that the Lord is good." The chapter entitled "What The Church Can Do" unfolds a truly practical plan to accomplish the awakening of America. The chapter "What The Reader Can Do" issues a personal invitation to receive God's Truth found only in His Son the Lord Jesus Christ. It is my prayer that this tool *Sunset of America* will be read and heeded by many who are searching for solid answers in their quest for truth and significance.

Michael A. Deblois
Colchester, Illinois

ACKNOWLEDGMENTS

Many helpers have graced my efforts in writing this book, and, without them, my task would have been unreachable. Some are still with me; one is in glory. To all, I offer my deepest gratitude, respect, and love. Thank you. Thank you very much.

Linda Conklin, former student and dear friend for over three decades, worked tirelessly reconstructing, rewording, rewriting the manuscript when I had grown very weary. Her input improved the manuscript hugely.

Others studied the manuscript and provided excellent advice. To these, I offer my deepest thanks. Dr. Robert Duhs and his wife Mary Alice, my cousin, provided excellent assistance, as did the noted scholar and close friend Dr. Jay W. Stein. My former pastor and dear friend Dr. Keith Miller provided sound advice, as did my colleague and a gentleman Dr. Robert Osmon--particularly in the area of learning theory. Darlos Loewenstein critiqued the manuscript and offered suggestions that hugely improved the book. Former student and a valued friend Tony Kozelichki was inordinately helpful. No one was more helpul than my dear aunt, Mary Crain, who critiqued the book and daily showered me with newspaper articles concerning education, many of which were used in the book. Her good sense was of immense help. Dr. Wayne Wiggens made suggestions that were significant.

Mary Ann and Jim Olson, former students from whom I learned, have affected me as no other friends ever have. They have shown me the character about which I wrote and identified as the *American Creed*, and they have shown me how to live the Christian faith. Their influence on this book has been huge. My dear friend Jim is now with the Lord.

My thanks go, also, to Jerry Klein, beloved fine art critic, columnist, and moral philosopher of the *Peoria Journal Star*, and Harry Whitaker, distinguished Superintendent of Schools in Peoria, Illinois, for advice concerning this book and permission to use their words and ideas.

Thanks also go to Hillsdale College for permission to use quotes from Dr. Ralph Reed and Dr. Balint Vazsony as published in *Imprimis*, the monthly journal of Hillsdale College.

I am grateful to the Lockman Foundation for permission to use the Scriptures in the book. Scriptures are taken from the New American Standard Bible, Copyright The Lockman Foundation 1960, 1962, 1963, 1968,

1971,1972,1973, 1975, 1977. Used by permission.

The most profound gratitude passes to my dear wife Joan G. Lindsey, who, in love, lifted me. Her good sense and intelligent evaluations were of immense help. Her loving influence on my life when I was near defeat reinvigorated me, and she encouraged me as only a loving helpmate can. The wonderful romance between a wife and a husband is a tremendous blessing of God, and I have been so blessed by Joan's love. My thanks go to her, too, for the dramatic photographic study of sunset in Key West, Florida, that appears on the cover of this work and profoundly influenced the title and direction of this book.

Alfred J. Lindsey
Macomb, Illinois

I am grateful for the influence of my family during my formative years, for their devotion toward my own spiritual development. I am especially grateful for a godly grandmother, Mrs. Eleanor Chase, for her sacrifice in my early years each Sunday in taking me to our little church on the hillside where together, often just her and I, we had our class time and I was taught of God's love. When I was promoted to the next grade, she earned a promotion also as the teacher.

I will be forever thankful for the influence of a variety of godly men who have impacted my life along the journey. Dr. Ron Surels unknowingly challenged me to answer the call of ministry as a senior in high school. Rev. Carl H. Smith allowed me to see in his life a passion for preaching the Word of God. Dr. Wendell Babcock, Professor of Bible at the Grand Rapids School of Bible & Music, Grand Rapids, Michigan, was and has continued to be a faithful listening ear and prayer warrior. Professor Bill Brew instilled into my life a strong work ethic when it comes to sermon preparation, and the challenge always to remember that "Ministry Equals People." Chris Bremer and Lance Brower have proven to be faithful friends who stood by me when I lacked a full understanding of what true friendships were all about. Dr. Robert and Mrs. Ruth Gray, who served as mentors, friends, spiritual examples to my wife and I during our ministry internship. They provided a legacy of what true servant shepherds are to be. No others have so impacted our lives in such dynamic ways. Rev. David and Mrs. Beverly Levy are ministers of encouragement who challenged us to seek God's best and avoid disappointment. Dr. Lyle Murphy is a man with whom you can ride the river. He and his wife Jane are wonderful trophies of God's grace.

Special thanks goes to the church board of the Argyle Bible Church, who caught a vision for this work, encouraged its progress, and believed in its purpose.

Michael A. Deblois
Colchester, Illinois

Chapter One

SUNSET OF THE AMERICAN DREAM

From Homestead, Florida, Route 1 winds south over the Gulf of Mexico to the Keys, where beauty and majesty live. Hues of the sea shade from blue to green, from azure to indigo. The sky is more lovely than a child's dream, and fluffy clouds, like wisps of cotton, float lazily by. Just to the right, the pelicans skim the water, and, in the distance, sea gulls soar. A porpoise breaks water, while, on the beach, nervous sandpipers scurry here and there. Sailboats dot the horizon, and fishing boats hurry to port. At the south tip of the road and, indeed, of America, is Key West, lovely beyond comparison, where the sunsets are said to be the world's most exquisite.

The stage is set. Now are the moments before twilight, and the seekers wait, gazing intently across the ocean into dazzlingly bright sunlight. Moments pass. The drama begins, more elegant, more breathtaking, more splendid than the imagination can conceive. The sun descends regally, ever so slowly, then more rapidly, and, finally, more quickly than a breath. The sky is aflame, until, finally, and ever so slowly, it dims, darker, still darker, and, at last, utterly black. As magnificent as any sunset in the world, it is finally gone, and left is sweet reverie that is the residue of such beauty, along with the comfort that morning's daybreak will come again, prelude and promise of a new day. Morning will come, as it has for eons of time.

But will it for man's most fervent and cherished dreams? Will it reappear for humankind's greatest nation? Now it is twilight. Can the dawn be called back? Can America and its golden dream be saved?

This volume will answer that question with hope; however, many have surrendered to hopelessness. That America is deep in social, political, and religious crisis should be clear to any thinking person. Something has gone askew, for grave problems multiply in geometric progression. Multiplied billions of dollars have been lost in vain attempts at social engineering authored by the federal government. Judicial efforts have been no more successful, and attempts by the states have born little fruit. Vast programs to deal with poverty, violence, gangs, other crimes, race, ethnicity, decaying families, divorce, and a myriad of other problems have grown steadily worse, resulting in growing numbers of sociologists, economists, and theologians throwing up their hands in hopelessness and despair. Many Americans are confused and angry, rightfully sensing that a frightful lostness and pessimism hover like a horrible nightmare over the land. The historic confidence of Americans has, all too often, given way to nihilistic hopelessness and existential lostness, and many of these people stand shaking their fists at the sky in utter exasperation.

Everything is not wrong. Indeed, much is laudable. Built on *God's Word* and the foundations of the American agreed-on values, the *American Creed*, social and political miracles abound. Material comforts have made life easier, and economic prosperity is a model for the world. Medical breakthroughs have proven miraculous. Science and technology have excelled, and knowledge multiplies. Freedom has, for now, driven communism to bay, and employment has remained high. Schooling has stayed relatively inexpensive and available to most people. Freedom of religion is admirable, as is due process under the law. Inflation has decreased, and times are good.

But a nation, like a fine home, is no better than the foundation on which it is built; and, in America, the substructure is crumbling. Every day, in most every way, the foundation is destructing.

Yonder is America and its hallowed dream; it is so magnificent there in the dusk framed by the fiery horizon. But the sky is growing ever darker. The collapsing foundation, the moral base representing Christianity and the *American Creed*, is the cause. Can the dawn be called back? The very future of humankind hangs in the balance; the foundation, held together by the Christian values and behaviors on which it was built, absolutely must be reconsidered and reinvigorated, else the golden dream of mankind is in deep peril. A terrible sensate age lurks.

But who or what is at fault? Where does the blame lie? Indeed, is it possible to locate the political and social malefactor in the nation's education, in the complex of its various and varying sources? Any worthy evaluation of America's grave problems must focus on why the forces teaching Americans have accomplished such a tragedy, and, having done so, provide a remedy.

The book has, as its primary objective, the salvation of the American Dream and the rebirth of its Christian moorings. The recommended solutions will focus on the three most important historically conservative institutions: school, home, and church. Operating as we shall recommend, they can call back the dawn and lead the effort to overcome the educational elites, the humanists who are educating the nation toward a new and appalling radical dark age. But America can, once again, shine through the darkness, birthing the dawn of a new and wonderful day when the dear land, once again, will be the shining light upon the hill. The twilight can evolve into the light and warmth of day, and the American Dream, the political hope of humankind, can reignite the hopes and dreams of the entire range of Americans.

The most handy institution to blame is public schooling. Currently, a hateful, brooding rage is directed toward America's schools, both from an unhappy general public and, particularly, from believing Christians. The schools are not innocent; however, the legitimate explanation of the problem lies far beyond classrooms. Public schools are no more nor less than a social extension of the American majority and of the communities financing them. Schooling, then, has the cardinal objective of mirroring the majority society; thus, America's social plight is reflected in the schools. What happens in the classrooms must be a result of the larger social order, a sure fact that should be understood if one is to consider the failures and successes of the public schools that are far more products than instigators of any evils. Turning to the dark side of public education was partially a result of a social revolution in the late 1960's and early 1970's whereby unacceptable behaviors became enthroned in the halls of higher learning and because of other powerful behavior-modifying forces.

The grave distress apparent in American society is widespread--similar, in many respects, to the manifest problems shared with the rest of the civilized world. Some sociologists believe that the difficulties stem from a confused world teetering between historical epochs. The deep problems in America, however, have their own overriding causes. The greatest nation in history, sanctioned by God, showered with blessings, and committed to the most noble ideals of the western world, has eroded as its character diminished. Make no mistake, the United States was firmly committed to Christian ideals as well as the precepts and principles of Greece, Rome, and Europe, in general. Beyond a doubt, these were the finest and most noble beliefs in man's history, and never ever should Americans apologize about their political and social underpinnings.

Nobody has understood this better than Gunnar Myrdal, who, in *An American Dilemma* (1944), explained that by some huge and amazing miracle America had formulated the most notable and grand consensus value system in the history of man. These magnificent values were the result, he wrote, of Christianity, English common-law, and the ideals of the Enlightenment. Here, in the magnificent consensus values shared by a huge majority of Americans across the groups comprising the nation, lies the nation's political greatness. Co-existing, though, were low-level values that directed behavior in less than admirable ways. The extraordinary consensus high-level values shared by most Americans were often in direct conflict with their actions to profit or protect themselves, and this presented a problem of huge proportions.

Though there were huge disagreements between groups, the American consensus valuations, perhaps better identified as the *American Creed*, bound with hoops of steel the many peoples of the post-colonial period, but such agreement is far more complicated in an increasingly complex social order. The escalating complexities resulting from the industrial revolution had a profound effect on America and elsewhere in the civilized world. The power of modern technology was loosed, and the world was never again the same. The overwhelming forces of specialization, urbanization, industrialization, and long-distance communications radically altered the economic, social, and moral arrangements by which Americans lived.

The agreement that had united the nation in a sense of social community suffered dedicated attack; the high-level values were in deep jeopardy. From farms and hamlets, the people congregated in the great urban areas where jobs existed, radically altering the concept of community and its attending consensus which partially gave way to a new community of vocational groupings, each tending to define right as it profited from the valuations. The community of moral agreement was seriously damaged, and informed scholars identified this as the beginning of the demise of consensus values. They argued that the *American Creed* had given way to the values of the many vocational groups.

In the years that followed, and to the present hour, the required agreement has been under siege, as the soul of the United States hung in the balance. Without the consensus creed and its Christian ideals, social problems multiplied. In most cases the nation had the knowledge and often the financial means to resolve the dilemmas; but there is no solution without agreement on objectives, procedures, and desired ends. If, indeed, the decision-making process is based on each interest group's view of right as the method by which it will profit, there is no hope for effective problem solution.

Social health demands a society in which social institutions are closely related but, even more important, in which certain basic beliefs are shared. Without such accord, a social order soon finds itself plummeting toward crisis, and so it is in the United States of America. The critical truth is that many in positions of power and influence are happily accepting the misguided efforts to destroy the very consensus that is the nation's social greatness, and the result is a sensate social order focused on the senses rather than virtue.

But what does all this mean to the believing Christian who accepts the truth of *God's Word*? Initially, it becomes clear that the *Bible*, the single most important influence in the *Creed*, becomes less and less important as an influence on the social order. And when man refuses God's truth, he invariably turns inward, to himself, the worst of all places. Man, not God, becomes the measure of all things. The worship of man is well identified as humanism which is, no matter claims to the opposite, a religion. As the measure of values and actions, this religion flowered when the physical and natural sciences and the scientific spirit adopted the ideal that man without God can solve all problems. Do not believe, however, that humanists should be demonized, a serious error made by many Christians. The humanists, though wrong, are often good people with noble goals. They should and deserve to be treated with dignity, respect and kindness.

The public schools typically follow the consensus of the times. Accordingly, they began espousing the humanistic doctrine and disparaging Christianity. The Supreme Court, the Congress, and the President, along with many other leading institutions, were culprits in the public school shift. It was man's age, now identified by liberal writers as the post-Christian era, and schooling bought into much of this philosophy being taught by educators far more powerful and effective than the schools. It is, then, no wonder that Christians and other thinking people have become disgruntled and distressed about public schooling.

Many disaffected Americans were slow to comprehend that this development was simply reflecting the society which was financing the enterprise. One of the most worrisome failures of the evangelicals in battling humanism in the schools is their refusal to face this truth. The schools have not been seized by a humanistic minority; they are a majority. If the schools were in the hands of a secular minority, the problem would be far easier than it really is to solve. Unfortunately, the time when believers were a majority is now past, and the dilemmas of an age identified by some as the post-Christian era are far more difficult to solve.

The distressing development became increasingly worse as the nation moved into the late 1960's and early 1970's. Flexing his muscles, man worshiped himself as he corrupted what he touched. It was a sad, sad era.

About the same time throughout the world, those without authority and influence, the have-nots, rose up in righteous indignation, demanding a full share of power and opportunity in their respective social orders. Had the movement been grounded in the *Word of God* and the attending values, it would have been a more noble endeavor than it was, however. In America the resulting Civil Rights Movement became a powerful contributor to socialistic humanistic reconstruction. In this regard, political action became a huge factor, as law, fashion, and legislation supported and backed the minority demands, a development that was commendable. Ancient and pervasive inequities cried out to be addressed if, indeed, the United States were to live up to the code that so distinguished the great nation.

But all social movements have their down-sides. Influenced by the self-worship and the developing narcissism and hedonism displayed in the era, the subgroups committed themselves to succeeding at all costs and to procuring what they perceived they had coming--and much more. The *Creed* suffered significantly as the tenets that had so influenced behavior were abandoned. *Noblesse oblige* (the nobler you are, the nobler you are to others) was ridiculed and under attack. The new rules were every group for itself, every person for himself. The *Creed's* avid demand that one should serve others, that in a sense one was his brother's keeper, became outdated, as giving and sharing became ideals of long ago.

A dreadful and primarily unforeseen effect of the new rules was the multicultural movement in schooling and in the social order itself. Though seldom mentioned as a primary failure in education, it may well be the most serious error of all. Products of the Civil Rights Movement, ill-advised humanistic psychology, and pop-top philosophy, the misplaced claims for multiculturalism and for pluralism are destroying the consensus that made America greater than any nation. Substituted were polarization and factionalization (named by some *fractionalization*)--unwavering and lethal routes to the scrap heap of history.

To the Greek writers of tragedy, man's tragic flaw was *hubris*, that is to say, his excessive pride. This imperfection led, as it always must, to the selfishness which is diametrically opposed to Christian doctrine and the Creed. As a result, narcissistic self-indulgence became a virtue. Witness the misguided psychology of the self and its infectious effect. Bookstores bulge with publications asserting the self along with using others for one's gain. Christian values and the *Creed* itself seem to fall into the oblivion of the past as its admonitions are taken less seriously. Selfishness has no inclination to hear that one should turn his cheek, that it is better to give than to receive, that one should help those in need. These precepts and most of the planks of the *Creed* gave way to the huge egomania of the time and bred an orgy of self-gratification masked as the milk of human kindness.

To comprehend adequately the current perceived failure of the many forces of education and, in a larger sense, of America itself, it is important to understand that this pride leading to selfishness is in bitter antagonism to Christianity and its attending values. The *American Creed*, then, is under direct assault as the man-centered social philosophy invades every institution of the nation, including home, church, and school.

The great American institutions failed to parry the thrust. Family, church, and school too often follow the philosophy of the time. When conservative foundations crumble, the social order is in deep jeopardy. Add the terribly negative forces of the mass media, the peer group, humanistic philosophy and psychology, as well as the multiplying evil forces of the period, and the problems stalking the nation become apparent.

Any solution to these manifold problems requires that America turn back to its *Creed* and, though misguided laws make this impossible in the schools, bow to receive Jesus Christ, the Savior of the World. The first of these is a secular hope; however, its success makes the trip to the Cross shorter--and this is no little factor.

Such a resolution demands that the school, the home, and the church each accomplish its respective job in educating youth. The failure of any of this crucial triad dooms the effort--and, most certainly, wounds the *Creed*. Without the success of these three crucial institutions, the dilemma will most surely become an implacable crisis.

In all of this the cardinal requirement is the consensus *American Creed*. Every child, every person, must comprehend and accept the *Creed* as the social foundation for problem solution, and this involves the studied will of the decision-makers as well as the involvement of each person in the decision-making process.

THE TRUTH ABOUT AMERICAN EDUCATION

Any nation or society educates its young to be what it expects them to be, to equip them to fit well into the social order and the majority culture comprising it. The youth are to be prepared to accept the consensus high-level values of the social order and to act upon the verities. The skills needed in the marketplace are to be mastered, at least to the degree each student is able; and recent discoveries, as well as new insights, are to be learned. Historically, these were education's goals, and they should not have changed in the current era. Now, however, the taxpaying public which owns the schools is unhappy with the education of the youth, and the growing wrath directed towards schooling is, beyond any doubt, unique in the nation's history.

The focus of the concern is directed toward the public schools, perceived by a growing number as failing institutions. Indeed, schools shoulder the blame not only for scholastic shortcomings, but for nearly all societal ills, including sex deviancy, alcohol and controlled substances, failing discipline, increased crime, lack of patriotism, falling test scores, driving problems, immoral behavior, violence, and a host of other dilemmas.

As a result, the public schools are increasingly judged to be failing institutions, and certainly they have earned their share of criticism. Invariably, however, the accusers are erroneous in assuming that schooling and education are synonymous. Nothing could be further from the truth. It is vital to comprehend that schooling is but a part of education, the failure paling before that of many other societal forces. This is surely apparent when there is an understanding that, by the very nature of what they are, public schools must reflect the social order owning and financing them. One reason that schools have failed to reach public expectations is that they have unwisely reflected the worst of American society. This, of course, is a momentous error, but it is predictable given the other forces educating the youth and the mood of the time.

A multitude of sources educate, some conservatively, some liberally. The most important of these, and entirely decisive to the proper education of tomorrow's adults, are the homes, churches, and schools, which must be the crucial and moral forces that mediate between the highest-level values as well as behaviors and the other forces of education that are frequently far from exemplary or moral. The triad of home, church, and school share a like commitment to teaching what is right and good and to inculcating habits and experiences which prepare young people to do battle with societal forces, so alluring, that may ruin both their lives and the American way.

The most important of the positive forces are the home and church. The failure of either or both of these institutions makes proper schooling impossible. But the success of these two would allow the schools, operating as they should, to fulfill what taxpayers demand and expect. The schools, building on home and church, have the moral and social authority to hold firm on the consensus *American Creed* and to withstand the other, and more powerful, forces of education.

But what are the contemporary sources of education in the nation? Already mentioned are the trio of home, church, and school; but these, as indicated, are only a portion of education. Tremendous power and authority reside in the following forces: mass media, peer group, political climate, psychology and philosophy, laws, and the economy. Surely, it should be no surprise whatsoever that these societal factors are profound educators of youth and that they have power and allure that schools, homes, and churches too seldom offer.

The forces just identified are, of course, not always negative. Sometimes they are worthy; however, in the current era they are often terribly damaging. The worst of these presents a significant concern to America, its dream of hope, and the education of its youth. If the home, church, and school fail in their historic goals, the American social order will fall deeply into crisis, a fact that is necessary to understand in evaluating anything whatsoever about education in the United States.

Unfortunately, there is mounting evidence that under the liberal, anti-God forces of the era the institutions of home and church have too often fallen to the negative forces. The left wing of the church long ago turned to a corrupt concern with man rather than God. Also, it should be apparent that the home is in shambles. What, then, can public schools do? The cards are surely stacked against them and ultimately against the social order itself. Indeed, schools alone, no matter their methods, cannot call back the dawn; nor can they, by themselves, be the cause of the American crisis. Though often terribly wrong, they remain but one of many such forces--and less damaging than most.

This is not to suggest that the schools are blameless. Quite the opposite is true, but the failure should be kept in perspective. Nonetheless, and even under current conditions, schooling can be a positive force; but an entirely different focus is required, one that may be, given present forces of society, impossible to reach. In the meantime, Christians (and other thinking people) will stand in abject wonder that the great nation is dissipating, dissolving before their very eyes, that a nation under God is becoming a nation under man.

As indicated, solutions lie far beyond the schools, but they can turn the attention of the nation back to the homes, and, in a certain manner, back to the churches. Together, these three powerful forces can redirect America.

PUBLIC EXPECTATIONS

When a social order is moving into crisis, a confused and enraged citizenry demands more of its institutions. With the home in shambles and the church too often dedicated to psychobabble and philosophic meandering, the people turn to schooling which they own and can control. At such a time the demands on schooling increase so that the institution must endeavor to meet objectives for which its employees were never professionally prepared.

This signifies a serious breakdown and surely results in the unreachable demand that public schooling solve the nation's social problems. Such a charge invariably fails, as it has in America; and the situation is made much worse, primarily because time is taken from the procedures historically demanded of schooling. It is a Catch 22.

In all of this, the schools are not blameless. In the days following progressive education, they increasingly turned their attentions to social problems. Professional teacher organizations had typically felt a need to go beyond academics to preparing the whole child for the social order. This was worthy, but it went too far. It was ever stressful to conservatives and evangelicals, but it seriously grieved many thinking people when the social order, attempting to remediate its social failures, demanded that public schooling become the nation's primary source in solving them.

The results have been disheartening and deplorable, no matter the dedication and efforts of the schools. Certainly, the enigmas of poverty, sex, poor job preparation, drugs, alcohol, violence, and ethnic and racial problems join a host of societal problems in surviving every effort of the schools. Most of these problems grow increasingly worse--some in direct proportion to the amount of federal and state monies spent in the schools on their remediation.

By themselves, schools will not and cannot author any effective solution to the terrible social dilemmas. Ultimately, taxpayers must understand this and refrain from demanding the unobtainable from the schools. Also, the schools themselves must face the reality that they have limited ability to solve social problems; and that they must focus on what they can do, what historically have been their goals, and what teachers have been professionally prepared to do. The schools cannot take the place of home and church.

Although the schools cannot and will not lead the nation into a social utopia, they can help pupils become successful, contributing members of the nation. The objective is the realization of this goal for the overwhelming majority of students. The fact that schools, in their rush to solve social problems, forgot this fact partially explains the rage that many taxpayers feel. Part of this was schooling's fault; part of it was not.

Educators nourished in the university cradle of liberalism and humanism were programmed to believe that they could utilize the public schools successfully to remediate America's most persistent social problems. They believed, then, that schools should broaden the curricula to consider problems formerly thought the province first of the family and then of the church. Believing that the family had either failed or that they were intellectually unequipped to deal with the problems, educators supported broadening the goals to include the social problems. They meant well and, in a way, were to be applauded.

In quite another manner, however, it became clear that they were interfering in areas where they had no right whatsoever to challenge home and church. The sorry result of this development was that time spent on the historic and academic aspects of schooling was horribly limited. Worse, the religion of man was used as the value system endeavoring to solve social problems. Nothing should have been more disturbing to believing parents, and the efforts of humanistic educators have continued to grow until, in the present time, schools have become a very real threat to concerned parents.

The schooling profession was responsible for the second, and more important, reason for the unfortunate social focus. Unfortunately, and much of this is surely political, the nation has a way of changing social problems into educational ones. In this regard, the argument that the schools had no choice in the social objective deserves consideration. Public school decision-makers could, at great cost, have refused the efforts of politicians to shift the blame for their liberal failures to the schools. They could have argued firmly for their historic mandate, basing their position on the will of the taxpayers; and perhaps they might have won. At least they might have slowed this crushing social momentum. That could have happened, but it did not. Now, it very well may be too late, for there is overwhelming evidence that a huge minority or a small majority of taxpayers has accepted the ideal.

Consider the results. Have the schools improved the sexual behavior of students? Has the issuing of condoms aided in any manner, save legitimatizing fornication? Has the divorce rate been lowered? Has driver's education reduced the number of teen-age auto fatalities? Have counseling programs built on man's worship of himself lessened the trauma of the era for the youth? Has teaching the multicultural tomfoolery benefitted either the minorities or the majority? Have liquor and narcotic problems decreased? On and on, the list grows, and the answers are more than disappointing.

Thinking people well comprehend that when schools invade the areas belonging to church and home they are sure to fail, not only in solving social problems but also in fulfilling the very obligations historically expected of them. Much of the problem results because there is too little time to attend to all the goals. As the schools focus on problems that are really not theirs, reading, math, English, science, and other scores tumble--to a point embarrassing when compared with those of other civilized nations. Time, indeed, is a critical factor.

Teachers knew this was so, as they worked long, long hours--no matter the claims of critics of the schools who speak out angrily even though they know nearly nothing about the school environment or who judge everything in terms of what they see in California and the inner cities of the great urban areas. In this teachers are not to be faulted. Many of the group sensed the wrath of the public as a result of the fact that they were asked to do too much in too little time. Many taxpayers were incensed at the schools, too often for the wrong reasons. As they watched America crumble, they lashed out at schooling and teachers, and they were partially correct in doing so. Teachers had indeed made momentous errors; however, the failure to work hard was not among them.

Teachers were stunned. Having tried so hard to accomplish all things, their collective sense of worth tumbled as they worked long, long hours and months trying selflessly to meet the needs of youth. The problems were made worse by the growing failure of the homes and churches to meet their requirements in educating the youth. Schooling's good days had passed; a sense of defeat pervaded teachers' lives. Faculty lounges were filled by dazed teachers, underpaid hard workers, newly loathed.

As a result, teachers moved to unionization for the protection of their interests. This, too, enraged the public, which had been conditioned to believe that teachers were above such self-interest. Reflecting this rage, Americans demanded accountability of their teachers. In desperate reaction the teaching profession rushed to measure learning, much of which cannot and should not have been measured. Behavioral objectives invaded schooling. Teachers were evaluated largely on how well these objectives were reached by the students--too often a simplistic way to evaluate the unmeasurable. The very success of such a procedure depends on the location of the school, family, motivation, socioeconomic class, ability level, and a host of other variables. The measurement was largely political, unprofessional, and professionally useless. At the same time, beginning teachers and graduates of teacher programs were required to pass state-mandated tests to be certified for teaching, a purely political action; and the results were all but useless in predicting the success of teachers. Millions of dollars were thrown to the winds in this failed political endeavor.

Let the teachers have their due. They are being roundly attacked for the wrong reasons; the barrage is misdirected. Indeed, teachers, most meaning well, are dupes of a system grounded in the religion of man. They have been educated in universities teaching this view, and their churches all too often join the others in accepting and preaching the humanist agenda. They mean well; but they are, at that point, unwitting enemies of the American common good.

It is, of course, tragic that these people are simply dupes of a system that has turned from God. In many respects victims of the man-worshiping social order, teachers cannot understand why they are perceived as evil by believers. Moreover, they may very well reflect the majority beliefs in the post-Christian era. This believers have trouble accepting, but they must come to this realization if the humanistic faith is to be adequately contested in the schools. Otherwise, the focus is directed to the ideals of another time.

Unfortunately, research does not indicate how people learn nor what their natures are. The two huge unanswered problems provide adequate proof that schooling is far less than a scientific endeavor. If it is to meet public expectations, there must be unimpeachable knowledge of man's nature and how he learns. Thus, schooling is an inexact endeavor, doing, usually, the best it can with huge weights of the two unanswered questions millstones around its neck.

All of this leads to the pendulum swing of public school curricula from one extreme, the liberal, to the other, the conservative. Schools move, in their seasons, from veritable prisons, bastions of traditional schooling based on behavioristic teaching, to child-centered playgrounds, conceived to stroke egos of the youth and to teach them primarily through abstract means. The pendulum of schooling fashion swings to and fro, following the varying forces that affect the institution. In this, the homes and churches are as guilty as the schools.

SOCIAL RECONSTRUCTION AND THE SCHOOLS

The history of educational thought in America is filled with the notion that public schooling should be a tool of social reconstruction--that it should rebuild and improve the social order. Years ago, Professors George S. Counts and Gerald O. Rugg achieved international fame in authoring a liberal, socialistic model for the schools that they claimed was democratic. Earlier, John Dewey also had a profound effect upon the schools. Liberals were often thrilled with the notion, while conservatives cringed at humanistic, anti-God programs that influenced the schools.

The problem of authority is important. Who should have the authorization to set school policy in reconstructing the social order? Thankfully, this power does not belong to the federal government. The *United States Constitution* allows it minimal influence, and this by funding some programs and releasing information. No more than seven percent of public school funds come from the federal government. The judicial branch of government does influence profoundly by court findings concerning the redress of constitutional rights perceived to be denied the youth. Current public interest in national testing and standards is unlikely to have teeth, and those willing to accept the ideal had better think twice before allowing the federal government power that is not constitutional. Allotting such influence to the federal government should be resisted like the plague, for schooling urgently needs to stay away from national politics. Constitutionally, the power that does not belong to the federal government belongs to the states. This means, then, that the legislated power of schooling rests with the states; however, in authoring and mandating school curricula and procedures, some states perform far better than others. Where a child is reared does make a difference. From a certain point of view, this leads to fragmented programs of reconstruction. But there is a powerful equalizer in federal law and court decisions concerning constitutional rights. It remains true, though, that states rather than federal bureaucrats should have a far better sense of what their students need.

If this is correct, then communities would also know better than state bureaucrats what their youth need. Hence, in America the states have wisely chosen to delegate much power to the local communities, whose property taxes are the single largest financier of public schooling. From a practical and political view, the people, the taxpayers, own the schools, and it is for their world that youth must be prepared to succeed. These people who pay the taxes and thus own the schools will, in fact, have their way with what they finance, a proper ideal because the moral power of educational authority belongs to them. And it should be made perfectly clear that the schools really have no right whatsoever to reconstruct the American social order because, given their power base, they can only reflect it. The public will rightly allow them to go little further, and this is good.

Like many others, this problem is political. Democrats and liberals typically desire that the power be in federal hands, while Republicans and other conservatives want the power in the hands of the people, as far away from Washington as possible. A retired democratic congressman recently pointed out that Republicans criticize government as the enemy of freedom, while the Democrats believe government is the answer to our problems and prefer the politicians they know to the consumers who are beyond their control.

But many have spoken in glowing terms about federal testing of both students and teachers. While conservatives have a rightful sense that schooling is slipping away from the taxpayers who finance it, the federal education establishment is growing, even though, in reality, it has little power unless a misinformed public gives it more.

The authority in all areas of schooling, including any efforts to reconstruct the social order, rests in the hands of the people. They must not let big government take this power from them. To the utter consternation of political and cultural elites, any answers to schooling lie in representative democracy; and this is so, concerning schooling and all else, in the federal, state, and local arenas. Americans, losing sight of this historic truth, are abdicating their power to government; herein lies one of education's most horrible problems.

The reader should be aware that federal interference in schooling based on anything but constitutional guarantees interpreted by the Supreme Court remains a huge failure--even when the programs seem to make sense. In President Johnson's *Great Society*, there was a protracted effort to assist the poor in schooling, and billions of dollars were spent to overcome environmental insufficiency. What came of the efforts? Test scores plummeted. Poverty was not alleviated. The results were disappointing, at best. Crime flourished. Racism was not solved.

In all truth, it was quite a magnificent effort by the federal government. Some of it was political but much was well-intentioned. Why, then, did it fail? First, the federal government has less vision about what people need than do the local communities and the states. Why would any thinking person believe that Washington bureaucrats, trapped into *inside the belt-line mentality*, could solve schooling's problems? If there are rules for the success of schooling, a cardinal one should be: Keep schooling out of the hands of federal bureaucrats; keep it in the hands of those who perceive locally what the problems are and what the youth need.

Nor can taxpayers believe that America is truly a Christian nation. Any accurate appraisal of the schools must surely perceive that contemporary

Sunset of the American Dream

America is Christian in name alone. The truth of the matter is that Christians are living in enemy territory--and it is this that the schools reflect. Any analyzing of the dilemma by believers must begin with this understanding; then intelligent plans can be made. Though a huge plurality say they are Christian, the behavior of the people very often militate against their claims. To be sure, they believe themselves to be Christian; but, *God's Word* being true and trustworthy, many are no more than followers of the religion of man. Further proof rests in the fact that those who believe the truth of the *Scriptures* are frequently identified as crazy fundamentalists.

It is clear, then, that a huge percentage of people claiming the name *Christian* are simply humanists who select from the *Bible* those ideas and ideals which they prefer. Believers may be sure of this; they are living in enemy territory, and it is in this very locale that American education, a minimal part of which is schooling, resides. Many evangelical writers evaluating the schools do not understand this truth. The problems, in fact, are far worse than they suppose. It is absolutely essential that this be understood in analyzing education's problems.

CONSENSUS: *THE AMERICAN CREED*

The political and social answer begins with the hallowed *American Creed*. Born of the struggle and pain of the old world, informed by the great seminal minds of antiquity, grounded in biblical truth, fathered by the suffering of the downtrodden yearning to be free, paid for by the blood of heroes, a set of values and actions emerged in America that shook and changed the world. Born gloriously was man's golden dream: the consensus value system in the United States identified as the *American Creed* (sometimes known as the American Ethos or American Tradition). This *Creed* is precisely what has made America the *shining light on the hill*, the political hope of mankind, the value system leading, finally, to the cross of Jesus Christ, the Savior of the World. Dr. Ralph Reed said of America:

> It is a nation held together by a common bond and a common vision–a bond of common experience and a vision of uncommon greatness. America is George Washington's *common country*, John Adams' *glorious morning*, and Abraham Lincoln's *inestimable jewel.*

> America is also a nation in which one becomes American not by accident of birth or by ethnic heritage, but by *subscribing to an idea.* No one truly becomes a Frenchman merely by moving to France. No one becomes a Spaniard merely by moving to Spain. But America has lifted its lamp

beside the golden door of entry to immigrants of all races and all nations and bids them welcome to what Irving Howe called *the good country*.

It is not blood or marriage that counts but a vision–a vision of a society based on two fundamental beliefs. The first belief is that all men, created equal in the eyes of God with certain unalienable rights, are free to pursue the longings of their heart. The second belief is that the sole purpose of government is to protect those rights.

But the common bond, the *Creed*, is under direct attack by American institutions, including the public schools that, too often, have no knowledge whatsoever of their tragic error. The most serious mistakes of these schools are evidenced in their current efforts, particularly multicultural programs, to make war against the *Creed*. Sad to say, also, home and church have too often joined schools and powerful educational elites in this debasement of the nation.

AMERICA'S VALUE CRISIS

The most serious symptom of an American political crisis is the breakdown of confidence in the *American Creed*. Whether called the overarching culture, the unspoken assumptions of an age, the cultural core, or the consensus high-level values, agreement among and within the many groups comprising the social order is required for a healthy, productive nation. It is, in fact, this basic agreement that defines the word *society*. Further, a great society agrees on noble, humane ideals within the framework of freedom. America, then, is a great social order as long as the *Creed* is maintained and followed.

Surely, the absence of value agreement makes effective societal problem solving all but impossible, and this can lead eventually to the collapse of the social institutions, school being one, and to chaos and anarchy. In the age of abject selfishness and self-aggrandizement, when groups and individuals raise their fists for power or open their palms for the dole, consensus agreements diminish.

Any solution must rest on rediscovery of the agreed-upon high-level values that are part and parcel of the *American Creed*. But does there remain such a consensus in the nation? And even if there is a diminished commitment concerning the *Creed*, is there still a measure of belief in the noble values that earlier united the vast majority of Americans? If there is, as this book will explain, there remains a very real hope for bringing this nation and its institutions, school among them, back from the abyss.

Sunset of the American Dream

If America is united in its noble creed, it will stand; if it is divided, it will fall. True when asserted centuries ago, the words remain absolutely dependable today. No matter the humanistic claims from the halls of ivy or other areas of the liberal establishment, America must be united. It follows, then, that any action driving the people into dedicated groups opposing the *Creed* is an act of intellectual treason.

The fashionable romantic assurances concerning America's pluralism and the resulting practice of groups maintaining their own unique qualities may sound well to the unthinking or the angry disaffected, but--and mark this well--without consensus on noble values there is no hope for the United States, save intervention by God. Just examine the record. Note what happened in the former Soviet Union when majority agreement disappeared, and consider America's Civil War. Look at Quebec; then recoil in horror at the Balkans.

But there is still another position taken by the romantics preaching against the *Creed*. Pointing the accusing finger at America, they proclaim that the nation is not, nor ever was, worthy. These people continue by enumerating the evils that they claim typified the nation. There never were, they assert, admirable consensus values. From the very beginning, they insist, the nation was fatally flawed.

These ideas, shared by many in the universities and politicians as well as preachers of liberal persuasion, are false. Yes, like every social order in the history of humankind, there were atrocities and other sins that were worse than terrible. Unfortunately, given the unredeemed nature of man, this has been true in every nation's past. Nonetheless, this is a noble country, founded on the highest ideals and based on Christian truth. Something very special happened in the United States of America; however, cultural pluralists, political and religious liberals, self-interest motivated groups, and multiculturalists play fast and loose with the sure fact that America was, from the very first, a great nation. Humankind's longing for freedom and hope for a better day did not look toward Africa, Asia, or a Hispanic nation. Instead, the dream focused on the United States, which was and is man's greatest political hope, and, surely, more than important in proclaiming the cause of Jesus Christ.

From America's early days, the consensus values, the creed of the nation, stood as a beacon for those longing for freedom, justice, and dignity. And the good news is, no matter claims to the contrary, that the *American Creed*, whose roots lie deep in the Christian, Jewish, and secular traditions of Europe, is still alive and continues to represent the consensus of the majority of Americans. Perhaps commitment is weaker than it once was in the selfish rush of each group to get its own; however, the essential core remains--and this is exceedingly good news.

Everywhere at once in the early 1990s, democracy and freedom won huge victories. No matter the beliefs of Marxists, socialists, and political as well as religious liberals, men have demanded freedom and justice, ideals that blossomed and flowered in America. What remains, and this is no little demand, is for the United States to live up to the planks of the *Creed* and to teach them as the truth. Tragically, the institutions of nation, home, church, and schools are failing immensely in this regard.

The *American Creed* was shaped by the great and humane philosophies of antiquity, particularly in Europe. The wise thinkers and philosophers of the ancient Greek and Roman world had a profound influence, as did the seminal minds of the Reformation and the Enlightenment. None of these, however, had the influence that the *Holy Bible* did: *God's Word* became institutionalized in the *Creed*.

This, of course, rankled unbelievers, as it continues to do today, but it is also an important reason for the strong current Christian concern about the *Creed*. They quite rightly claim that morality is important but that salvation is the primary Christian message and that the *Creed* does not lead to salvation. Thus, they often submit, any teaching of morality, even Christian, misses the point; it does not, cannot, lead to salvation. Such teaching, some believe, aids the humanistic cause, reasoning that is compelling, but further consideration is required. In this self-seeking humanistic era, morality is increasingly under attack. It is a long, long walk from man's base values to the Cross. Alternately, it is a much shorter trip to the salvation experience if the *Creed*, with its Christian foundation, is taught.

Let no person deride the *American Creed*. Its noble beginnings are to be celebrated as a miracle of humankind, and it must not die in the selfish onslaught of humanism gone mad.

There are those, however, who claim that the arguments and bad feelings among America's social, racial, and ethnic groups are so serious as to render any agreement ineffective. Such a claim is shortsighted, and accepting this view is to believe that America is sinking into the scrap heap of history. It is not, then, the complete breakdown of the *Creed* that typifies America's most pressing problems; rather, it is the absence of a method of inquiry that uses the *Creed* in problem-solving, particularly when there is apparently little or no agreement among the problem-solvers. The joining of the planks included in the *American Creed* and a method of decision-making based on democratic procedures is necessary for effective, humane problem-solving in the nation; moreover, such an approach could be of immense political value for the teeming millions in the nations of the free world.

But is there still time? Is it too late? While shorter than one would hope, there remains some time. From now forward, though, rapid, dramatic changes must be made; and these required modifications must climb over the backs of a huge number of societal forces that, unchecked, will make the task impossible.

The *Creed* can once again bring the many groups together in worthy consensus values, restoring, before it is too late, a sense of community, or, more precisely, of being part of a society, that is to say a group of people sharing common ideals, beliefs, and hopes. The disparate groups, the warring factions, can be brought together, but the clock is ticking, ticking toward midnight as the selfishness of the humanistic age is all-pervading. The job may be impossible, but this simply means that renewed, dedicated effort is needed; the land of the free and the home of the brave is sinking in the quicksand of humanism. The conflict, and that's what it is, must not be lost before the battles are fought.

THE AMERICAN CREED: THE POLITICAL HOPE OF MANKIND

Following are the planks of America's hallowed *Creed*:

(1) Recognition of the moral worth and dignity of people
(2) Freedom coupled with the restraints to maintain it
(3) Equality that means worth and dignity for people
(4) A social order so conceived and so operated that every person can grow to the fullest level of his capabilities
(5) A perfect union, one and inseparable
(6) Representative government operated as a republic and with a Congress representing the will of the people
(7) Government for the expressed purpose of serving the people
(8) Governmental power derived only from the consent of the governed
(9) Protection of the electorate from governmental excess and inequity
(10) Power of all branches of federal government limited to the *Constitution*
(11) The innate right of all citizens to life, liberty, and the pursuit of happiness within the law and acceptable behavior
(12) Freedom of religion
(13) Dedicated belief in the sanctity of the historic family with the belief that the family is the nation's most important institution and the understanding that the traditional marriage vows are sacred
(14) Respect for practical wisdom
(15) The crucial importance of honesty and integrity

(16) The work ethic with the understanding that success comes from work, study, and application
(17) An equitable system of law protecting the populace from crime and dishonored contracts
(18) The existence of adequate armed forces to protect the citizens and nation from threat to the *American Creed*
(19) Laws that allow an accused person every right to prove his innocence
(20) Personal responsibility of each person for his actions
(21) Due process under the law for all people
(22) Dedicated belief in the preeminence of the American republic with the willingness to become one with the majority and participate in democratic process for improving it
(23) Free economic enterprise within the bounds of fair play
(24) Assistance for those absolutely unable to help themselves
(25) The belief that murder is wrong
(26) Honoring mother, father, and family
(27) Fairness in dealing with other people
(28) Cruelty as unacceptable behavior
(29) Undue coveting as unacceptable behavior
(30) Dramatic limitation of government in lives of Americans
(31) Courage to meet life's problems
(32) Willingness to forgive
(33) Disdain for arrogance
(34) Loyalty to family, friends, church, and nation

DOES THE *CREED* REALLY WORK?

It is no surprise that the existence of the *American Creed* based on its consensus high-level values is considered by many liberals, particularly those holding radical political philosophies, as either a figment of imagination or a dangerous ploy of the wealthy to trap the poor in the lower class. Leftist-leaning intellectuals, particularly in the halls of ivy, often agree, as do numerous disaffected persons.

But, surprisingly, it is also being heard from conservatives, and this is cause for significant concern and thoughtful consideration. These people have typically held the line, demonstrating a passionate faith in the *Creed*. They well comprehended that consensus bound together America, bringing together the many groups and representing, at its highest levels, humankind's best and most profound political hope. But now many serious conservatives wonder if the *American Creed* and its consensus value system has been swamped by self-seeking humanistic selfishness gone mad.

These people have good cause to wonder, but further analysis allows an answer to the question. The problem has always focused, it should be remembered, on the depth of commitment to the *Creed*. It was Myrdal who explained that in Americans there was a constant battle between their noble, high-level consensus values and their low-level ignoble and shameful behaviors. In this regard, one could maintain an absolute belief in the *Creed*, yet behave badly. Many will rightfully identify this as hypocrisy, a disease shared by all human beings. Knowledgeable scholars romantically wrote that Americans were so deeply committed to the *Creed* that even when their interests were at stake they would honor it. But that is the question: When man's interest is at stake, will he continue to honor the *Creed*?

This was graphically demonstrated in 1998 when the President was being investigated for adultery, lying, and possible obstruction of justice. How did Americans react to the charges? Indeed, a huge number (over sixty percent in polls) rallied behind him, amazed at the flamboyant ability to compartmentalize morality and civic duty. They claimed that morality, truth, loyalty to one's mate had nothing to do with his governing, and there was more than a hint that marriage vows, made before God and man, were of a better time. When such evil is accepted as right, the very existence of the *Creed* as a powerful social force for good is rightfully called to question. Witness the feminists falling all over themselves to back the President because he favored abortion and other radical female positions, an apt example of selling out right for personal gain and defining deviancy down, even accepting the murder of children. Far, far too often, people forsake what the *Creed* has taught them is right for personal gain. This has always been true, but under engineering of the media and humanistic permissiveness of the age the problem has hugely multiplied in geometric progression. As a result, America is a nation in grave crisis. Man's great hope, the American Dream, is in deep jeopardy. Indeed, immoral leaders breed an immoral society, no matter the prosperity of the social order.

Properly taught and learned as a result of instruction in school, home, and church, the Creed will surely improve behavior dramatically, although when personal interest is at stake the nature of humankind will still, and all too often, tilt behavior in humanistic, self-seeking ways. It is rather and finally Christian salvation that is utterly required. On this rock hope abounds, for man's nature needs changing so that even when self-interest is involved he will turn to what is right.

Even with the Creed imbued in the code of behavior, a hierarchy of values exists in every person. Certainly, self-preservation is at or near the top of the list, and values comprising the Creed, though deeply held, often yield to self-interest.

Note, for instance, two presidential elections. A man who is deeply morally flawed (and this perhaps for the first time was common knowledge prior to elections) and whose behavior and ideals were often clearly opposite the Creed was twice elected President of the United States. How in the world did this occur? The first time the economy was in jeopardy and people feared for their jobs and future. At the time of the second election, times were relatively stable. Given the hierarchy of values, the results are understandable--even though voters may have abhorred his values and behaviors. They voted for their pocketbooks and this should not be a surprise.

This does not mean the Creed is dead, but it does raise doubts about commitment to it. Fervent dedication is needed to contest such dangerous attacks at the Creed as occurred in the late 1960's and early 1970's, a shameful period when the youth went mad, led by those who struck viciously at the heart of decency and the *American Creed*. The feeling by wiser people that the American Dream had surrendered to adolescent temper tantrums, anarchy, and criminal behavior was understandable--and they were right. These coddled youth were assuredly not, as the romantics and enemies of the American Dream claimed, noble, although many of them did not participate in the shameful behavior and were admirable young people. The radicals only success was ignoble: the dedicated attempt to trash and destroy the *American Creed*. They thumbed their noses at the very values offering political hope to the nation, substituting, instead, hate (which they called *luv*), anarchy, and chaos.

For a time there was no stopping them. Every single American institution failed to slow their inexorable race toward hedonism, narcissism, and immorality. None failed more than the universities, many of which genuflected to them and, more than is usually understood, led the insurrection by motivating the youth to criminal behavior. In this higher education reached its lowest ebb. Even where faculty were not accomplices, the student tantrums and criminal behavior confounded them; and, tragically, they all too often surrendered to the students instead of having them arrested and prosecuted as should have been done. The very picture of university and college administrators and teachers cowering before students continues to loom large in the taxpayers' minds, and higher education has paid a bitter price for its handling of the situation. The planks of the *Creed* were attacked viciously by the youth. What should have been tomorrow's hope, the hateful, coddled youth, were a most destructive force in damaging the *Creed* and thus the nation.

Finally, many wrote that the nightmare had passed. When President Nixon abolished the draft one summer, the problem moderated dramatically. Then

Sunset of the American Dream

the supposedly noble mentality of the youth was exposed; their self-seeking selfishness became clear. The danger of being drafted was gone, and the evil movement was all but forgotten. The lack of their commitment, short on character, long on threats and bombast, had embarrassed the romantics and leftists who had so praised their behaviors, vision, and dedication. It seemed that, although wounded, the *Creed* had weathered their attacks.

But an annoying problem remained. What type of world would these narcissistic, hedonistic anarchists build when and if they matured? What, indeed, would happen to the *Creed*? Many being college graduates, they would be well represented in decision-making positions in the social order. If they could forsake their pledge not to bathe regularly, dress properly, gain some decorum, and--oh how painful this was to them--learn to work, perhaps, it was thought by many, they could still be functioning Americans and, if miracles still be possible, societal and business leaders.

Two decades passed. Many of the unwashed, those who had not too severely damaged their brains with whatever they smoked, injected, drank, or breathed, who were not in jail, who had deserted the streets, seemed to return to the real world. They wore the proper clothes, improved their hygiene, married for a while, forsook their pledges not to bring children to the evil "Amerika," and even, amazingly, went to work. Many joined liberal churches, the PTA, service organizations, and other such groups. Some people breathed sighs of relief. Perhaps, they hoped, the *Creed* was safe. Maybe, just maybe, it had survived the hate of the radical youth.

This was, of course, wishful thinking. The *American Creed* had been severely damaged; the problem was not remediated. It did seem to many that Ronald Reagan was elected because he was perceived to stand firmly for the *Creed*. It seemed to have withstood the barrage of the 60's and 70's, but the deep problems were not solved. The youth were not yet in positions of power. Now they are, and, finally, their day has come. This, not the 60's and 70's, has become the fabled Age of Aquarius.

The wall of decency, of commitment to the *American Creed*, is constantly being pushed back toward the jungle. The unwashed have stirred, heady with power to influence and alter, but the *Creed* stands in their way. Smoother now, speaking the language of the majority, seemingly more moderate, they maintain much of the old idealism. The *Creed* is under attack. The hippie mentality, now matured and hence more dangerous, bids fair to damage seriously the *American Creed*.

There can be no question but what the *American Creed* has been done much damage in the new Age of Aquarius. Likewise, it should be clear that the disaffected youth of the late 60's and early 70's were a symptom of a far greater problem: the victories of humanistic thinking, the worship of man rather than of God. Add the affluence, selfishness, and arrogance of the movement and a clearer explanation emerges. This does not mean, though, that the *Creed* was dead; however, it does magnify the terrible problem of humanism, the religion in direct competition with God's plan.

Let politicians, teachers, theologians, judges, attorneys, professors, and other decision-makers beware. When the chips are down, when the money is on the table, when the *Creed* is trampled, the people will eventually be heard. The price for standing against the *Creed* is, rightfully, defeat, and this is very good, indeed. Though diminished in the current era due to the educative forces analyzed in this book, the *American Creed* is alive, and it gloriously continues as the political hope for the nation and the family of man.

Nonetheless, there is conspicuous evidence that it is diminished. It must be revitalized, as the schools, homes, and churches do battle to save it. The *Creed* must be taught by these crucial institutions as a fervent social faith, for it is an important political hope with the power and authority to unite the population in building a better social order and in solving the many problems eroding the very soul of the nation. Moreover, the Creed is a wonderful foundation for the next step: Christianity. Despite victories by naysayers to the *Creed*, morality is not dead. There remains guarded optimism, but only if American institutions make teaching the *Creed* a cardinal objective. Schooling absolutely must face this problem directly, as must the home and church. This is education's very most important political calling, for, in the final analysis, it is character, as defined in the *American Creed*, that may very well generate a new vibrant society standing again as the *shining light upon the hill that cannot be hidden.* It is not the final answer, but it is a crucial step in the right direction.

Chapter Two

NIGHT GATHERS: MAN'S OWN RELIGION

This is education's crisis hour, as it is America's time of choice. What happens in the next short period is critical, a fact that Americans should well understand. The contest is precisely the battle of two religions: God's and man's. The strife in America, and thus in schooling, though few people understand it, is between these two views of the very nature of truth itself. Which, in fact, is the proper religion/philosophy on which humankind should build its hope? Christianity or humanism? That this question is even asked indicates the depth of America's crisis.

Believers obviously select Christianity, and this formulates their entire sense of how the youth should be educated by American institutions. Parents can select a church where Christian truth is taught, and they have the responsibility to bring up the youth in the faith. But they most often do not have the choice of where their sons and daughters attend the public schools. This being so, they must understand that most schools stand firmly for the humanistic faith.

Any informative discussion of the matter must begin with an historic examination. During World War II, the epic struggle between freedom and fascism raged; at the same time, the bloody battle between fascism and communism was waged as Hitler warred against Russia. Hitler and his evil Fascism were defeated, although the political philosophy looms as a distinct political threat at all times. At war's end, though, the seeds were sown for the bitter conflict between communism and democracy. The resounding clash of these two great forces lasted from the end of the world conflict until the amazing fall of the Soviet Union and, really, European communism in 1992.

During these contentious years, many believing Christians joined others in judging communism to be a horrible evil. These people were quite right in identifying communism as a formidable evil faith looming to battle the religion of Jesus Christ for the hearts and souls of humankind. Numerous believers felt that Marxism was a world-wide demonic plot, reaching to the highest echelons of the American government, that must be contested on every front--from politics, to the entertainment industry, to the World Council of

Churches, to liberal churches, and, surely, to the public schools. The effects of the struggle were felt across the nation in the hamlets, towns, and great cities.

Many humanists, the university, church, and mass media liberals, were in a state of shock as their socialist/communist dreams evaporated, but they still found time to ridicule those who had battled the humanistic nightmare. The battles had been noble, indeed, even if there were a measure of paranoia. Of this believers were sure: The Christian faith is the only hope of the world and of fallen man. The people were, beyond a doubt, correct in uunderstanding that communism was a terrible threat, and that it had to be battled. Finally, the evil world religion had fallen.

But was this great conquest over godless communism the total victory that believers had hoped for? The answer is both *yes* and *no*. An evil force had been, at least for the foreseeable future, defeated; however, the genuine enemy was humanism--and it remained untouched. Because the victory over communism was/is no more than a win over one wing of humanism, the contention goes on between the religion of God and the religion of man.

It is to be seen in every facet of life, sadly even the church, and it is the very organizing principle of public schooling. The taxpayers cannot control the mass media, the peer group, and most liberal institutions. But the taxpayers do own the schools, and they have every right, indeed, obligation, to do honorable battle against the humanistic movement in the schools. This is critical because the humanistic doctrines are from nearly every source indoctrinating them. It should be said, too, that the people can control their churches, and it is incumbent upon them to rid themselves of humanistic, unbelieving pastors. To a degree, then, they can affect both the schools and the churches they attend. These are no little hopes in the battles against humanism.

WHAT IS HUMANISM?

The American Encyclopedia, 1983, defines humanism in this manner: "[It is] an educational and philosophic outlook, that emphasizes the personal worth of the individual and the central importance of human values as opposed to religious belief." In 1933, the *Humanist Manifesto* asserted, "Humanism is the faith in the supreme values and self-perfectibility of human personality." *The Encyclopedia Britannica*, 1983, suggested, "In recent years the term *humanism* has often been used to refer to value systems that emphasize the personal worth of each individual but that do not include a belief in God." Much of the history of the philosophy/religion was quite glorious. The roots of the movement were in ancient Greece and Rome, and

Night Gathers: Man's Own Religion

it was very popular and influential in Europe from the 1300s through the 1500's. The greatness of man, his philosophy, literature, and art, grew and grew, making of him a kind of god. The influence still permeates the arts and higher education, indeed, the very ideals that influence widely the highly educated and the socially elite.

This philosophy/religion has a most profound influence on the nation. In fact, the word *humanities* is the goal of the educated person in arts and sciences. The studies typically include philosophy, language, history, the arts, and *humanized* religion. Included, also, is a dedicated effort to find the meaning in life, but increasingly the theological has been left out as a possible answer.

But how, many ask, can such a noble seeking after truth and knowledge be viewed by Christians as evil? After all, they might reason, the humanists mean well, and they are approaching their search as scholars and gentlemen. Any reaction against this noble philosophy could be a reactionary, ignorant attack by Christians who are guilty of stereotyping. No, evil, they would assert, is not to be found among the humanists; they are what education works to produce.

Nonetheless, humanism is the great evil in America, and it is particularly dangerous because it seems so right. Man is at the center of all things, and all answers result from his ability to solve problems. He is himself a god who has no time whatsoever for the God of the *Bible*. Through devoting himself to his perfection, he can make a perfect world by studying what man has accomplished. The biblical truths may be beautiful literature, but they are not the *Word of God Almighty*. God, they believe, is irrelevant or non-existent, a product of man's fertile imagination. Man, not God, is the measure of all things.

If men do not worship God, they have primarily two other choices: to worship themselves or nothing whatsoever. Great social orders cannot be built on self-worship or quitting. If there is no hope, men are miserable as they dejectedly wait for life's end and nothing more. If they believe in themselves alone, morality fades away, as they too often define right by the way they profit from their actions. Add to this the rationalization of their own evil thinking and behaviors, and the portrait of a nation at crisis is drawn. Moreover, any honest person, no matter how moral, surely recognizes the depravity of his own nature. He should surely recognize the evil just below the surface waiting to be drawn forth in certain situations. Any intelligent study of history supports this claim, and it largely explains the fall of great civilizations.

Man without God is lost, no matter his claims. Existentialism and nihilism would, if man were God, be worthy explanations of the universe, but there is no hope without God; hence, humanism can in the long run only destroy social orders. Man's hope began on a cross about two thousand years ago, and with the Messiah, the Lamb of God Who took the sins of man on Himself to save all men who take Him as Savior. Humanism, destroyer of social orders and men's souls, offers no lasting hope whatsoever.

The humanistic faith is packaged so nicely, presented so reasonably; but every word of it, every action, everything, attacks God's truth. And it is the very organizing principle of the schools and too often of the homes and churches. It is no wonder whatsoever that humanism is quite rightly identified by believers as the great problem. In the schools, humanistic instruction abounds in ways that most people fail to recognize. From morning to night, from day to day, from week to week, from year to year, it is drummed into the minds and habits of the students at school. The problem is far more serious than nearly anyone knows. The many evangelical writers who evaluate schooling's problems typically point the finger of accusation at possible federal control of schooling, but they overrate its power in the present time. Humanism is the essential problem, not only of the schools but of the nation itself, particularly since the homes and churches have so often joined the schools in proclaiming its authenticity.

HIGHER EDUCATION

Universities and colleges extol an almost mystical belief in the *liberal arts* and in the *humanities*, both coming from and ever linked with humanism. One of us was a student and professor in a large state university for over five decades and heard daily the deification of these two words issued by professors with the same awe and respect that Christians feel for God. Perhaps the most important lesson was that the humanities with all the claims about the greatness of man, surely do not produce humane persons. Indeed, in higher education, there is more backbiting, hate, envy, and smallness of character than in many professions. The vaccination of humanism is impotent. If man is to be changed for the better, there is only one cure: a trip to the Cross of Jesus Christ--and college education, all too often, moves him in the opposite direction.

Higher education is a prime wrongdoer for the reasons just analyzed and because its humanistic faith is often in direct disagreement with the *American Creed*. Moreover, the professors, too often divorced from social, political and theological reality, live and hide from reality in the ivory tower, itself far removed from the real world. In spite of those liberals who write that the nation be controlled by *experts*, that is to say university theorists, the truth is that such persons must not make policy for the nation. Disaster would ensue.

The dangerous socialistic, humanistic anti-American sentiments displayed by many dreaming utopian dreams from the shelter of the academy must be resisted by every thinking person. Their research should be received, studied, and, when useful, utilized by non-academics in the decision-making process. Beyond that, the university humanists have little worthy to say about politics or morality.

IS HUMANISM A RELIGION?

Christians had high hopes that the U.S. Supreme Court would finally rule that humanism is a religion. The High Court did make that ruling, but tempered it by declaring that the religion could be taught in the schools because it is part of the consensus American value system. If, indeed, the Court's decision had been otherwise, every area of school content could have been contested as teaching religion; believers would have had the ammunition to halt the humanistic excesses in the schools based on the *First Amendment* to the *Constitution*.

Nonetheless, there is reason to believe that a humanistically oriented schooling would not anger many who claim the name of Jesus Christ. Mounting data makes clear that multiplied hundreds of thousands of people who claim to be Christian subscribe to many of the ideals and values of humanism. Many, in fact, attend old-line churches which formerly preached the gospel of Jesus Christ and now stand firmly for humanistic philosophy and psychology. They still use the language of Christianity, but the words actually have humanistic meanings. They have sold out the faith to the humanistic religion. These people would very likely support the humanistic procedures in the schools, while asserting and believing that they are Christian. Among these, believers fighting the school procedures would seem to be radicals and religious fanatics.

It was predictable yet tragic that the High Court failed to understand that humanism is a religion subject to the *First Amendment*. If not, then consensus Christianity, itself a religion, should be taught in the schools. Like any religion, humanism has a stated dogma, perhaps best identified in John Dewey's *Human Manifesto* and Paul Kurtz's *Human Manifesto II*. Important planks of the doctrine are atheism, evolution, amorality, self-centered man not needing God, and a socialistic, one-world view of the planet. All of these, of course, are in direct opposition to the *American Creed*. Atheism denies God; man, then, must save himself. Evolution holds that the biblical interpretation of creation is false. If God is not to be trusted and man is, then amorality and immorality are predictable. Virtuous man, who perceives himself a god, could hardly do wrong. Certainly there is no sin. Autonomous, self-made man is a cornerstone of the religion. Basically good, corrupted only by institutions, he is the measure of all things. Hence, humankind is responsible to no authority save its own admirable conscience. Because acceptable values are what each person defines them to be, absolutes are an outdated concept. Such a philosophy leads to ruin.

How are the planks of humanism apparent in schooling? Too often, they appear in these teachings: evolution is a fact; youth are their own authorities; values are relative; there is no supernatural; morality should not be part of public schooling; the youth have the right to read and listen to whatever they want; a world view is better than patriotism; socialism is preferable to private ownership; and man's reason is the highest level of hope.

Again, however, there are numerous public school Christian teachers, believing churches, and Christian parents who represent a valuable underground to work against the humanistic schooling. They labor with dedication to teach that there are two views of creation: the biblical and evolutionary--and both are theories, not science. They conduct their instruction to show that the children are not their own authorities. They teach the *American Creed* as the truth, and the youth learn that there are absolutes. They legally teach in their classes that Christianity was an important factor in American history. They speak in favor of morality in sex. They limit reading to those works supporting the *American Creed*. Finally, they proudly and correctly teach the superiority of freedom over all other types of government and the importance of patriotism. Some teach all of these things; others just some. Make no mistake--they are heroes.

PREPARATION OF TEACHERS

The humanities, liberal arts, and colleges of education typically control the state-directed agenda in preparing teachers for the public schools. This is so because colleges of arts and sciences, the humanities departments, are comprised of so many academic specialties that by sheer numbers they control university politics. To the utter chagrin of these departments, colleges of education are included by state law, though liberals are working fervently to remove them from the picture. There is bad blood between the two groups, with the exalted humanities professors looking down at colleges of education, as they issue attacks at *trade school mentality*. The colleges of business, medicine, and others having some connection to the real world typically have fewer faculty and thus less political power, thus placing the influence in the hands of the people less aware of the real world and more likely to be disciples of humanism.

Faculty mind set is also important to consider. Liberal education (humanism) often leads to the ideal that an earned PhD allows a knowledge of all things, and a sense of superiority and arrogance is fostered. These faculty believe that they must operate and control the college or university, and administrators are distrusted, even hated. Faculty, many of whom cannot change a tire or do much of anything away from the halls of ivy, lobby to run the entire university--even though they are no more than mere employees. Leadership is denied and decried.

The very nature of professional preparation constantly narrows their teaching and research so that they become true experts in a narrow aspect of a specialty. To stretch themselves beyond this preparation is arrogance.

This in part explains why the power war is ever waged in higher education. Unfortunately, politics, for which most professors have not been professionally prepared, become the first business of many, perhaps most, faculty as they endeavor to understand a real world, too often beyond their comprehension. This is so because they are operating in a university or college, most surely not at all like the real world; they often live in a socialistic environment, ever--and this should be terribly embarrassing--*politically correct* and as far from the American social order and its dream as socialism from democracy.

Neither research nor teaching is the main business of many faculty in higher education, no matter their claims. Politics are. Only one who has spent a career in the academic atmosphere could understand the stark truth of this fact, as the professors, forgetting the beautiful humanistic claims, scrap for what few benefits are available to them. Nonetheless, the romantic humanists have the votes and set the agenda--as the magical words *humanities* and *liberal arts* float like romantic zephyrs through the ivory towers, so very removed from reality and, far, far more important, from the kingdom of God.

It is no wonder, then, that in the overwhelming number of universities and colleges, save the Christian ones, students are immersed in the philosophy and religion of humanism. Yes, the universities have, indeed, prepared the beginning teachers for the humanistic agenda in the schools. But the blame transcends the institutions of higher education. Nearly every societal entity conspires to deify man, even the liberal churches. Consider the mass media, laws, politics, and the growing aggregate of societal forces that teach and enlarge the humanistic faith and philosophy. Ultimately, it should be no surprise whatsoever that the Christian parent is sending his offspring into enemy territory that dangles what seems so beautiful, so very reasonable, so sweet: the powerful religion of humanism.

SUNSET OF AMERICA
THE MULTICULTURAL, PLURALISTIC TRAGEDY

In the last few years, humanistic mentality, misreading man's nature and the greatness of the United States, too often cast its votes for multiculturalism, a grave error that has yet to reach its most dangerous levels.

Balint Vazsonyi, a survivor of Communism and Nazism and Director for the Center for American Founding, issued this warning in a 1997 speech at Hillsdale College:

> What is multiculturalism if not a redistribution of our cultural heritage?...We have been ordered by the prophets of social justice to replace our common American identity with multiculturalism. One cannot fail to notice the enormous importance the leaders of the social justice crowd attach to the eradication of American identity. They insist on bilingual educations and multilingual ballots. They remove the founding documents from our schools. They enforce anti-American history standards. They banish the Ten Commandments. Add to this the replacement of American competence with generic "self-esteem" and voluntarism with coercion. Consider the vast numbers of new immigrants who are encouraged to ignore the very reasons that brought them to America in the first place.

On the surface, at least, it seemed that the idea might have merit. Who, indeed, could argue with a procedure that would better prepare those whose primary language was not English to learn the new language more quickly and completely?

In this regard, a bill of goods was sold educators, politicians, and even minority groups, as well. Instruct the child early in his own language and build on it by studying his own culture, and the projected result will be the learning of English and the American culture more quickly, a supposition, incidentally, that was not supported by the bulk of research studies. The force of the movement came from the U.S. Congress, although it was actually the brain child of liberal university humanists and minority groups flexing new muscles developed in the civil rights movement. Politics were also critical; the growing numbers of blacks and Hispanics represented votes, more than twenty percent of the population. Liberal Democratic legislators joined by some Republicans, falling over themselves to court the voters, passed the Bilingual-Bicultural Act. Until the presidency of Ronald Reagan, programs for Hispanic youth were rarely funded unless the instruction was in the native or street language of the youth; and the programs reached far beyond blacks and Hispanics, including Asians and other groups whose numbers were growing in the nation. In fact, any non-English speaking group of twenty persons enrolled in a given school district was to be instructed in its own language. Such an approach, it was widely argued, would better prepare the youth for entrance into the American social order and would foster a far better self-concept.

But the historic objectives of schooling were in jeopardy. The very cardinal objective that characterized American schooling was forgotten. No longer was the goal to produce Americans, but to reconstruct the social order so that each ethnic and racial grouping's identity should be the central factor in a person's life and the nation's destiny. The goal had changed from producing Americans who accepted and shared the *Creed* that had so distinguished the nation, substituting, instead, enraptured claims for pluralism, the celebration of a few of the various social groupings comprising the nation.

This had occurred from and in the bilingual, bi-cultural programs. Many racial, ethnic, and gender-oriented groups understood that such teaching was political and thus a prime method to gain a platform of power. It was then that the movement turned unpleasant. The power grab was predictable given the morality of the times. The selfishness of the era authored the situation--even though many of those posturing for new power felt that they were forces of good. Nothing could have been further from the truth.

The multi-cultural aspects of schooling changed dramatically. No longer was it simply language. Then it was literature, social problems, history, values, and countless other social areas of ethnic, racial, gender, and other subgroups. The damage and danger were that the unifying principle of schooling, the doorway to success as part of the majority, was severely challenged. In deep distress was the historic and correct ideal to offer all groups schooling preparing them to become Americans.

This objective had been and remained noble, the goal being to take persons of varying ethnic and racial backgrounds and to make of them a new people, a great people, identified as Americans. This hallowed goal beckoned the disenfranchised and put-upon of the globe to the nation's shores, and it was clear that within the second generation of their arrival in America their ethnic and racial backgrounds had eroded hugely. People quite rightly identified themselves as Americans who shared in the creed of the nation. The primary calling of the schools in working with the minority young people was to prepare them for full acceptance into the middle-class social order. Families and, sometimes, churches continued to teach the old ways--and this was as it should have been. In each succeeding generation, however, the old ways diminished--and this was good. They became Americans, and this, too, was as it should have been, no matter the claims of ethnic romantics to the contrary.

Many Americans have an abiding interest in and aversion to this horrible multicultural development. As written earlier, the *American Creed* is substantially based on Christian ethics and behaviors. It is more than important that the *Creed* remain in force; at least the Christian values would, more or less, remain in place. The humanistic free-fall into the scrap heap of history would be delayed.

Also, the acceptance of new aliens into the nation has changed significantly. Formerly, the huge percentage of new Americans came from Europe, a people who shared the Christian heritage. Now relatively few Europeans are accepted, and those who come from other parts of the world are often not Christian. If their own ways were taught in the classrooms, the Christian influence would surely decrease. To be sure, freedom of worship is an important part of the *Creed* and surely the right of all Americans--and it should be. Yet the Christian base of the nation is severely threatened if the schools veer from the Christian values influencing the *Creed*.

Moreover, and this is very important, multicultural programs do not have the blessings of the majority of Americans who will, as indicated earlier, have their way with the schools they own. The arrogance of elites who control the schooling establishment in forcing multiculturalism could promise defeat for the misadventure, but, for this to happen, concerned Americans must become personally and politically active in attacking the movement.

It can, then, be written with authority that the rapidly growing program to teach multicultural pluralism, particularly ethnicity as a desirable societal goal, is a grave error, both for the nation and its minority groups. No concern in the public schools is more important, for surely the lesson of history is that unchecked diversity in the social order, the cancer of increasing lack of agreement between the peoples comprising the nation, leads to social crisis and chaos. It does, indeed, become a self-fulfilling prophecy of dissolution and defeat.

For the first time in its long history, public schooling can cause lasting harm. If the multicultural misadventure is not halted, the American republic could be forced to surrender to factional and tribal turmoil and lostness; crime, now epidemic, might very well become an implacable war in the streets.

CONSENSUS

The need for agreement among the people comprising the nation has already been analyzed. It is, therefore, shocking to understand that it has all but been abandoned in the current headlong rush to multiculturalism. If this

Night Gathers: Man's Own Religion

were the only charge against the movement, it would be quite enough to abolish the effort. And surely the pluralistic nightmare transcends the schools reaching to every institution in the nation. All the elite educating forces chipped away at the *Creed*.

The cost is too much to pay when American institutions, in this case schooling, champion ideas leading to separatism. A primary goal of schooling, then, is to instruct toward agreement among the many peoples and groups comprising the nation and to teach them a decision-making process using the *American Creed* in areas where there is not agreement.

THE BEGINNING OF MULTICULTURALISM

It is profitable to examine more carefully how the movement developed. Several forces fueled the school programs, including federal law and legislation, humanistic philosophy and psychology, a confusion about the values that had distinguished America, and substantial affluence.

Joining others, these factors led to changing goals in preparing teachers for the public schools. In all of this, the universities and colleges where the immoral authoritarian *political correctness* had been established took the lead--to the eternal shame of higher education. The philosophy of this development includes a huge abhorrence of the United States and its dear dream. Humanistic to the core, the movement represents a firm commitment to keep God out of the schools, to hate capitalism, to distrust the great, ennobling American documents, to preach that all evil is relative to the situation causing it, to be socialistic (often Marxist) in political orientation, to have complete disdain for believing Christians, to believe that the federal government should control all things, to rewrite American history to identify America, particularly the men, as a nation of murderers, criminals, and rascals, to believe that America is certainly no better than any other nation (quite likely the worst of them all), and to deny the biblical roles of men and women.

In the late 1960's and early 1970's, numerous university faculty shared a smoldering loathing of America. Their attacks often focused on distrust of the agreed-upon American values, the planks of the *Creed*. Such business appealed to adolescents aflame with emotions of revolution against their environment. The professors played to their idealism, attacking the *Creed*. The teachers posed consensus as corrupt or nonexistent, and they recommended cultural pluralism as necessary and crucial for ethnic groups. The obvious result of this instruction was to convince many gullible students that the *Creed* was an empty social ideal and that every group should do its own thing. In such university programs the seeds of the multicultural tragedy were sown; and, unfortunately, the weeds, the tares, have sprouted and prospered. The liberal professors were even more successful than they had hoped.

But there were also good, well-meaning people who out of guilt or love were dedicated to helping minority youth. Dedicated to ego-building in students, they often assigned ethnic students to study their origins and taught them the importance of a pluralistic social order made up of neighborhoods and ethnic islands in the cities, each celebrating its own origins and cultural values; and all of this was to replace the consensus *American Creed*.

Unfortunately, however, noble intentions often do not lead to admirable results. So it was with this effort. As indicated earlier, research does not support the efforts. Surely, these educators have not understood the serious societal problems in the former Soviet Union, Quebec, the Balkans, or modern Ireland. Their study of the American Civil War must have been lacking as well as their reading about ancient Athens and Sparta.

The problems are far more complex than they suppose, reaching to the very core of human nature. These teachers believe that a study of minorities will result in an understanding and appreciation of these groups. School can, then, legislate peace and love between the various groups in America. One wonders why this approach does not more often succeed, why, for instance, race problems at universities are said to be worsening. The multiculturalists typically refuse the research findings in social psychology that the individual person or group is far more often accepted by other groups if believed to be "one of us," that is to say like those in the group to be joined. This being the case, the multicultural steamroller is moving on shifting sand, acting to hurt badly the very people whom it is endeavoring to help. Because such school programs lead to separation and second-class citizenship, the romantics are gambling with the futures of minority youth; and they are doing damage to the nation, as well.

The movement had begun with blacks, where it stalled after some years because separatism was the worst plan in a time when the doors opened to them. After long and sometimes bloody battles, blacks tended to become practical. Yes, black was beautiful, but they came to understand that the goal must be to gain middle-class membership in order to succeed. For a period in the late 1970's and early 1980's, good sense returned; the young black youth were prepared to succeed in middle-class America, a move in the right direction. But dissident voices still cried out for separation and warfare, and they were heard. As a result, too much time was spent on black history, literature, culture, and street language. This ethnic extremism extracted a terrible price: the omission of schooling preparing the youth to join the middle-class American culture and the majority society. A powerful lesson had been learned by many in the black community.

But the lesson had not been so promptly learned by other minority peoples and separatist groups. In the middle 1970s, a similar romantic schooling philosophy gained status for Hispanics, women, homosexuals, American Indians and other disaffected social groups. To the surprise of those who understood the situation, many of the multicultural groupings in America were not included. Left out were socioeconomic classes, religious groups, geographical regions, vocations, and religions. In many or most cases, each of these was more important than ethnicity, race, or gender, a fact pointing to the unfortunate political nature of the multicultural misadventure. After the black separatist surge in the schools of the late 60's and early 70's had given way to good judgment and practicality opening the door to the marketplace, the Hispanic phase began with optimistic claims for multicultural school programs. Here the multicultural movement gained power. To knowledgeable educators, multicultural came to mean multi-Hispanic, and a dreadful narrowness invaded the public schools. The lessons learned from the black separatist schooling were all but forgotten, the purpose of schooling obscured. This situation became worse when blacks rediscovered the earlier demands, and women, American Indians, homosexuals, and other groups coveting political action and power demanded a piece of schooling's multicultural agenda.

Other ethnic groups which were not included must have stood in wonder that they were left out and surely must have understood the political nature of the senseless movement. Irish, Poles, Italians, Sicilians, Greeks and countless other groups did not study the literature, history, and ways of their people. This truth alone indicates the lack of integrity and the political nature of the false movement.

WHAT ABOUT BLACKS AND HISPANICS?

One of the claims of the romantics is that blacks and Hispanics had tried to become one with the American middle class but they had, to a large degree, been shut out. Thus, the argument rages, the *American Creed* has failed. It is true that these two peoples cannot point to success in the same way or to the same degree as many persons of European heritage; school programs based on teaching the consensus *Creed* have not resulted in optimum equal opportunity and/or achievement. It is further so that they struggled in a racist social order in which Americans were certainly not living up to the *Creed*.

Many young, rightfully impatient, blacks rediscovered the idea of separation, a position in disagreement with Dr. Martin Luther King's demands that his people must be allowed, as the *Creed* promises, full acceptance into the American social order. Many blacks, though probably not a majority, lost patience. Separation seemed best to them, and, for many of them, rage exploded. Also, many of them turned to an Afro-centric view. They believed that they were Africans, not Americans; and the culture of Africa, greater than anyone had earlier supposed, was to be the focus of their study and reasoning. The preserving of the African culture was to be the first business of schooling.

This alliance with Africa is ludicrous. This is so, first, because on the African continent, huge and pluralistic, there are countless cultures; certainly there is little or no homogeneity. The claim that there is (or was) an overarching African culture is patently false. Secondly, a huge percentage of blacks are Americans by any definition of the word. Many go back six to ten generations. Though horribly militated against by racism, they have helped build this nation. It makes about as much sense for a black to believe that he is African as any person to base his ethnicity on the claim that he is a Garden of Edenist. The success of blacks lies in their identification as Americans--even though they have legitimate cause to feel wrath toward the whites who misused and mistreated them.

But the black multicultural programs have resulted in schooling that is unacceptable. It is predictable that many blacks would hate whites--that there is reason for doing so. Slavery is boldly attacked, and it should be. But the truth should be known, and it is often disguised in the attempt to rewrite history. Slavery is typically identified by multiculturalists as a white conspiracy. Though there is much blame to be levied, the fact is that blacks themselves captured their brothers and sisters, sold them to Arabs, who sold them to American whites. In no way does this justify the horrible racist slavery that subjugated the blacks. Every nation has its shame--and this America certainly did and does. In large part, the United States was living a lie, disrespecting the *Creed*. It should be remembered, though, that the defeat of slavery did not come from any African culture, but from the morality and judicial system of the United States. And from the time of Abraham Lincoln, there has been a wavering yet basically steady improvement in the social situation for blacks. Always, in all social orders, barring a rapid change in life conditions, such change comes slowly. This is a shame, but it is true. And it surely remains true that blacks in this nation are American, not African; and they must, if the nation honors its *Creed*, be allowed the opportunity to compete, succeed, and gain admittance into the majority with the right to earn the dignity and success that is their constitutional and moral right.

How then is the door to equal opportunity and citizenship to be opened to blacks, and for that matter to Hispanics as well? Governmental actions provide the legal machinery where constitutional rights are not allowed. In this legislation and Supreme Court decisions are important and necessary. But another solution, and about this you may be sure, transcends governmental actions and legal machinery. It happens as the minorities become attached to the majority, as they become one with them, as they become an integral part of the majority society and culture.

They must, in fact, conceive of themselves as Americans, not Africans. Until this happens, no amount of governmental laws, social engineering, claims of the romantics, or any other actions will lead to a lasting solution of the terrible racism directed toward black Americans. Every action of the schools (and every American institution) must be to open the doors of middle-class membership to all groups. For this reason, any prolonged efforts in schooling to feature ethnicity is an action in disregard of the best for the entire scope of minority students.

Also, it is important to understand that many blacks in the last thirty years have entered the American middle class. They have most often succeeded because of their entrance into the majority social order. These middle-class blacks have not sold out to the enemy, the *white devils*, as some segregationists claim; instead, they have sensibly accommodated themselves to the social and cultural environment in which they will compete and live. They have, to a large degree, joined the American majority middle class. The wisdom of this choice is demonstrated in their ability to succeed in the nation's marketplace and to enjoy dignity as Americans.

Those who claim that entering the American middle class social order is selling heritage for security may accurately be seen as racist, a form of selling a culture and race apart. The fact is that minority people are living in America, a nation with an overriding national social order and culture. The nation has many subcultures, of which ethnicity and race are but two. The youth have typically understood the importance of becoming Americans, as have their parents. It is liberal politicians and hate groups which preach otherwise that are doing serious damage to the very people they claim to represent. And becoming part of the majority, blacks and Hispanics have power to influence the majority, building, at least in theory, a better social order. Witness, for example, the effect of black music and athletics on American entertainment and sports, the influence of Latin foods on American dining, and a host of other ethnic influences on the social order. Such developments allow minorities not just to influence the majority but to add to, join, and enrich it.

Moreover, and this many multiculturalists refuse, much of what has been identified as ethnic is, in fact, more accurately identified as socioeconomic class. What the romantics refer to as black culture, or ethnic culture, actually should be better identified as social class. In the black multicultural school programs, there is wide agreement that the ethnic culture should be taught the youth. But what black culture? Upper class? Middle class? Lower class? It may surprise the reader to know that, most often, lower-class black culture is taught, romanticized, and considered to be *the* black culture. The result is a tragedy, for lower-class black culture programs present a hidden culture of poverty that will often seal the youth into a life of failure. Such programs discard the key that unlocks the door to lasting dignity, which is upward mobility into the mainstreams of the majority.

Hispanics have become as politicized as blacks in demanding a multicultural program for the youth, an ideal that is also deeply flawed. Hispanics, too, must prepare themselves for membership in the American social order. Most Hispanic parents understand this, but the outcries of radicals excite the mass media, which, in turn, makes it seem as if the few revolutionaries actually represent their people.

In this regard, the problems become huge; there are numerous Hispanic peoples in the United States, several of whose cultures differ. Among these social groupings are Mexicans, Puerto Ricans, Cubans, Haitians, and others. There are often ill feelings between these peoples, and, in the great cities, bloody warfare. They need all to be Americans who share a common culture.

SCHOOLING FOR JEWISH YOUTH

The situation has been far different for Jewish youth than for blacks and Hispanics. The Jews have been the most mistreated of all peoples in their long history. If blacks and Hispanics say that their physical appearance has made it nearly impossible to succeed in America, a similar problem exists for the Hebrews. For decades before World War II in America, they suffered terribly, perhaps worse than blacks and Hispanics since the war.

Jewish parents, however, did not demand that the schools teach Hebrew heritage. Rather, they felt that their children must be socially prepared to compete and excel in the majority society, a lesson learned in the painful trials of their people. Schooling was to serve the purpose of enabling competition on a fair basis with others, not on the basis of having their Jewishness taught to them in public schools. The result has been the outstanding record of persons of Jewish extraction serving with distinction in the most demanding of professional roles: in law, medicine, theology, business, and the arts.

Central to the Jewish success in America was the role of the public schools in bringing the youth into the American society and culture regardless of national origin, race, or creed. From the family, the synagogue, the peer group, and weekend private schools, the Jewish people received instruction, coupled with justifiable pride, in their heritage. From the public schools, they expected and received a full immersion into the values, ideas, and skills of the American culture. It is clear why the multiculturalists choose not to talk about the Jews.

WHAT ABOUT ASIAN YOUTH?

Nor do the multiculturists want to talk much about Asian students. In many respects, their parents' views of schooling are similar to those of the Jews. Subject to terrible treatment in the days when they were hired to build railroads and to labor for minimal salaries, they quite rightly, over time, understood the crucial importance of entering the American culture. The fact that part of their cultural heritage included the work ethic was a compelling reason for their success, and the demands they made of the schools were practical. Indeed, they demanded that the schools prepare their children to become part of the American social order and that the youth be held to high, demanding academic standards. At home, the youth were taught to excel. The result was the remarkable success of these people, whose achievement is absolutely amazing, and this is not to suggest that their upbringing and education negated their Asian backgrounds. But, properly, this instruction occurred in home, worship, and peer group. This is, of course, education as it should be.

THE MELTING POT AGAIN

One of the popular arguments for the teaching of ethnic backgrounds is the teaching of aliens who are arriving either legally or illegally in the United States in unprecedented numbers. It must be remembered, however, that the problems of educating new Americans is neither new nor unique in the nation. Recall, for instance, that in 1890 one-quarter of Philadelphians and one-third of Bostonians were foreign-born; and by the turn of the century eighty percent of New York residents had been born abroad. The success in educating these people to fit well into the society and culture of the American social order, particularly in the second and third generations, has been a highly successful model for the free world. Schooling played an important part in this amazing success story, and it was accomplished by endeavoring to educate all people to be Americans and to have the values and skills to fit well into the social order.

In schooling the approach was called the *melting pot* which now, to the terrible detriment of both new Americans and the nation, has fallen into disrespect. The multiculturalists absolutely hate the melting pot ideal, substituting what is sometimes named the *salad bowl*.

The *melting pot* must be rediscovered and implemented in the nation's schools, churches, and families. From the early days of colonial America until the 1970's, the ideal of the nation was to build Americans. The notion--and it was surely correct--was that America is a very special nation, better than any other. New Americans, then, were to leave their alien cultures at home and to become the great new breed of people called Americans. Aliens understood this and honored it. Why not? America was their land of dreams held fast by the *Creed* with its important Christian influence. God had touched the United States in a special, beautiful manner. Americans were a great people, and the social order along with its institutions guided the new Americans into the nation--and this was good. The schools were to do everything possible to meld each person into being an American. Old ways were left at home. This view of schooling was noble and, more importantly, right. Though not eliminating hate and racism, it helped even the playing field for minority peoples.

But the counterculture in the disastrous late 1960's and early 1970's did profound damage to the melting pot ideal. As indicated earlier, the worst of the youth of the era did what may be irredeemable damage to both schooling and the nation. Frightfully ignorant of America's greatness, they tried to trash the very nation that was the beacon of hope to humankind. Since, as they foolishly reasoned, America is a cruel, authoritarian nation, schooling must not be allowed to become a melting pot producing more selfish, unworthy people. To build Americans, they believed, was to perpetuate the evil capitalistic society. Many of them, deeply admiring socialism and, too often, communism, dedicated themselves to destroying the very *Creed* that had helped build man's greatest nation. Another important reason for so doing was to attack the religion of Jesus Christ, for a Marxian, by definition, hates Christianity, seeing it as Marx did, "an opiate of the masses."

And for the present, they have won victories; the greatest damage of all their gains was the debasement and weakening of the melting pot theory. Instead, they spoke vigorously about the *salad bowl*. Romantic claims rhapsodized the silly title. After all, they insisted, a melding is like putting all sorts of beautiful vegetables into a blender, the result being a grayish, ugly color; and this, their strange reasoning went, is symbolic of the *melting pot*. Ah, but the *salad bowl* is beautiful. Nothing is changed. There are the gorgeous red tomatoes, beautiful green lettuce, magnificent orange carrots, and all the other impressive colors of the vegetables. It is a veritable rainbow of beauty. And then there is the strange analogy of this salad bowl with schooling: All people, they claim, are beautiful, like the vegetables in the salad. They should not be melded into anything. Their very differences are wonderful, and, in a pluralistic nation like America, they should remain what

Night Gathers: Man's Own Religion

they are. No capitalistic social order, certainly not an evil nation like America, has the right to make them something they are not. Should these romantic humanists succeed, the United States will be deep in crisis, its golden dream spinning toward the scrap heap of history.

This would be a tremendous victory for radical humanists. Based on their false notion of man's innate goodness and right action, the nation would be in shambles, its Christian base all but destroyed if God permits the humanist victories. The *American Creed* would be dead, and the nation would be thrown back into a social jungle of each group fighting each other. Mankind's greatest social order stands on the edge of the abyss leading to the scrap heap of history. And the salad-bowl schooling practices, primarily the disastrous multiculturalism, would be a major cause of the failure.

All of this is not to say that the *melting pot* was an unqualified success. There were profound failures, particularly with Americans of non-European backgrounds; however, overall, the victories were quite grand. There is no justifiable reason to turn to pluralistic schooling based on ethnicity and race. Instead, the *melting pot* is the schooling model that is worthy of being intensified, updated, and reinvigorated to complete the task so well begun.

The *melting pot*, properly understood and implemented, offers much hope, not only to ethnics but also to the range of multicultural people. The new Americans must join all other multicultural groupings to build a people who share in allegiance to the consensus *American Creed*. They must surely all be educated by the schools (and all American institutions) to become Americans who with pride, love, and tears of joy become one with the most notable *Creed* that has beckoned the dispossessed of the globe. America must not be ripped apart by radical pluralists; the nation must not be driven into angry groups fighting with each other. And using schooling to help gain this terrible goal intensifies the frightening travesty.

Famed social prophet W. O. Stanley perhaps verbalized it best in his book *Social Foundations of Education*:

> Our common values are of the utmost importance. They are the only threads which are holding us back from the brink of disaster. If our gravest problems are to be solved at all, they must be solved in terms of our common ultimate values. There is no basis for adjustment. Indeed, the danger is that in the struggle of opposing programs the loyalty to common values will be lost, that class struggle will degenerate into class war. Then men would come to deny the principles of human dignity and of democracy in the interest of programs to benefit certain classes.

MORE MODERATE VIEWS

There are those who will claim that the preceding section overstates the danger of multicultural programs, that it is quite possible to take a moderate view that will not attack the consensus *American Creed*. Such a program would begin study with an ethnic addendum by starting instruction in the language and culture of the student. The other would focus on a comprehensive instruction of nearly all of the ethnic cultures and socioeconomic classes, geographical regions, races, vocations, genders, and other areas truly representing multicultural. The second of these is quite different from the typical multicultural agenda, and there is some reason to believe that it might be worthy.

Concerning the first of the views, there is deep trouble. A political hue and cry of the first magnitude has accompanied attempts to begin a child's schooling with his ethnic language and culture. If acceptable research should substantiate that the child would more quickly and effectively be absorbed into the American mainstream in this manner, such an approach might be acceptable. If, however, such documentation does not exist, there is no acceptable reason for teaching the child in his own language and culture. At present, the weight of supporting research does not support the method.

The second of the views deserves further consideration, for on the surface it seems a good idea that Americanized students study the various subcultures comprising the whole. The serious error displayed by the romantics is that they focus only on the ethnic when, in fact, far more important are socioeconomic class, vocational groupings, regional differences, age influences, and sex roles. Any multicultural study should include all of these in depth. How very shortsighted it is to examine only or primarily the ethnic. If only one of these were to be taught, it should be social class, which is the most important factor to be considered, and surely the religious aspects should be examined in depth. Actually, most of the multicultural programs in the nation turn out to be exercises in multiethnicity. Worse, many are just multi-Hispanic and/or multi-black, misrepresentations that may very well be fatal to the current chic of cultural ethnic schooling.

Even if teaching the entire range of multiculturalism to all students is a good idea, a huge problem exists: Is there enough time to accomplish the study? Make no mistake--the romantics are not willing that there be a fleeting examination of the many aspects of the subject, particularly the ethnic. The result would be so complete a study of the subcultures as to represent a herculean endeavor.

Meanwhile, the taxpayers who own the schools voice dissatisfaction with the institutions, demanding student success in reading, writing, math, speaking, job preparation, higher-level reasoning abilities and other survival skills–as well as requiring the moral teachings to build worthy people prepared to accept and live the *American Creed*. Add the multiplying demands made of schooling and the problem of time becomes exceedingly important. Reeling under the barrage of demands the schools are asked to attempt far more than they can possibly attain, and this is a primary cause of the perceived failure of schooling. There is simply no time for a complex immersion of students into the various subcultures as a major emphasis in schooling, the ethnic being only one. Time is surely a factor that must limit and slow even the moderate plans of the multiculturalists.

WHAT CAN HAPPEN

A thesis of this book is that the American social order is the best in history. No nation has been or can be perfect, but the United States, despite cruelties and inequities, is man's golden dream; it is the finest that has ever been and surely, surely, surely is worth saving. Any endeavors that can damage or slay the dear dream must be resisted like the plague, and the multicultural movement is a serious political and social threat to the *Creed* and thus the nation.

It is no wonder that those unhappy with America so often are multiculturalists who are led by the leftist philosophy of the *politically correct*. Indeed, these are the hordes who often hate America. Humanists to the core, and this includes the liberal churches as well, they are the crowd wanting God out of the schools, deploring capitalism, distrusting the great American documents, believing the socialistic and/or Marxist ideals, hating believing Christians, asserting that the federal government should control all things, rewriting history to make America and its heroes evil, and shouting that the *American Creed*, if it ever existed, is dead. If these people are successful in destroying the *Creed*, America may well be doomed. The brilliant ploy of the political multiculturalists to drive people and groups into disparate factions, what is often named polarization, may finally win the day; and, with that victory, the United States will be in deep jeopardy.

There is also the numbers game militating against the *American Creed*, itself, as indicated earlier, a byproduct of European culture. Unfortunately, most new Americans do not have a European background. Huge and cataclysmic problems are evidenced in the changing population of Americans that, unanswered, also may doom the American dream.

Given the dire political situations in the huge population centers where ethnic problems abound, it may well be true that any hope lies in the smaller areas far away from the urban areas. In most smaller towns, the *Creed* is not under political fire. In many of these places, the American dream is alive, if not perfectly well. It may very well be that the small and middle-sized communities are the ones to lead. In them the *Creed* can be held as the truth; the *melting pot* can operate. The successes of these schools in these communities must be so pervasive that they will stand as a beacon of hope in a nation under siege by those who would destroy it or, worse, those who would try to help but in the very doing destroy it.

If the dedicated multiculturalists had their way, the dear land would be *fractionalized* and driven into angry confronting camps, each fighting the political wars to get what it desires. When the groups live together in the urban inner cities, conflict and violence will occur. It could, probably would, be a war of extermination in the streets, as varying ethnic cultures come into conflict. The *fractionalization* must not be allowed to happen. And, unhappily, multicultural efforts are fueling such a social order. Like many humanistic solutions, the false notion of human nature, motivation, and behavior make serious problems worse than they originally were. No more infamous example is available than multiculturism.

Chapter Three

ELITE POWER FORCES: GOVERNMENT AND MASS MEDIA

The varying forces that influence education and, indeed, every nook and cranny of the nation have been partially listed and analyzed. Often perceived as reasonable and humane, these forces are primarily, if not completely, personifications of humankind's judgment that it holds the answer to all things--that God is dead, nonexistent, or irrelevant. The resulting disregard for *God's Word* has resulted in a humanistic culture based on values far removed from *God's Word* and the *American Creed*. Moreover, because the vital conservatising forces of home and church have too often joined schooling in promoting actively the pagan religion of humanism, believing Christians can view this only as a grim societal crisis.

WHO AND WHAT ARE THE INFLUENCERS?

Any evaluation of societal situations has to begin with the sources of power. Sociologists would often identify these influencing educational forces and persons as cultural elites. These elites are the primary sources influencing the values and behaviors of the social order; thus, their authority must be analyzed in depth. The failure of many writers to evaluate education's problems with insight is often seriously damaged by the refusal to analyze the location and exercise of power, that is to say the elites who make policy and formulate attitudes. In explaining these factors, we will scrutinize two critical questions: Who are these cultural elites? And how precisely do they influence the education of America's youth?

Important to note is that the elites who hold such enormous influence are most often not of average, middle-class social position or mentality. For the most part, they are upper-middle or upper class. It would be predictable, then, that they tend to be more liberal in political, personal, and religious matters. They are not as likely to support the planks of the *American Creed*, which is but another way to indicate that their values may differ considerably from those of most Americans. Certainly, they would far more likely attend liberal, unbelieving churches--if they attended at all. At the same time, they would be disproportionally represented in liberal, leftist politics. The world they perceive is not the one most Americans accept. It should be no surprise, then, that the American people are often incredulous at the decisions of the Congress, the moral corruptness of Hollywood, the antisocial hate preached by rock and rap, the leftist rantings of the media, or any of the liberal pronouncements of the humanistic elite, but perhaps none so anger the people as ill-used governmental power.

THE FEDERAL GOVERNMENT

The U.S. government, bound by the *Constitution* and its amendments, is comprised of three branches, each a check on the other: the judicial, the legislative, and the executive. Since congressmen are elected by the people in a representative democracy, the will of the electorate is supposedly represented and protected from governmental excess. Unfortunately, however, the desire of the founding fathers, as indicated in the *Constitution*, to limit the powers of government has been shunted aside in the race toward socialism and governmental control of the electorate. It is fair, based on the earlier identification of the elite, to question whether or not the will of the people is being represented or the desire of the founding fathers is even considered. This of course questions whether or not the *Creed* is being forsaken.

It is, in fact, fair to wonder whether the elites who make governmental decisions really perceive what is going on outside the Washington, D.C., beltline. Having very often come from a population differing from the *typical* American and imbued with the liberal mentalities of other governing elites, their allegiance to the *Creed* must be distrusted. To many of them, liberal, humanistic goals seem both prudent and correct. Indeed, they are far more influenced by the siren song of humanism than by the *Creed* or the claims of Jesus Christ. This Americans must understand.

Since the time of Franklin Roosevelt, a graph would indicate a wavering yet steady descent toward increased governmental power moving toward socialism, the enemy of Christianity, and in the direction of humanism. Only the persuasive style and vision of President Reagan slowed the movement. Perhaps needed in Roosevelt's time, the movement away from the intent of the founding fathers seems to represent the desires of the elites more often than those of the electorate.

For many years now, the United States Congress has had a liberal, humanistic bias, with Democrats typically in power. For the most part, then, liberal decisions were to be expected--no matter the feelings of the electorate. The Supreme Court, the judicial branch, has, since the days of the Warren

Elite Power Forces: Government and Mass Media

Court, been, more or less, liberal, many justices actually acting on the ideal that they are to write law rather than to interpret the *Constitution* as it was written.

Also, the bully pulpit of the President is a powerful tool. Witness the influence of Franklin Roosevelt, John Kennedy, and Ronald Reagan, among others.

Federal Court Decisions

In almost the entire range of books evaluating the schools, the power of the courts, particularly the U.S. Supreme Court, is not considered or is grossly underestimated. A huge number of the attacks at public schooling are, in fact, misplaced and should be directed toward the courts. The schools are thus bound by judicial decisions and, save breaking the law, are often not able to meet the demands of the local taxpayers. Of particular concern are the most sensitive problems facing the schools. Among these are discipline, censorship, free speech, and other rights of students, including all constitutional rights allowed adult American citizens. The courts rather than the schools determine policy in these matters.

The argument that the courts are the most important governmental influence on the schools can hardly be questioned; they are the final and defining human judgment on the contested matters. The force of law is a powerful factor in schooling. Supposedly, this exercise of strength is not political, as Supreme Court members decide a case on its constitutional merit. Such a claim, at best, is only partially correct, and this makes many decisions less than admirable. Politics are most surely at work. It is no surprise that liberals and conservatives vote quite differently, and it is likewise no surprise that women often vote differently from men.

Therefore, and this is a critical fact to be considered in later chapters, Americans should understand and act on the fact that who is appointed by a president to serve on the Supreme Court may very well be his single most important action to assist or harm America and its various modes of education. Who the president is remains utterly crucial; this very fact demands that believers join other thinking Americans in becoming political. The failure to do so is a serious blunder.

Consider the attendant problems. Conservative jurists most often are committed to the ideal that the calling of the Court is to base the findings on the meaning and intent of the founding fathers who wrote the *Constitution*. Judge Bork, perhaps the nation's foremost jurist, was lynched by Congress featuring ultra-liberal Democrats Kennedy, Metzenbaum, and Biden, all of whom--given their records--should surely sit in judgment of no man in any matter. The giant Bork was vilified by those who believed that the Court was to reinvent the *Constitution's* meaning. The feeling that meanings of the *Constitution* should be reinvented is a wholesale surrender to humanistic doctrines.

In public schooling, *Constitutional Amendments I and XIV* are the primary areas where the Court (or federal courts) enter the fray. The *First Amendment* reads: "Congress shall make no laws respecting an establishment of religion or prohibiting the free exercise thereof."

The *Fourteenth Amendment* submits:

All persons born or naturalized in the United States and subject thereof, are citizens of the United States and of the state wherein they reside. No state shall make or enforce any law which shall abridge the privileges or immunities of citizens of the United States; nor shall any state deprive any person of life, liberty, or prosperity, without due process of law; nor deny to any person within its jurisdiction the equal protection of the laws.

The Court's interpretation of these two amendments has resulted in a quite amazing influence on all American institutions, particularly schooling. Bound by the Court decisions, the schools braced themselves for the firestorm of criticism and attacks, much of it from Christians who blamed them rather than the judiciary branch of the government.

But a serious mistake is made if one believes that all of the High Court's decisions are wrong or absolutely anti-Christian. Some of the findings are helpful to Christianity and the *Creed*, and some are so misunderstood that believers have incorrectly reacted, say, for instance, in the notion that the *Bible* is banned from the public schools. It is fair to suggest, also, that though politics are a factor given the religious and political affiliations of the jurists they are not subject to the huge interference of interest groups--and this makes the Court less political than the legislature.

Any extensive examination of the effects of the judiciary upon the public schools would result in many volumes. Given the goals of this book, however, a look at some court decisions and cases is helpful. For an excellent comprehensive examination of this data, an exhaustive study of John W. Whitehead's *The Rights of Religious Persons in Public Education*, published by Crossway Books, Wheaton, Illinois, 1992, the source from which some of the following material came, is useful.

One of the areas of schooling roundly denounced by many believers and other conservatives is the lack of discipline and control of students. Such accusations are too often levied at the schools rather than the legalities

Elite Power Forces: Government and Mass Media   63

affecting the situation. Yes, the mass media is guilty--and this all-powerful force surely is a more influential teacher than the schools. But even the tremendous power of the media pales before law--that is to say the Supreme Court and federal courts. The schools are not nearly as guilty as many critics believe and claim; rather, they are more nearly victims.

The Supreme Court had a profound effect on discipline in the schools, and the reader would do well to contemplate how he would have voted on the cases discussed in the rest of the chapter.

The 1969 Tinker v. Des Moines Independent School District landmark decision was absolutely crucial. The Tinker children, who wore black arm bands to school protesting the bombing of Cambodia by American forces, were sent home from school until such time as they removed the arm decorations, a demand they refused to meet. They brought suit against the school system, and the case was eventually heard by the U.S. Supreme Court. The High Court ruled that the youths had been denied free speech. In a fateful pronouncement, one that led to the student power movement and made discipline something quite different in the schools, the Court demanded that a youth did not leave his constitutional rights at the door when entering school. The Pandora's box having been opened, students' rights hugely increased; teachers' rights in dealing with the youths declined dramatically. The right to control students was much diminished. Student rights and license became increasingly important, and a spate of other court decisions continued to strengthen the power and rights of students, a move that reflected the humanistic philosophy of the era. And parents, so often disaffected with the schools, were not bashful about using the new legality to attack them. This may seem reasonable to the reader, and perhaps it was, but of this be sure: The door to chaos in the schools had been opened. Discipline was much, much affected.

This and other decisions did not strip all the rights of teachers to control and discipline; they simply made it far, far more difficult. Court rulings made it clear that student behavior was not to jeopardize keeping order and discipline, nor were the rights of others to be invaded. But a measure of control had been lost, and this made all the difference. The parents, believing what they were taught by the media, turned in anger toward the schools. In another age, a student was punished at home when corrected at school. Now the parents may choose to seek legal redress from the schools and teachers. And the schools stand, hands manacled by law and fashion, wondering why they have become the enemy. Having wondered, though, they must then turn to their humanistic doctrines that have eased discipline in the race to build healthy egos--too often forgetting the balance required to mediate between the two. Some, but not nearly all, of the blame belongs to schooling. Even here, though, the schools are following the philosophy and psychology of the era. Witness, in fact, the influence of Dr. Spock, of the humanistic psychology of Carl Rogers, and of the many humanistic influences of the era. School people can argue, and with more than a little reason, that they are reflecting the child-rearing desires of huge numbers (perhaps a majority) of people.

More important to believing Christians is the notion that court decisions are strongly biased against Christianity. Beyond a doubt, this is true. The court's findings trample the desires of the founding fathers who indicated in the *First Amendment* that the state should not force a religion upon the people, nor should it do harm to religious freedom.

The various decisions by the High Court concerning religion in the schools took huge liberties with the intentions of the founders, but the judiciary did not take everything away. Whitehead lists the six specific procedures deemed to be establishments of religion in the public schools:

(1) state-directed *and* required on-premises religious training, in McCollum v. Board of Education;
(2) state-directed *and* required prayer, in Engel v. Vitale;
(3) state-directed and required *Bible* reading, in Abington School District v. Schempp;
(4) state-directed and authorized posting of the *Ten Commandments*, in Stone v. Graham;
(5) state-directed and authorized "periods of silence for meditation and voluntary prayer," in Wallace v. Jeffree; *and*
(6) state-directed and required teaching of scientific creationism, in Edwards v. Aquillard.

These decisions remain a terrible disappointment to believers, an affront to those who believe *God's Word*. The Court had turned its back on the Savior of the World and men's souls. The nation was and is in jeopardy, and the founding fathers would surely have bowed their heads in shame and disgust.

There are, however, windows of opportunity in the schools. In the Shempp case, for instance, the finding made clear that religion can be taught in the schools--but objectively. Religion can be taught about; it cannot be taught as a truth. It is this fact with which the schools must live--and this sad situation surely is not the responsibility of the schools.

But the schools overreacted, making the situation far worse than it might have been. Many Christian leaders, joining one of the authors in disgust at the turn of events, fought the teaching of the *Bible* as literature. However, it was what was left in the public schools--and, in truth, it is surely a much shorter walk to the redeeming Cross of Jesus Christ for those who have read the *Bible*, to those who have been exposed to *God's Word*. Let God Himself speak through His Word, and this the parents must monitor carefully. It is all a poor bargain for the children of Christian parents; however, it is not so bad as to let *God's Word* lay fallow in the public schools.

The schools were so fearful (and sometimes so happy given their humanistic foundations) that they all too often eliminated everything Christian from the schools, and in this they lied about the history and literature of the nation. To teach American literature and history without considering the Christian influence on the nation and the critical importance of Christianity in the *American Creed* was grossly dishonest. The students simply were not told the truth about their foundations, a momentous failure in the schools--particularly when they are able, under the law, to tell the truth.

In 1996, President Clinton, who had earlier bitterly railed against teaching Christianity in the schools, indicated that a wide range of religious experiences including Bible reading, private prayer, statement of religious beliefs by students in homework and artwork assignments, religious clothing and messages, student discussion of religion, and, most importantly, lessons about the role of Christianity in literature and culture were acceptable in public schools. Unfortunately, the President did not comprehend, or chose not to, that the courts have not always protected religious freedom in the schools; they have all too often refused the meaning cast by the framers of the Constitution and its amendments, particularly the First Amendment. But if Clinton were correct, a huge amount of the blame must be directed toward public schools.

Teaching about religion and the truth of history, though, is influenced by other court decisions. A federal court set the following guidelines for schools teaching about religion: The school board should maintain absolute control of materials and those faculty who teach the subject; the teachers should be state-certified and prepared to teach the subject in question; and they should not answer questions about their respective views on religion (what happened to free speech?); the class should not be required of all students; and the school boards should insure that the teacher is objective. This ruling was not all bad, for, at least, teachers had to be prepared and could not disparage Christianity.

An important fact potentially useful to Christians when they question school policies is that humanism, by any logical definition, is a religion, as indicated earlier in the book, and should be considered a religion subject to the same constitutional limitations as Christianity. This should be the Achilles' heel of humanistic schooling, and it was the method to contest humanism in the schools. For this reason, the Smith v. Board of

Commissioners of Mobile County decision was by all means an utter tragedy for Christians. A lower court decision that certain books being used in the Mobile County schools were promoting the religion of secular humanism and were thus not acceptable was overturned. The reasoning was that the books were indeed promoting secular humanism but--and here the Christian cringes--the values were said to be "fundamental" and "a major objective of schooling."

Imagine that, the court agreeing that secular humanism represents the American value system; think of the ramifications. Judicial decisions are far too often the result of politics and fashion. As charged, the schools are licensed to teach the religion of man as the truth and the truth of God as nothing more than literature.

The Christian writers who point the finger of accusation directly at the schools for teaching humanism should reconsider. As analyzed above, the schools must teach humanism and not biblical truth unless there is a dramatic conservatising of the High Court. But some humanistic areas are vulnerable to *First Amendment* court cases. As an example of such areas of humanism, meditation, channeling, visualization, and other areas of New Age join witchcraft in perhaps breaking the intent of the *First Amendment*. Such cases will continue to find their way into the courts--and they should.

All of this is to indicate that it becomes very difficult to teach values, save those humanistic ones that "are a major objective of schooling." This is very important, indeed, because this book will eventually recommend that the teaching of the consensus *American Creed* be a cardinal objective of schooling. Court cases make clear that the *Free Exercise* clause of the *First Amendment* will not allow the denigration of a child's heritage and beliefs, a problem that is intensified by the multiplying numbers of students who do not come from a European background and the multicultural programs driving the youth into angry and conflict-laden ethnic and other interest groups. At the same time, though, the courts have approved the teaching, even the indoctrination, of the public values that unite the people "in a comprehending loyalty," no matter their particular backgrounds. Existing, also, is the doctrine of free speech that makes such instruction difficult, necessitating two cardinal objectives: first, making absolutely certain that the values held up as true are, in fact, consensus American values, and, second, allowing a decision-making process that involves all of the youth, no matter the background, when there is no agreement. Such a procedure, analyzed in detail later in the book, should effectively answer *First Amendment* challenges, but the values based substantially on Christian foundations cannot be presented as Christian.

All Supreme Court decisions have surely not been damaging to

Elite Power Forces: Government and Mass Media 67

Christianity. For instance, the 1925 Pierce v. Society of Sisters finding resulted in the right to send children to private rather than public schools. In like manner, the 1930 Cochran v. Louisiana State Board of Education decision made possible, under well-defined conditions, the use of public funds to purchase books for children in religious schools, while the Everson v. Board of Education finding made it legal to use the public funds for busing students to religious schools. In recent years, there has been a spate of decisions favoring Christians. Christian clubs have the legal right to meet on school property if other clubs do. Evening religious meetings for the public can legally be held if other groups are allowed the right.

The United States Congress

Bills passed by the Congress join the Supreme Court decisions in profoundly setting policy in the public schools. In President Johnson's term, astounding sums of money were made available to the schools. In the desire to build his *Great Society* and to eliminate poverty in America, Johnson and the Congress relied heavily on the schools. And, following the Civil Rights Movement, billions upon billions of dollars were allocated to the schools along with the accompanying federal demands. Part of this was political, but much of it represented a sincere dedication to helping the poor. Even a conservative Christian might have supported many of the bills. A powerful lesson from the experience should, however, be remembered forever: Schooling will not and cannot solve the great social problems. The answers lie far beyond the nation's classrooms and the amount of money made available. Universities declaring that they can solve problems of poverty and social dysfunctions are simply lying, naive, or ignorant, a fact proven by the failures attendant to the funding of the bills in Johnson's era. Much of the money was thrown to the winds. Government will never, can never, solve social problems through the use of the schools whose very function is to reflect society, the best of it.

But the federal government does indeed achieve its elite influence in the schools through legislative efforts, and this believers should take very seriously. Governmental power in schooling, not mentioned in the *Constitution* nor desirable, is nonetheless real. The Elementary and Secondary Education Act (ESEA) was passed in 1965. The powerful effect of congressional bills had begun in earnest.

The ESEA was comprised over time of many titles. The first of these, Title One, made available at the start $1,000,000,000 for the economically and culturally deprived, but this was just the beginning. Less than a decade later, the total cost exceeded $40,000,000,000. Disconcerting to taxpayers is that a huge majority of this sum was spent on teaching reading as test scores plummeted in the skill.

Title Two made $1,000,000,000 available to media centers and libraries for commodities like audio-visual equipment and books. Title Three furnished $1,000,000,000 for supplementary educational centers and services. Title Four furnished multiplied millions for research. Title Five made available $25,000,000 to state departments of education. It did not end there. To mention just a few more of the congressional bills demonstrates the power to influence schools even more dramatically. In 1970 the Environmental Education Act was passed to make huge monies available for environmental schooling and research. In the same year the Drug Abuse Education Act made substantial sums available for varying programs dealing with the terrible problem. On and on the spending went.

The Headstart Program, started in 1964, was one of the most ambitious of all the efforts. Noble, if not a little political, the bill was based on the notion that poor children could be helped considerably if preschool programs helped them catch up with their more successful counterparts. Part of the program allowed them a hot meal. Nearly every imaginable procedure was used--from utter governmental control to wide choice by the various centers. It was (and is) a huge, huge effort based on the idea that changing the environment of the child will result in a significant social and academic gain for the youth. In all honesty, it seemed like a good idea; for this reason it became a sacred political cow.

And what was/is the result? There is scant evidence that it has helped at all, if one considers the parts that have been statistically tested. About the best that can be said concerning the areas measured is that they result in a small increase in success that disappears later in school; and the youth not involved in the program, those who do not come from poor families, do not seem hurt. There may be sense in the claim that the program does much good--but it has to be in areas that are not yet measured. Certainly, the meal helps, but the huge monies invested in Headstart could finance a much-expanded food program. The problem concerning the notion that changing environment of children will solve most of their problems will be considered later, but there is no question that Headstart was and remains an admirable effort--even though the results are very disappointing. Nonetheless, the program can, for political reasons, hardly be touched. At some time, though, unless positive and verifiable results appear, taxpayers will rise up, demanding different approaches to assist the youth needing such help.

But from where will such programs come? Can bureaucrats inside the Washington, D.C., beltline provide such assistance? There is little or no reason to believe so given the results of the multiplied billions thrown to the

Elite Power Forces: Government and Mass Media 69

winds. And never forget that every dollar from a governmental source results in less control of the schools by local taxpayers who own the schools and by the state which has the legal right to control them.

The governmental influence in the schools is considerable because it is dangling substantial monies to them. Make no mistake, however--what the federal government pays for, it owns and will direct. Never forget this. Schools do not have to buy into governmental programs and thus pave the way for losing the right to help local students whom they know and understand in a manner that a bureaucrat in Washington, D.C. never ever could. Why didn't the schools *just say no*? The answer, of course, is money, big, big money.

The reader may either favor or abhor the governmental interference, but this is not the point here. What is demonstrated is how the huge elite force of government influences schooling when Congress passes bills that finance schooling. Much that grieves taxpayers concerning the schools is, again, the result of Congressional action, and the schools should be free from attacks in these areas. To be considered, also, is the sure fact that for most of the recent past the Congress has been controlled by a liberal humanistic group; thus, for the American conservative, every influence of the U.S. legislature has been suspect.

The Executive Branch

The President of the United States is an important elite affecting education--but in a different manner than the Supreme Court and the Congress. In many ways, though, his influence sets the tone for the legislative and judicial. Perhaps his greatest power, in this regard, is the nominating of new Supreme Court judges. These judicial nominees must be accepted by the U.S. Congress. It has been true for some time now that the legislative branch has been overwhelmingly liberal. Reagan had some success in dealing with them because of his amazing popularity, and he thus was able to make appointments that, at least at the time, seemed conservative, although some proved terribly disappointing.

The President also has the power to influence by his personality and popularity. The position is fraught with power to influence the entire social order, including the public schools, homes, and churches.

Likewise, the President must decide whether or not to sign the bills sent forward by the Congress. This is power to derail the hopes of senators and members of the House of Representatives; often this dooms the humanistic, liberal bills that affect the schools. Now and then, though, they override the veto and still get their ways.

Finally, there is the President's willingness or unwillingness to enforce laws already existing. Many of these men were very slow to enforce integration, and this slowed the intention of law. Dragging his feet, the President can delay and delay implementation of judicial and legislative pronouncements.

The Political Party in Power

Already, the vast differences between the values of Republicans and Democrats have been determined. The primary difference turns on the Democrat's belief in the power of centralized government and the Republican's faith in the democratic power of the people operating with far less governmental influence. The first tends toward socialism, the second, democracy. Of course, some Democrats are conservative, while some Republicans tend toward liberalism. Obviously, the party in power in Washington has a profound effect in setting public policy and values attendant to prevailing actions, congressional bills, and court decisions.

Democrats, typically far more liberal, work day and night to place the power in the hands of legislators rather than the people. The judgments are to be made by a liberal governmental elite, a philosophy far divorced from the *Creed*, Christianity, and other great American documents. If the schools and other American institutions are to overcome the present crisis, power must be reinvested in the hands of the people, in personal responsibility rediscovered, and in the dramatic downsizing of liberal governmental control. Who is elected to every national office makes a huge difference, not only in education but, also, in all areas of American life. Failing to realize this objective may very well doom any hope for solving America's most persistent and serious problems, schooling being but one. The lesson is now clear: Socialism has failed. Marxism has failed. Freedom has won! And why was this not emblazoned as headlines in every American newspaper? Could it be that the liberal papers were pouting at the victory of freedom and the attending *American Creed*?

State and Local Politics

Whether one is a Democrat or Republican is less important in state and local politics. At that level issues often become more important than national political symbolism. There are far more likely to be liberal Republicans and conservative Democrats. This is to say that Americans must surely become aware of the political beliefs of candidates for every office, from state level to the crucial school board elections. Politics are a very important elite force

Elite Power Forces: Government and Mass Media

affecting schooling and education, in general; and it is vitally important for voters to understand this.

THE MASS MEDIA

The mass media is the most powerful of all educating forces in the United States. Not school, not the peer group, not the family, not any other influencer is as successful in educating the youth (and all Americans) as this powerful force. And that very education, as earlier analyzed, too often is more than damaging, standing firmly against the *American Creed*, Christianity, decency, the great American documents, including the hallowed *Constitution*, and the remarkable pronouncements and letters that so distinguish the western world. Those involved in this gigantic endeavor and who profit from it predictably urge that their medium is responsible only for reflecting the social order, not formulating it. At its very best, such a claim is weak, and absolutely incorrect at its worst.

The media does both: It reflects society and it formulates thinking independently of what it reflects. In both cases it stands accused of the most horrendous of crimes: the attempt to destroy the *American Creed* and its values and to delimit the Christian faith.

It is no excuse whatsoever that the elite of the media do not understand that they are, in fact, accomplishing this terrible moral crime. What they formulate is all too often the complete disregard for the *Creed* and Christianity. What they reflect is, also, all too often, badly chosen, reflecting the very worst of the social order; and it inexcusably presents perversion as moral. The media panders to the evil, accepts it, and falsely thinks, in the strange way too often wrong is rationalized, that the nation is served well. It might, had it been different than it was, have chosen to reflect the noble, the conservative, the Christian; but it selected, instead, the debauchery, wantonness, and degradation, all too often presenting them as typical and thus acceptable. Part of this was a result of the very strange liberal mentality. Most of it, however, was reflecting the worst of the social order because it sold well.

But what is the mass media? Though there are quarrels concerning the definition of the term, a useful understanding is that it is a means of public communication that reaches huge numbers of people at the same time. Each of the areas comprising the mass media is identified as a medium, and all of these, as analyzed earlier, are profound educators of not only the youth but also every American, as well. Normally, the media is thought to be made up of television C.D's films newspapers radio magazines and books. Together, these mediums wield persuasive power and influence, which, is education.

Television

The power of television has been evaluated earlier, but a more precise examination of the medium demonstrates the huge problems it presents to the schooling believing Christians and many other Americans want for their children and grandchildren. Television does, beyond a doubt, accomplish much that is praiseworthy. The medium must be given its due. In some ways, it endeavors to be a positive force--but, even in this, thinking people must be ever watchful. In the programs for little children, a kind of smarmy humanism is portrayed as the truth. It must be said, however, that this may very well reflect the mood of the age--that is to say that humanism probably is, at some level, the value system accepted by many, perhaps a majority. The huge war against it, favoring, instead, the *Creed*, rages with the very political hope for the future of the nation in question, and television far too often allies itself with humanism and its excesses, while the American consensus value system is under a moral blitzkrieg.

A few examples make the point. Take, for instance, the epidemic problem of alcohol in the nation. Time after time in discussions concerning teaching the youth about alcohol, supposed experts smugly begin their dialogues with the assumption that the youth do drink and will continue to do so To often, plans begin with "responsible use" of alcohol. This must result in rhapsodic elation by those who brew the swill. How much of this foolishness about alcohol education is informed by the huge expenditures on advertising by the liquor industry? And how about discussions on television concerning sex education? Again, time after time, the position is that they are having sex and will do so no matter what. Teach them, the TV sets often recommend, to be responsible about it; then it is acceptable. Television spokesmen may claim this from morn until the signal dims, but God calls it sin outside of marriage. How often, save from a few Sunday morning sermons, does anyone hear that fornication is sin and that such behavior is wrong? How often do humanists declare that it is a destroyer of lives and homes?

The cavalier view of sex is seen again and again on the medium. Note the soap operas often displaying sexual license as perfectly normal and good--though, and this is to their credit, they sometimes punish severely those who break the code represented in the *American Creed*. Too often, marriage vows are held up to ridicule, as if they were values from another age. Watch the filth of the comic club programs; there is no rock bottom to their sexual decadence. Homosexual lifestyles are presented as normal--just another family style--no better nor worse than others. And the programs are focusing on one-parent families, presenting them as perfectly normal, when, in fact, they should be saying, as the research proves, that children of such families

Elite Power Forces: Government and Mass Media 73

are laboring under a huge disadvantage. Television, again, is pandering to its audience, the divorced one-parent homes. People, the medium assumes, must feel well about themselves, no matter what. Hence, says the tube, one-parent homes are just fine.

If television portrayed many of the homes as having succeeded to a degree because of the nobility of the one parent dedicating him/herself to the children, there could be little disagreement. To portray these homes as normal and wonderful, offering full opportunities, however, is a horrible lie, attacking both what research proves and the *American Creed*. It is as if the marriage vows did not count at all--as if humans were subspecies, who owed themselves rather than their children the best possible life. In this respect, the selfishness of many of the baby boomers must not be held as an example of anything--save what not to do. This, television decision-makers fail to understand or do not choose to acknowledge.

What about the television talk shows? Hardly experts in problem solving, hosts and guests babble without end. How in the world can viewers listen to and take seriously the advice and thoughts of actors and musicians, many of whom live lives of utter chaos and tragedy? Pray tell, what kind of advice can these people give–except on their acting or singing? Why in the world, save for money, could television decision-makers present mere entertainers speaking about things which they have no expertise. The artistic types, so divorced from reality and the *Creed*, can't teach anyone about anything, but being entertainers. Nonetheless, the taxpayers romanticize these performers, listening raptly to their preachments. The power of these people to influence, to educate, is immense, particularly in the areas where they can do the most harm: sex, patriotism, loyalty, God, liquor and narcotics, responsibility, and a myriad of other critical issues. The power to educate is huge; and, all too often, it is a direct attack at God, the *Creed*, and what decency humankind has learned in its long, lonely walk through time.

The adolescents are delighted at MTV. To an adult or, for that matter, a thinking adolescent, the music videos are appalling, seeming for all the world like nightmares inhabited by deadbeats from hell. Overt sexuality is everywhere. For adolescents, there are few more dangerous television offerings than those of MTV. Be assured that the medium is teaching about sex, violence, and many other dangerous topics. In almost all of these, it is anti-God, anti-*Creed*, and anti-decency. How in the world can the institutions of home, church, and school win over this influence? More will be said about the music of adolescents when recordings are discussed later. In all of this, however, the reader should recall the complicity of television, as preteens and their older brothers and sisters spend thousands of hours watching, learning, being educated by MTV. Is schooling responsible? Is the home? Is the church? Or is the media far more damaging? The schools make good scapegoats, but such reasoning makes the problem all the more difficult to remedy.

Increasingly, television includes expanded news, the reporting of which is roundly attacked by many conservatives. The charge is that a disproportionate number of the major television stations are controlled by political and religious liberals; hence, the conservative and middle-of-the-road positions are neglected, the result being a highly biased and unfair reporting of not only the news but the validity of America's high-level values.

But are these charges fair? Is the reporting of news on television a false educator in the nation? The answer to these questions is compelling. It is true, first, that attitudinal tests in schools of journalism have indicated a sizeable majority of people who view themselves as liberal and, second, that, rather than reporting the news, they desire to be a positive factor in what they believe is right and true. It is, then, predictable that they lean heavily in the direction of liberalism and they are, or would like to be, social activists. This would strongly indicate that the news on the major networks would tend to follow liberal goals. Everything being equal, the networks will probably present a biased, liberal agenda.

Newspapers

Most of the negative influences of television also apply to newspapers, for the power forces influencing journalistic endeavors are from the same elite places as those setting television policy. Indeed, a liberal, humanistic (often socialistic) elite controls most of the huge newspapers, a group far removed from the Creed and the very people reading their papers. How perceptive it was for a famed newspaper columnist to indicate that when he arose in the morning both a noted newspaper and the Bible were read so that he could "get both sides of the issue."

It is surely true that all newspapers are not embarrassments to the Creed; some are liberal, some middle of the road, and some conservative. Most of the large papers are humanistic and liberal; many smaller ones are conservative. Also, though this is all too rare, some papers endeavor to present all sides of issues–and these are to be cherished as are those who stand unashamedly for the planks of the Creed.

But consider some of the grievous damage done by newspapers. A mind-set based on a humanistic, existential, nihilistic, narcissistic view of the nation and its destiny is often perpetrated. One might look in vain for hope, as the negative is presented day after day to a people needing optimism. Often the news is slanted toward liberalism, humanism, and socialism as the Creed is

Elite Power Forces: Government and Mass Media

disparaged. Vile cartoons lampoon the President and other politicians thus attacking the very dignity of the presidency; and the arrogance in attacking politicians with whom the publications disagree is damaging. Violence and sex are featured and highlighted; they sell papers. Cartoons lampoon the American values, and advertisements sell alcohol and tobacco. Columnists define deviancy down. The list of damaging procedures goes on and on. Newspapers are hardly the positive voice they are thought to be by journalists; quite the opposite is true.

It does not matter whatsoever that the journalistic decision-makers think they are accomplishing what is right. In larger part, their efforts are hugely damaging to the nation and the Creed. They are, indeed, a primary educative elite teaching Americans how to live and believe, and far, far too much of the instruction they offer is completely antithetic to the American Creed and the Christian faith that established the nation.

CDs and Music

Tied into radio listening and television watching, CDs and tapes are part and parcel of the mass media and its education of the youth.

Music is a profound educator of the young. In a very real sense, it has ever been so. Each generation has its music, and often it raises the ire of parents and grandparents. Often, these adults make bleak, apocalyptic charges, claiming that the youth are being corrupted. In the past five decades, such sorrowful claims were made against jazz, swing, progressive jazz, and other music genres. The march of events suggests that the elders probably overreacted; hence, it would seem reasonable that the negative claims of the current naysayers are precisely what can be expected of adults.

Such a claim could not be more incorrect. This music is menacing to the souls of the youth and to the nation. It does not merely represent a new sound; at its worst, America and its noble dream are utterly repudiated. Even more horrible, Christianity is lampooned and selfish humanism (and often New Age philosophy) is extolled. Killing is defended. Violence is recommended. It seems the world has gone mad, and the horrible music is a powerful detriment to the nation and Creed, particularly vile gangsta rap.

Parents should not be deceived when their children indicate that they do not listen to the words. First, they do know the words whether they know it or not; studies of subliminal advertising make this very clear. Second, even if the dangerous words were not heard, the youth are subjected to the beat, said by some to be satanic. Most of the rock music has the beat of sexual intercourse. In his book, *The Closing of the American Mind*, Alan Bloom has remarked that "rock music has one appeal, a barbaric appeal, to sexual desire--not love, not eros, but sexual desire undeveloped and untutored."

In reviewing the results of adolescent music concerts, Jerry Klein, revered columnist of the *Peoria Journal Star,* wrote:

> Alas, romance seems to have vanished and we have this kind of raw sex, accompanied by primal screaming and a couple of thunderous chords loud enough to vaporize the brain and obliterate any moral restraint. Some of this is little more than a barbaric appeal to engage in sexual intercourse.
>
> Yes, yes, I know, I am way behind the times, a dinosaur, a curmudgeon. But that is where I intend to remain, resolutely and proudly. Too much of this up-to-date world has become mired in garbage and sleaze. Too many people mistake sewage for self-expression, and odious sludge for art, and I have no intention of being one of them.
>
> The end result, I fear, is to encourage a world with lots of sex and very little love, uncommitted fornication rather than conjugal affection, domination rather than partnership, conquest rather than a mutual, committed and loving relationship. This is all yet another jarring illustration of how the vaunted sexual revolution has become positively revolting.

A huge body of adolescent music attacks the very foundations of both Christianity and America itself. Go back to the early days of rock and roll; listen, for instance, to the fabled *Woodstock* album. Said by some to be an almost religious record demonstrating that adolescents had reached a higher plane of compassion and love, it was actually extolling a neo-humanism focused on the popular urging of the day, "Tune in; turn on; and drop out." Forget the *American Creed,* the best that has been said and thought in man's lonely walk through time, and become involved with the counterculture. Use narcotics to expand the consciousness, and drop out of the majority culture. Sprint nude through the fields. How is that for a noble comment by and for the youth? Brainchild of adolescent music, it spawned and reflected a generation of youth in the late 1960's and early 1970's who were disastrous to both Christianity and democracy. And it must be remembered that these youth are now adults, many middle-aged parents and grandparents. Many of these youth, now wearing suits and working in jobs at which they formerly sneered, continue to accept a portion of the evil philosophies of their era. What will they teach their children about the music and its claims? The answer may already have been issued, for, in 1994, their children again assembled at *Woodstock,* and in 1999's Woodstock they became vile criminals.

Elite Power Forces: Government and Mass Media

Much of the music of today's youth has become far more undesirable than that of their parents. Enter acid rock, rap, and other musical disasters. It should be indicated that there is some such music that recommends a moral world; this is the best of it. Parents, grandparents, teachers, pastors, and Sunday school teachers should listen closely to it, at the same time comprehending that it assumes religious status with many of the youth and that too often it supplies their heroes. Think about the purveyors of adolescent music, who, like deadbeats from a horrible nightmare, often have more power than family and church in formulating the youths' life philosophies and behaviors.

Moreover, the music speaks of delightful things to teenagers. It is narcissism. It is pro barnyard sex. It is anti-establishment. It is anti-parent. It is anti-America. It is do one's own thing. It is murder. It is violence. It is anti-authority. It is pure hedonism. It is anti-God. It provides ghetto youth a forum for violence. These developments represent heady philosophy for adolescents, but there is an enemy: Mom and Dad stand guarding the gates, endeavoring to work against the new and wonderfully permissive world of youth music. As Professor Bloom has so well written, "The inevitable corollary . . . is rebellion against the parental authority that represses it." And make no mistake; the parents cannot stop their children from listening to the music. Indeed, they can manage the situation at home and can hope to teach better taste, but the youth will still listen. It cannot be stopped.

A pandora's box of evil is opened. The mind of the youth may be corrupted. And even when the child needs so much help from his/her parents in this regard, Mom and Dad often, because they are perceived as the enemy in terms of the new permissive freedom, lose control of their children's moral and religious upbringing. Often not the fault of the parents, the situation is a frightening development. One may properly wonder if the school, home, or church have anything like the power of adolescent music in educating the youth.

This is particularly so with the acid rock and "gangsta rap" music of the present era. Rap music is particularly damaging, for, at its worst, it educates ghetto youth to lash out in rage against the system perceived to have trapped them in abject poverty. It recommends gangs, power, revenge, hate, and murder. One performer opined for the murder of police. Others advocate indiscriminate sex, using the females called "hos" (whores) in the music only as sex objects.

The hate and violence of alternative rock and rap are powerful teachers. Listen to lyrics about carrying weapons; hear the threats. It is most dangerous education as it attempts to legitimize rebellion and violence. But liberal humanists often faun over the disgraceful music, sometimes identifying it as legitimate literature of protest. This is the way, of course, many liberals reason. Man is not evil, only the institutions that have corrupted him. This is not the way most Americans want their children educated and that includes youth of all ethnic groups. Why is there not a music that tells them to work hard, succeed at school, forgive, and master the skills and ideals that will open the door to middle-class membership and the resulting acceptance into the majority? That's the kind of song needed to educate them for success, but seldom is it written and sung. It doesn't sell well.

Adolescent music is indeed a primary educator of the young. It teaches them about sex, the social order, hate, violence, and a host of other incendiary topics. This becomes horribly frightening when schooling's failure to teach the *Creed* is considered. If the primary education that students receive about violence, sex, and other crucial areas comes from adolescent music, the nation is in deep jeopardy.

Movies

It is difficult to place the various media into niches, because films are a big part of television. The television viewer spends many hours, of course, viewing films. Any positive or negative assertions about television must be substantially based on films.

Like television in general, films are both good and bad. At their best they are exquisite instructors; however, it is disquieting to note that the best of these films were likely to have been produced in earlier decades. Think of the films that entertained and taught the planks of the *Creed*. Recall *All's Quiet on the Western Front, Ben Hur, Quo Vadis, The Sign of the Cross, Mr. Smith Goes to Washington, Gone with the Wind, My Friend Flicka, To Kill a Mockingbird, Snow White* (and many of the other Disney films), *All the King's Men, High Noon, Shane, For Whom the Bell Tolls,* and hundreds of other great and useful instructors of Americans. Co-existing were lesser films, many B-grade movies that at least taught the moral truths.

There was a feeling among some film makers in earlier decades that art had the responsibility to build better, more worthy people and social orders. As these feelings have eroded under the onslaught of humanism with its attending selfishness and self-aggrandizement, films have degenerated all too often to ennobling evil.

Arty, creative types often chortle at the thought that movies (and, indeed, all art) should have a moral purpose. Instead, they assert, art is art and not therapy for the soul. Critics would identify this as formalistic criticism, the study of form as the final judge of worth. Is a comedy a comedy and not a moral criticism? Add to this the false idea that humanism is right and true, and the walls of decency tumble.

It has happened in Hollywood and in all areas of American life. The floodgates were thus open, and the glitter of the big screen remained a powerful teacher--but then the religion of humanism and its attending depravity gained center stage. Yes, there were still some fine films that taught the right things. But the erosion to the immoral and the amoral became a flood: the dam was broken. Though there were rating systems, supposedly to aid parents, filth gained respectability in the cinema profession; and the race was on. Civilized values were under siege, and many people loved it, couldn't get enough. Like those in the ancient Coliseum, they shouted for bread and circuses--and there they were (are) in living color: sexual copulation before their very own eyes, nakedness, violence and blood, existentialism and nihilism, human suffering, and degradation of Christianity. On and on the list of film evils grows and grows. The film producers played with relish to the depravity, and the people lapped it up.

What manner of education is this to young men? Testosterone is flooding into their adolescent systems. Their imaginations soar; they are sexually aroused. If it's portrayed in film, it must be acceptable. The hot blood is running, and they are on the edge. In its sex education programs, does school provide instruction so compelling? Does the home? Does the church?

But it is not just in matters of sex and violence that Hollywood accomplishes such effective instruction in evil. In almost every area of decency that comprises the *American Creed*, the film makers (and other areas of the arts) attack so very artfully and effectively. Can the public schools match the instruction of these master teachers?

Those accepting the *Creed*, though, know that films and all teaching approaches should focus on the moral. The job of art, and all areas of teaching, must be to build better people. Faulkner agreed in his Nobel Prize address to young authors. It is as meaningful to young teachers and to parents, as well:

He must teach himself that the basest of all things is to be afraid; and teaching himself that, forget it forever, leaving no room in his workshop for anything but the old verities and truths of the heart, the old universal truths lacking which any story is ephemeral and doomed--love and honor and pity and pride and compassion and sacrifice. Until he does so, he labors under a curse. He writes not of love but lust, of defeats in which nobody loses anything of value, of victories without hope and, worst of all, without pity or compassion. His griefs grieve on no universal bones, leaving no scars. He writes not of the heart but of the glands.

These are powerful and informing words coming from a man who did not claim to be Christian, yet he understood the crucial importance of the American consensus values being the very center of what is demanded in building, educating, a better people. Too many artists, including film makers, are writing "under a curse," and the people, needing much more, are watching the very curse made appealing on the screen. Too often, school teachers join the film makers and other artists by surrendering to the claim that they have no professional right to teach morality. The gentle, sometimes massaging, sometimes jolting, brilliantly-made films continue to teach an evil agenda. Wrong seems right. American consensus morality, the *Creed*, having held back the jungle's advance, sifts like sand through the hourglass, faster, ever faster now. And it is twilight; behind it is the darkest night.

Books and Magazines

It is more difficult to identify books as a mass medium, but they are, particularly with the overwhelming appeal of paperbacks. Perhaps more than any other mass medium, the effect of books is hard to evaluate. For those who take seriously Faulkner's words and, more importantly, for those who write truly of the Savior, writers can have a wonderful effect on readers.

Witness the books displaying the words and wisdom of evangelical, believing Christians. Consider the praiseworthy Christian presses that produce such wonderful literature, ranging from deep biblical analysis to Christian novels. It is important to understand that there is Christian literature for every purpose, every reading situation a child, adolescent, or adult can face. One wonders why the crowds are often so small in Christian bookshops. If the literature in these shops is not purchased for the youth, a very important check of the rampant humanism of the day is overlooked. Indeed, there is a well-written, worthy, informing, and engaging literature written for the sons and daughters of Christian parents and for gifts to relatives and others.

Everything considered, most of what was said about films applies also to books, although it can be argued that books, on the whole, appeal to better educated and perhaps more intelligent audiences. If this is true, these works may be more dangerous to the Christian faith than films. But the same ideals and themes are apparent, some good, some terrible. In most, but not all, humanism remains the theme.

It is tempting to claim that the largest sellers, the blockbusters, are humanistic; but consider the amazing sales of Billy Graham, Alan Bloom, Hal Lindsey, and a host of Christian giants. Few are novels. It is, of course, the secular novels that are typically the largest sellers, save *God's Word*. Recently, however, adult Christian novels have become best sellers.

Elite Power Forces: Government and Mass Media

This is not to indicate that novels are the only area of concern. Note the psychology shelves at the bookstores. Every psychologist going the road has a chance to coin and sell a new (though none of it is really new) psychology. The psychology of the self, the anti-Christian assertion of the self, sells well. Books with sexual themes or how-to tomes and/or naughty pictures are everywhere. The frankness and blatant titillation of these publications, posing as science (which psychology is not), are an affront to believers and an ever-abundant impediment to the education youth should receive. Then there are the New Age areas of the bookstores (or the growing number of New Age bookstores); and these, so alluring to the young, loom as a terrible threat. And what about books concerning witchcraft and the occult? Indeed, danger lurks on the shelves of America's bookstores.

Perhaps the worst is pornography. Already discussed in the area of films, the problem is even worse in books. To be sure, there is well-written pornography thought by many to be great literature. Books like *Fanny Hill*, *Lady Chatterley's Lover*, *Tropic of Cancer*, *Lolita*, and others are often taught as worthy literature in university and college classrooms--but they are, and of this you may be sure, filthy and dangerous to America, its young, and the *Creed*.

Part of this has to do with Supreme Court decisions concerning the *Constitution* and free speech. The High Court has ruled that the work must be compliant with current "community standards" and must display "redeeming value." From the humanist point of view, who can say there is no redeeming value whatsoever in the books listed above? Hence, the door is open to abject filth finding its way onto the bookshelves.

Teens and preteens are overwhelmed with this dangerous writing, ground out often in paperbacks with lurid covers. And what do they read in this moral pigpen? Group sex is a recurring theme. Bestiality is everywhere. Lurid descriptions of sodomy and lesbianism abound. Often the reader is subjected to the torture and murder of a girl after she is raped. Sexual orgasm is the theme of the works, and this supersedes decency and love. Women are no more than playthings for men, and they are portrayed as nymphomaniacs desiring to jump into bed at any time with any man, woman, group of people, or animal. Engulfed with this filth that is most surely instructing them, Americans are being taught a perverted view of sex. Can schools match this instruction? Is the reason for the sorry state of marriage and divorce partially understandable? What happens when a young man fed on pornography discovers that women are not lining up to bed him and that there is far more to marriage and love than sexual orgasm? How much, added to the rank selfishness of the era, has this to do with the soaring divorce rates in today's marriages? What happens when he expects constant sexual enjoyment each day in every way and discovers that his expectations are unrealistic? Can the marriage survive--no matter the teachings of the school--and even the church? Pornography, whether it comes from books or films, instructs--and, too often, delightfully to the young.

This problem goes beyond filthy books to magazines ranging from soft core (if there, indeed, be such a thing) to the most lurid, and such magazines are big business. Hugh Hefner, former publisher of *Playboy*, formulated a philosophy on sex and life that was the direct antithesis to what the *Bible* teaches. Hefner pleaded for rank hedonism, narcissism, and sexual license for all. A Christian might well have named it dissipation and satyriasis with style on the road to hell--and that describes it well. Americans and others around the world made Hefner (and now his daughter) wealthy and powerful. The public longed for the accompanying pornography masquerading as hip and worthy writings. Magazines like *Hustler* and *Penthouse* gained huge popularity as they featured titillating pictures and writings. Many other publications joined these in what to the youth was compelling sex education. Certainly it left nothing to the imagination, and surely it excited their sexuality. Can the schools, home, and church match the power of this education? Are the schools, as so often charged, guilty of America's sexual morass? Hardly! At the very worst, they are just a little bit reproachable. But this little bit is far too much and needs to be rectified, and the schools must be a compelling source of good in the sorry situation.

Radio

This medium is less well-defined as liberal or conservative than most of the others, a fact that is true because people often listen to their local stations which can tend, particularly in the areas far away from the great cities, to be conservative. Witness the amazing popularity of the Rush Limbaugh program, which is heard on over 600 stations. Consider the popularity of Dr. Laura Schlessinger. At the same time, however, Howard Stern preaches his sexual views and profanity to many listeners--though typically to those who live in huge urban areas.

It is important that the youth be educated on what is happening in their own communities, and, in this, the local radio stations are invaluable. National news, perhaps from ABC, NBC, CBS, or CBN, may be tilted toward the left, but local reporters of the nation's news may not be. Civic educational efforts by local radio stations are an advantage.

The lurking danger is in the rock and roll music stations that, as analyzed earlier, are a problem of huge proportions. These stations, many broadcasting all the filth, murder, and mayhem, loom as an infamous educator of the youth.

Such education is surely most often in direct contradiction to the American consensus value system and the religion of Jesus Christ.

Computers and Cyberspace

The computer age has changed the face of America, resulting in social and economic revolutions that have influenced many writers to identify the last of the twentieth century as an information society. Partially true, such claims resonate joyously to liberal educational elites who, leaning far to the left, underestimate the crucial nature of manufacturing and selling goods. America, operating as it must, is a manufacturing nation and an information social order, and this must not be forgotten in romantic notions about computers.

But computers are powerful elite educators, and they have transported multiplying millions of people into cyberspace, a world with frightful connotations. It developed from cybernetics, which is the theoretical study of processes that control the electronic, biological, and mechanical systems. To cybernate is to control automatically by computer, and space refers to the time and content of the computer messages. The power of this elite force is both astounding and frightening. Control by computer is a fearful possibility, and cyberspace looms as both a force of great good and a distinct danger to the *American Creed*.

American is on-line in cyberspace. Increasing numbers of people are involved in Internet and the World Wide Web, and negative aspects of the movement loom as a gigantic problem to parents, churches, and schools. Degradation is there, and immorality lurks. The most graphic sexual debasement and utter disregard of marriage and family are there. Indeed, marriages are being torn asunder on-line as men and women share bawdy letters in cyberspace. Indeed, the power to educate in ways antithetic to the Creed boggles the mind.

The utter danger of this also has the power and authority to damage the youth in another way. Enchanted by this permissive, controlling mass medium, adolescents often spend far too much time hunched over computers when they should be developing mind, body, and spirit. They should interact with other youth, learn to share, play football in the neighborhood, work to develop their bodies, practice leadership skills and teamwork, achieve socialization and acculturation, and contemplate the world by lying on their backs studying the heavens. These take time that computers too often rob from them.

At the same time, though, computers offer much that is useful. A world of information is at hand, and a sophisticated knowledge of the instrument is a societal necessity. The defining problem is how to limit the evil and maximize the good, a goal that school, home, and church must define and teach.

Though on the surface, media and government seem unlike in their power to instruct, they are, in many ways, similar, both having largely yielded to the humanistic faith. Their power to educate dwarfs that of the schools, homes, and churches as these institutions too often operate.

Chapter Four

OTHER ELITE POWER FORCES

ELITE INTEREST GROUPS

There remain numerous other educative power elites as effective in the damage they accomplish. A careful examination of these is important in understanding America's deep and abiding problems.

In a democratic republic like America, interest groups surround every issue concerning the public. Always there are liberal, moderate, or conservative groups. Hence, the questions are approached from all sides. So it is with schooling. And who is to say that this is not America doing business as usual and as it should?

To conservative Americans, a very great evil is the National Education Association (hereafter identified as NEA).This is not to be confused with another NEA (National Endowment for the Arts), which somehow believes that artists are holy and should not be subject to the laws of decency. This interest group may be as damaging as any force to the *American Creed* as it displays rapture at a statue of Christ in a jar of urine and other such alleged art. But the educational NEA is the focus of this chapter.

The NEA is a powerful union wed to the welfare of teachers, but it is also much more. It is political, as it influences politics in the direction of socialism; always, it backs the most liberal politicians who, in turn, often promise to sell out to the group. It is also a teachers' union representing the interests of its huge membership. Finally, it is a professional organization, supposedly standing firm for democratic schooling. Actually, instead, it was/is ever pushing for an anti-God, socialistic social order grounded in the humanistic faith.

The long, checkered history of the NEA has been dubious from its very inception. Long the organ of the left and school administrators, the organization changed in the early 1960s, pandering to faculty and thus becoming, for all purposes, an active labor union for teachers. Part of this was a battle for power. The teacher unions were growing. Now there is a huge, predictable battle for influence between the American Federation of Teachers (AFT) and the NEA.

Of the two, the NEA is the primary target of conservative groups. The actual effect that the group has on school policy is less than conservatives suppose. The NEA is as predictable as liberalism itself. Always, it follows a self-seeking ultra-liberalism far removed from the *American Creed*. Always, too, there is a socialistic cast to the group's thinking. They will prosper more with liberal politicians than with conservatives, demonstrating, again, the importance of politics in saving the *American Creed*.

The objectives of the NEA on its 1992 resolutions is instructive. The very statement of pure *political correctness*, the goals stand in abject disagreement with scriptural truth and the *Creed*. Part of the list, of course, endeavors to accomplish the typical business of unions, protecting members.

This is worthy of careful examination. The overt attacks at school choice are certainly self-seeking. Private business, vouchers, or tax credits, the group claims, peril the public schools; hence, they attack. For the same reason, home schooling is under siege. Predictable, also, is the demand for increased early childhood schooling and expanded counseling. More teachers would be required, but the home would lose more power and authority. The grossly incorrect demand that those with AIDS should continue to meet with students day to day is ludicrous. Just think: A few years ago teachers had to have their lungs x-rayed. Any sign of tuberculosis resulted in the teacher being removed from the school environment. Now those who could infect the youth with the HIV virus, reasons the NEA, can stay. Insanity multiplies.

Even more serious are the philosophies espoused by the labor union. Sex education, the job of the home and church, is to become more important; moreover, the parents are to be disenfranchised as the teachers railroad every whim and desire without legal redress. Abortion is approbated. Sensitivity to homosexuals is a goal, and counseling for these people is to lead to acceptance of their actions. Indeed, the "diversity of sexual orientation" would often focus on presenting homosexuality as an acceptable lifestyle, no better nor worse than others, though God makes clear that such a lifestyle is sin. The "right to reproductive freedom" opens the doors to adultery, fornication, abortion, and nearly any sexual deviation.

The biblical explanation of the destinies of men and women and their natures is utterly trashed. Sexual stereotyping, most often scriptural, is under direct attack. Affirmative action, which makes no attempt to consider excellence, is recommended. The schools' most dangerous misadventure, multiculturalism, is, of course, approved, as is global education, most often a means to attack America--or to whitewash its greatness as the political hope of mankind.

And anything the schools want should be taught to the pupils, no matter the desires of the parents--those who own the schools. (1UThere is o be no censorship. Indeed, there must be no interference, neither moral nor legislative by the home.

To cap the miserable situation, the NEA wants *extremist* groups out of the schools entirely. Who are these terrible groups? They are those who disagree with the NEA's pro-humanist, anti-Christian claims.

Is it any wonder that home schooling and private Christian schools are increasingly evident? And is it any wonder that Christians attack the public schools, for, surely, they comprehend that schooling is not meeting the needs of their children. So often it stands directly against much that parents endeavor to teach.

The most fearful aspect of the NEA is that its labor union increasingly has the power to radicalize increasing numbers of teachers in a time when they are buffeted by angry taxpayers. The old cliche of any port in a storm is useful. Many will go where they are appreciated and represented with some power. They are being driven into unions, even though the labor movement nationally is declining rapidly.

But critics who claim that the unions have made anarchists of teachers are only partially right. In some places, particularly in the great cities, this is so. In the hamlets and middle-sized communities of the nation, the touch of the NEA and other unions is less. Many teachers who belong to a union, whether it be the NEA, AFT, or a local group, have little interest in it. They would like better salaries and working conditions, but the objectives of the union are foreign to them.

Of far more threat are the political ramifications of the NEA as it endeavors to influence education through the use of radical politics. In this, there is reason to fear the group.

The AFT has similar ideals, but it is far less likely to affect national politics concerning schooling. It is, first and foremost, a labor union more adept at local influences than the NEA. It knows how to use power, bombast, and threats, and it has brought home to teachers many victories concerning working conditions, salary, and redress of unfair, illegal mistreatment. Local unions typically gain less dramatic victories, and many work closely and cooperatively with the local school boards.

It is the NEA that looms as the greatest threat--and this because of its political agenda. With a liberal president and congress, the NEA would be a distinct and terrible menace to those who send their children to public schools. This elite force, having done some damage, can, in a favorable environment, become an important factor uniting government and schooling in a socialistic, anti-God system that could, over time, destroy the *American Creed* and, indeed, the nation itself.

In the give and take of the American system, numerous groups endeavor to persuade. It should not surprise, and, really, it is the political process that has made the nation a very special place.

Conservative groups have had an important impact on the schools--and will have even more in the future. Dr. Pat Robertson built a huge and effective conservative organization to do battle against the liberal forces. Working with Robertson, Dr. Ralph Reed and the Christian Coalition, representing over a million members, had a profound influence. These groups have enjoyed huge successes affecting local, state, and national elections. This organization could eventually rival the NEA in power and influence; it could neutralize the NEA ideology. The Daughters of the American Revolution has been a force, as has the John Birch Society--so attacked by the liberal media. Believing churches have been a huge asset. Consider the power of the Moral Majority under the leadership of Dr. Jerry Falwell in promoting conservative Christian views. Witness, also, the amazing successes of Dr. D. James Kennedy, famed pastor of the Coral Ridge Presbyterian Church in Ft. Lauderdale, Florida. The influence of Dr. James Dobson in his *Focus Upon the Family* is immense. These are but a few of the elite conservative forces laboring against the anti-Christian ideals of groups like the NEA.

But democracy is at work. Liberal church groups and unbelieving churches speak out vigorously for the humanizing of schooling. Nearly any artist type with a soapbox cries out against the *American Creed*--and certainly against anything Christian. A powerful influence has been producer Norman Lear's *People for the American Way*, a group opposing anything that hints of Christianity and much of the *American Creed*--although it must be said that the group has moderated its stand a bit. The American Civil Liberties Union's actions, supposedly to insure constitutional rights, have attacked anything Christian and much of what is right and decent through the courts. Again, though, all of this is part and parcel of the democratic process. Each group has every right to be heard.

Still, the NEA looms as a terrible threat, not as it now operates, but when liberal politicians are in power. With victory this group could lead the quest that would place schooling in the hands of Washington bureaucrats (the very worst place it could be). This elite force is, indeed, much to be feared.

Another powerful interest group is Planned Parenthood. Harry Whittaker, for many years distinguished Superintendent of Schools in Peoria, Illinois, explained the perverse power of this movement on his administration. Its liberal agenda, particularly as it applies to abortion and sex, is a powerful elite force antithetic to the Creed and perhaps as damaging as the NEA. In nearly every way, this group stands against the Creed and Mosaic Law.

THE PEER GROUP

Of all the elite influences setting policy to educate, none is more important than the peer group, particularly during the junior and senior high school years. Too often during this period, much (perhaps all) of what the home, church, and school have taught as right and true falls before peer group ideals. To many parents, it seems as if their sons and daughters have gone mad--that they have sold out all that is good and decent to groups of adolescent and preadolescent youth who come very close to knowing nothing. Many who claim to know the ways of these youthful minds assert that this is perfectly normal--that the behavior represents no more nor less than an admirable assertion of freedom and a healthful breaking away from the home and parents. The person is simply growing up. At its very best, however, this is but partially true.

But psychologists issue numerous statements that demonstrate the inaccurate nature of their endeavors which often do not represent scientific knowledge. Just shop around, and almost any notion of motivation and behavior finds a comfortable home in a psychological theory. It is very important to comprehend that much of what such people, including counselors, utter and write is based upon what they feel rather than proven knowledge. Make no mistake; much of humanistic psychology, counseling, and psychotherapy is at complete odds with the Creed and biblical truths and must thus be viewed as incorrect and dangerous by believers.

Nonetheless, there is compelling evidence in social psychology that the peer group becomes of paramount importance to youths during the teen years. About this there is little disagreement. The quarrel is whether or not such behavior is inevitably damaging to communication with the home, and that is absolutely unacceptable under any conditions. The humanist may nod his head in approval of much peer group behavior and thinking that should be contested by most Americans--and, indeed, must be battled.

It is important to know the mind set of many who write of normal adolescent behavior, particularly the humanist prattle. Distrusting any value system based on the *American Creed* and claiming that teaching about right and wrong is inherently teaching religion, they base their fondest hopes on the beneficent nature of mankind, innately good and led astray only by institutions and environment. And, at the same time, for some inexplicable reason, the inexperienced youth are thought to have endless knowledge. But from whence comes this profundity and acumen? It cannot come from experience or a wide fund of knowledge. The person, they say, must discover what he already knows. This claim is, whether or not they understand it, central to much humanistic psychology; thus, much unacceptable behavior is accepted as normal and acceptable.

Adolescents most surely are not given the knowledge of all things, and in their group affiliation desires they must continue to maintain their dialogue with home, school, church and remain decent, no matter the values and behaviors of their group. This view seems ridiculous to many sitting in decision-making positions in the public schools who have been foolishly brainwashed to accept the humanistic psychological explanation for human motivation, values, and behavior.

In truth, the power of adolescents is precisely what their parents (and other adults) operating within the law allow them. They are neither mature nor wise. Some educators will argue that everything must be relevant to them and that they have a sound sense of what they need; hence, the peer group develops this good sense and judgment based on relevancy. How foolish and shortsighted this is. Yes, they have some notion of their current interests, much of it, incidentally, narcissistic and hedonistic, no matter the teaching and training from home and the church; however, they can have little or no sense of what will be relevant when they grow up. Adults know far more about this than they do, and this the liberal humanists too often fail to understand.

Still, because the peer group looms as powerful educator of the youth, any solution to education's problems must focus on the group's influence on its members. Parents, school, and church must turn their dedicated attention to dealing with these groups. The power and motivation of groups is well represented in social psychological studies. Attitudes are formed more effectively in groups than alone, and people, particularly adolescents, have strong desires for affiliation with their peers. Add the study of mob behavior, and any thinking person should understand the tremendous power of such groups to influence behavior and ideals of their members. It is, then, crucial for the adults in power to extend every effort to locate the youth in the best possible peer groups. Even this is a gamble, for the character of any group can be terribly misread by adults, but the efforts must be made. So much is at stake.

Many mothers who were students of one of the authors through the years indicated that the peer group would not be a serious problem for their children. In most cases, the children were in elementary school; perhaps most often toddlers. This naive thinking by the mothers that the ideal home and church would overcome peer group influence is too optimistic. Yes, the home and church are crucial, and they increase the possibilities that the youth will locate with less damaging peer groups. But there is a kind of madness that sets in with many teens and preteens, and it is most often informed by a peer group--often of the parents' scorn. The best that many of these mothers can hope for and expect is that their sons and daughters will not seriously damage their lives in this life stage and that they will, when mature, return to the ways of their upbringing. But parents must not underestimate the overriding power and influence of the peer groups.

They are, perhaps after the mass media, which largely influences their excesses and foolishness, the most influential of all the educators during the teen years. How in the world can schooling stand as the effective teacher that the peer group is? And how, say, in matters of controlled substances and sex, can the schools match the preachments of the group? How responsible is schooling for youth behavior in these areas?

HEROES

Because the peer group and its mentality is inextricably linked to its heroes, it would be difficult, indeed, to overestimate the effect that such perceived champions have on young people. Certainly, for many of them, such people are profound teachers, instructing them in their very philosophies of life and in the behavior they should exhibit. The peer groups are frequently built around a person, often a young, anti-establishment member of an adolescent singing group--although they are influenced, too, by other media figures, often sports participants.

Many readers of this book could share how a person or persons influenced their lives. Until the late 1960's and early 1970's, the situation usually presented few serious problems, although even then many parents were annoyed and distressed at the hero worship. How this changed, starting perhaps over twenty-five years ago. The rock musicians, many of whom should have claimed the slogan, "Hate society; be disgusting," became heroes and models for hundreds of thousands of adolescents. They burst tragically upon the scene standing in abject antithesis to what most Americans wanted for their children. They were filthy; untended hair hung down their backs. Narcotics, they babbled, represented a new and wonderful hope to escape the horrible American world. Barnyard sex, often shared in communes, was an important new social movement. They identified their disgusting behavior as the *new morality*, while their mothers and fathers sighed--well understanding that it was most surely the same *old immorality* that had broken so many hearts, homes, and lives through the years. No one over thirty was trusted, and work (the Puritan work ethic) was, of itself, thought evil. The political affiliation with their heroes championed the Marxist-Leninist ideology. Ho Chi Min, Castro, and Stalin were huge heroes of the youth; and students, influenced by their heroes, dutifully carried copies of *The Redbook* by Mao Tse Tung in their hip pockets. Often they went into ecstasy quoting heroine

Jane Fonda, who was reported to have said, "We all should drop to our knees and thank God for communism."

Hero emulation as a good system of education had broken down. A trip to the bedrooms of many adolescents in the era would have found posters of the following on their walls and ceilings: "Che" Guevara, the Marxist-Leninist revolutionary; Jane Fonda, friend of the Viet Cong; Jim Morrison of The Doors; and Janis Joplin, who drank herself into an early grave trying to ease the pain of being an American. Mick Jagger, preening satyr and the very personification of rebellion, shook his buttocks at the youth, and they accepted the act as truth--which must have amused Jagger. Then there might also have been posters of the Beatles, who bred disobedience and rebellion in the youth. Sulking Bob Dylan preached anti-establishment themes and would surely have been represented on the wall.

The fact is that these antiheroes formulated a most effective revolution based on hero worship. Add to that peer leadership and procedure to evangelize the dangerous foolishness, much of it anti-American, and a social problem of huge proportions emerged. It is profitable, indeed, to examine the late 60's and early 70's for the worship of antiheroes. In the current era, the problem is somewhat different, but, still, the media breeds sorrowful heroes. In any era, the youth must surely have worthy heroes, men and women who stand for high-level values and worthy behaviors. But one must properly ask if the school is guilty for the damaging heroes that the youth accept. The schools are, of course, largely innocent. They continue to teach about great persons: Abraham Lincoln, George Washington, and the rest of the list of admirable historic and literary characters. Unfortunately, though, the lure of the mass media and the resulting youth culture have far more power than the school in the matter. Neither the home, church, nor any social force has as much power to instruct adolescents.

But liberal professors in the colleges and universities joined hands with revisionist historians to dismantle the respect for many heroic persons and the accompanying myths that had provided such positive heroes.

Myths are of primary importance in providing heroes to the young people. One understanding of the word is that it refers to a person who represents a highly admired cultural ideal or a powerfully shared emotion. The person displays heroic qualities which may have been magnified to make him greater than he is, and stories of his life, often much exaggerated, make of him a model for the youth. The tales focus on how good or admirable we might be and are thus a powerful force for good in educating the young. Someone, however, will submit that teaching a lie is evil. Why, they will ask, should Thomas Jefferson be held up as a model if he fathered children with his slaves--and even left these children nothing in his will? Ben Franklin was a womanizer; so was Eisenhower. The revisionists take pride in attacking the noble examples educators have held up for the youth. Indeed, the critics are most surely wrong.

In all of this, maturity is a factor. As we build heroes, we do not lie; rather, we focus on and enlarge the admirable values and behaviors to help build foundations in the *American Creed*. The wonderful tales of Washington chopping down the cherry tree and tossing the coin across the river have no basis in fact but tremendous value in teaching the values the great man held. So it is with Abraham Lincoln, Winston Churchill, Martin Luther King, Jr., Nathan Hale, Patrick Henry, and with hundreds of other historic figures. We have used myths to build a great people.

But we do not stop here; for when the youths reach a certain level of maturity it is incumbent that the truth be understood so that they comprehend their own natures. In every person, there is the continuing battle between good and evil. Sometimes good people, heroes, behave terribly. This, too, is crucial for students to learn--but later. Then it is not a silly and cruel debunking, but a comprehensive understanding of human nature. If Thomas Jefferson did battle with his dark side, then the students, admiring positive values learned from the great man's life, are steeped in the nature of man and the very battles that each of them, in one way or another, will face.

Yes, myth has tremendous power and validity in presenting proper heroes and admirable high-level consensus values to students. It builds the significant and admirable value system that must be part of the very foundation they utilize to measure right and wrong, both when they are very young and, later, when they come to terms with their own behavior and that of their fellow men. This is essential in teaching the consensus *American Creed*. Those who in their smugness or political agenda strive to destroy heroes, the great myths that build character and values in students, have done much harm to the students who need the valuable foundation of admirable consensus American high-level values--precisely what has made this nation so admirable.

For the myths to have salutary significance, however, the hero must--and this is crucial--stand for admirable consensus values. Rock stars most often do not. Rap stars do not. Heavy metal stars do not. Fascists and Communists do not. So many of the persons appealing to the youth in this era cannot help build the proper myth. These people are not a part of a satisfactory solution; instead, they are part of the problem--and they must be perceived as precisely that.

THE PARENTS OR THE STATE?

Much of any hope for improvement in the American institutions, school being one, turns on the power of the family. But who has the primary responsibility to raise children: the family or the federal (or state) government? Not so long ago, the answer would have been clear: the family. In recent years, with the increasing power of liberalism, the selfishness of the current era, and the lure of the federal dole, many have turned to the liberal dream of federal control in rearing the youth. In all of this, there is a notion shared by many humanistic liberals that parents are typically cruel, incapable, thoughtless, and uncaring. Fathers, they believe, are lurking to rape their daughters and to beat the children. Mothers are co-conspirators, and both are too ignorant to raise the youth. Somehow--and this would be laughable if it were not tragic--many believe that bureaucrats inside the Washington, D.C., beltline know what children need.

It must be noted that an important factor in this mentality resulted from the Civil Rights campaign, particularly from the women's movement--part of it from the selfishness of the baby boomers, part of it from very real financial need. Whichever, the children were under direct attack when mothers turned to the federal government, demanding federally run, free day-care centers and other governmental doles so that they would be free from their historic mandate: raising their children in loving, nurturing homes. This, of course, delighted the liberal politicians who rubbed their respective hands together with glee. The floodgates were open to increasing governmental control of homes and families. Indeed, the second family income and the feminist dedication to desert the home for the ego satisfaction of the marketplace opened the door to the government having a far greater role in educating the youth. As feminists shout, "Biology is not destiny," they must realize, then, that the fate of the family may be set by politicians.

The problem, though, far transcends the problem of whom is to raise children. It is, in fact, how much power the federal government will have in all areas of education, including schooling. Any effective solution of this terrible predicament demands that the power be taken from the federal government, as the *Constitution* consistently indicates, and returned to the people, particularly the family, America's most important institution.

THE FORCE OF SOCIOECONOMIC STATUS

This is a crucial factor in what transpires in the schools; however, it tends to be a local rather than state or federal problem. *Socioeconomic* refers to the social level and status as well as to the economic and financial positions of people who are typically identified as lower, middle or upper class--although there are many gradations between these three levels. It is absolutely critical to comprehend that socioeconomic level is a most important factor in a child's success. It is essential to understand that it is far more important than ethnicity or race in determining the manner in which a person lives. The terribly misguided multicultural school movement that focuses so often on just ethnicity or race could not be less effective or meaningful. Socioeconomic level is sadly and foolishly bypassed in the political demands of each group to get its own.

The neglected truth is that blacks, Hispanics, and all peoples behave primarily as those in their social class. Upper-class blacks and whites behave, think, eat, live, and worship very much alike. Middle-class ethnic and racial groups behave, think, eat, live, and worship like middle-class whites, and so it is with peoples in the lower class as well.

For instance, lower-class youth are far less willing to delay immediate gratification than are those of the other two classes. Violence as a means of problem solution is far more typical of lower-class people, as is gang participation. Sex begins at an earlier age for lower-class youth, and cursing is far more prevalent. Indeed, it is social class, first, that defines behavior and motivation. It is tragic and foolish that the multiculturalists pretend not to understand this.

This means that the very area in which a child grows to adulthood may very well define what the expectations and behaviors of the schools are. It explains, also, why racial integration and the ensuing busing have not been more successful. It is far easier, many would claim, successfully to mix middle-class whites, blacks, and Hispanics in the schools than lower, middle, and upper-class whites alone.

In this regard, children attending lower, middle, and upper-class schools should sometimes receive differing schooling. Upper and middle-class schools would, everything being equal, offer more college preparatory courses, while lower socioeconomic level pupils would study more often in programs preparing them for jobs after high school. Thought by many critics of schooling to be racist, this practice endeavors to prepare youth to succeed at what they will do after graduation. It fails at every level, though, if it does not prepare the academically able from every group for college success and those not choosing higher education to excel in the work world. The force of socioeconomic levels has to be evaluated in any accurate explanation of the elite influencers of schooling.

Part of the problem is money. In most states, though, this is changing gradually. The wealth of a given community's property is the most important financier of schooling. That is to indicate if the average price of real estate in a given community were, say, $100,000, the monies per student would be far, far greater than if the value were $15,000. If the wealth of the community, as evidenced in its property taxes, is high, it could result in a $7,000 or $8,000 difference per pupil in available monies for schooling. This being true, socioeconomic level is a powerful influencer of schooling.

Earlier, in the Rodrequez Supreme Court decision, the finding was that, since the *Constitution* failed to speak of the subject, schooling was not a constitutional right of American youth. Hence, it was legal to finance schooling primarily by the wealth of the community. Still, though, the powers not belonging to the federal government are the states. Hence, if a state constitution mentions schooling, it may demand that the wealth of the state finance schooling so that all students receive equitable sums, a battle being fought in many state courtrooms now. Even with this, though, socioeconomic class remains a dominant force in defining what will transpire in the schools.

This next area of discussion is most certainly not *politically correct*, and it most often is not discussed. It must be, however, because like socioeconomic groups tend, often because they have no other choice, to live in the same neighborhoods and areas. This is particularly true of lower-class people, and it becomes a serious social problem in the ghettos and barrios of the great cities. The lower-class folks are located in such areas because of some combination of environmental and genetic forces. The second of these areas is off-limits in *politically correct* discussions. Nonetheless, genes are a factor in what people are and become, and they must be considered in any discussion of powers that influence schooling.

Liberal educational theorists often join their governmental fellow travelers in claiming that learning is simply a function of time and effort. If a student is having trouble, the schools often supply more time and tutorial help; but learning is more than just a factor of time. Genetic ability is also crucial. For all of us, there is a limit to what we can learn and do, a truth not understood by many critics of schooling.

One of the trademarks of schools in the present era is the overwhelming assistance for disadvantaged students, a fact that has no peer in the history of schooling. A truly remarkable humane effort, it speaks glowingly of the efforts of the schooling enterprise. Indeed, laws and dedication of teacher and administrators have joined hands in the admirable effort. Japan, Germany, and other economic giants have not even approached the efforts of American schools in educating all students, and this must be considered in any comparison of the schools.

In these and other nations, the focus of schooling is on educating the very most gifted students. It is no wonder whatsoever that such nations produce high test scores, that American students do not at this time compete well with them. And so the reader, as well as all taxpayers, must consider this dilemma in depth.

There is not an infinite amount of money. Choices must be made.

Other Elite Power Forces

Presently, it costs over three times as much to school a mentally handicapped student as it does the other pupils. This, of course, means monies that could be used to educate an intellectual elite are utilized for all young people, with huge sums being spent on those who have the least intellectual abilities. In America, could anything else be done? Yet, the nation dare not allow other industrial nations to supersede it in intellectual leadership. In this abiding problem resides a major question for the nation and its schools.

A few years ago, people of good will believed that one of the most admirable goals (and indeed it is an important plank in the *American Creed*) was to provide equal opportunity for all American youth. That became a noble goal, and, prodded by legal fiat, enormous strides were made. It became clear, however, that equal opportunity was not obtaining equal results, something that many liberal politicians demanded. They were, of course, sadly incorrect in their expectations. This result was bound to have occurred and should not be evaluated negatively. All people do not have the same abilities, and so it is with intellect as well.

Since the beginnings of modern schooling, educators have known that learning and success in life are, to a very large degree, the result of both a child's environment and genetic inheritance. This fact suffered dramatically as a result of the genetic ideas of the monster Adolph Hitler, who endeavored to build a master race and to eliminate from the face of the earth the Jewish people, whom he perceived as hereditarily inferior. The genocide of the Jewish people stands as one of the terrible atrocities in the history of man's cruel walk through time, as evil as the contemporaneous butchering in America of babies in their mothers' wombs, many because of perceived genetic deficiencies.

After the defeat of the Axis foes, few people desired to speak of genetic inheritance at all. This profoundly affected all institutions, but perhaps none so much as schooling. Forgetting any thoughts of genetic inheritance, the schools turned completely, or very nearly so, to environment as the causal element in what a human being becomes. Hence, grandiose plans were made to build a great people and society by controlling the environment. Indeed, it was thought that if the environment were controlled, schooling could go a long way toward solving the problems of poverty and other social ills.

Part of this resulted from the humanistic environment in teacher preparation. Humanists often believe that mankind, being good and noble, becomes evil because of environmental factors. Just change the environment, and mankind will flower. Believing that naive, simplistic ideal, decision-makers in the schools worked hard to educate by changing the environment, particularly of poor, inner-city students.

If humans are some combination of their genetic inheritance and their environment, it is no wonder that the schools turned to environment; for they could, certainly not in the short run, affect the genes. To be frank, it is clear that this problem is to be solved in the bedroom and not the classroom. Ultimately, then, genetic theories would obviously not be embraced by the schooling profession, even though it knew full well that genes play a role in what people can do and will become. They were probably correct in placing all their hopes on the environmental ideal. This is all they could change, and, in the 1960's, President Johnson's time, they secured huge federal monies in attempting to change the social order by manipulating the environment in the child's life. It was as if truth itself were discovered in those days. The fact, now denied by many who were involved in the romantic movement, was that the universities, reveling in money made available by the federal government to build President Johnson's Great Society, promised that they could lead the public schools to achieve greatly, perhaps abolishing poverty. The universities preened and gloated with their new and exciting power. Yes, a wonderful new America could be built on changing a youth's environment, and they would lead it.

From this, an important lesson was learned: Don't expect the universities to solve anything that has to do with the public schools. The ivory tower mentality and its attending humanistic agenda exclude higher education from this arena. The extravagant claims, resulting, really, in nothing but failure, announced to the public the huge deficiencies of the universities and colleges; and, at this very hour, higher education, discredited, suffers terribly from the failure, particularly because the taxpaying public financed the folly to the tune of multiplied billions of dollars.

Higher education, though, can help. Perhaps the most important calling of the university, research, provides considerable significant information. Anyone making decisions concerning the education of the next generation should certainly discover the results of research in schooling, human motivation, social psychology, learning theory, genetics, and other areas pertaining to teaching students. Otherwise, the public school people themselves, armed with the results of the research, should make their own decisions. They are on the firing line rather than romantically secluded in the tower.

Research called to question the very humanistic gospel of environmental causality for most human behavior that the universities so embraced. Several findings profoundly affected knowledge of genetics, asserting that to place all the eggs in the environmental basket simply was oversimplifying a very complex problem. Studies of twins indicate a most surprising genetic influence in their lives. It became clear, to a very surprising degree, that many illnesses are of genetic origin. Other studies indicated that genes seemed to affect behavior of humans in a most emphatic manner. Still other studies found that school, focusing on changing the environment, was a poor predictor of success in a pupil's life; rather, it was the home from which he/she came. This, of course, suggested that both genetic inheritance and environment were factors. At least, it suggested that middle and upper-class homes produced more successful youth, and there is surely a very important genetic factor at work.

It is this factor that, in large part, explains many of the shortcomings of public schooling. Two huge problems are of critical importance: the situation in the urban inner city and the failure to educate children not achieving well in school.

In the 1960's a spate of laws, huge efforts in financing, and dedicated teachers focused on the problems of the inner cities. Primarily, the effort was on changing environment. The Civil Rights Movement led, among other things, to the worthy effort to desegregate schools, this, of course, partially based on the thought that a change in environment would result in optimum learning for black youth. Part of the movement was to bus the youth for racial integration. Busing, the result of research accomplished by James Coleman, was the product of humane and worthy motivation. The results, unfortunately, have been disappointing. The change in environment resulted in little more learning by black youth. Test scores, incorrectly identified as no more than a measure of culture, rose just a bit, and governmentally financed programs helped only a little. It is true that black test scores, significantly below those of whites, have risen a bit, which can allow some hope. Though the difference is still huge, it is slightly better--and this is a meager statement of hope for the environmental view.

The busing movement, mandated by laws with teeth, did mix the races although never to the satisfaction of the U.S. Department of Education or the courts. At this time, it has failed. The situation in the great metropolitan areas has become intolerable, producing what some sociologists have identified as a permanent underclass. Part of this was the result of busing limitations. There could be no forced busing across school district lines unless segregatory intent could be proven or unless the two districts agreed to the idea. What happened, then, was what some identify as *white flight* to the suburbs. More accurately, it was *middle-class flight*, and it was predictable. Successful people, not simply the majority, seek the better life. When they can afford it, they often move to the suburbs or country. But the results are serious indeed for the teeming millions in the urban areas, and one reason for this is the genetic problem, something that is almost never mentioned by analysts of the situation.

The inner cities are, of course, not all black. Hispanics, whites, and other groups are also involved; hence, any discussion of genes should not be considered an attack upon blacks. Still, there is an ominous problem grounded in what the child inherits. Those who move to the suburbs or country are most often educated people who have done well financially. These are most often people who have had the genetic ability to succeed in an intellectual arena, and such people tend to marry others with similar abilities. Having succeeded, they seek the better life, move out of the old neighborhood, and find a home among primarily middle-class people, often of other ethnic and racial backgrounds. This is not to say that there are neither bright nor capable people in these areas or that every successful person flees. It is to assert that genetics play a far greater role in poverty than is generally supposed, and this surely means that inherited traits play a huge role in the terrible plight of inner-city people and those residing in isolated rural areas. Changing the environment may help, but the genetic problem will not be solved; and, without this solution, the turmoil in the great inner cities will not be solved.

Schooling can continue to deal with environment and, hopefully, gain some victories, particularly as it equips the youth with the skills salable in the marketplace. To expect that schooling will solve the social problems in these areas is a false dream, and the taxpayers expecting such a result had better understand this. The social order, apart from the schools, must come to perceive that the most difficult solutions will come from sources other than the schools. But there must be an answer, for the problem is social dynamite that bids to destroy the nation; and any solution must take into account the genetic aspect.

As indicated earlier, there are those who insist that schools must go beyond equal opportunity to equal results. If the poor performance of the pupil is based entirely on environmental shortcomings, such a result might possibly occur; however, the innate ability of the child is a crucial factor, also. The belief by educators that environment alone is the factor influenced liberal legislators to attack schooling because equal results were lacking. In the early 1970's, there were those who claimed that all children were born *tabula rasa*, their minds a blank slate. Many of these people believed foolishly that each child, properly educated and schooled, could be Einstein or Beethoven. Such fuzzy thinking affected many of liberal humanistic persuasion. It was here that the *equal results* thinking gained strength, and it did damage to the schooling enterprise.

This belief led to an assumption by many curriculum-makers that learning was simply a function of effort and time. This is to say that nearly any child can learn anything if he endeavors to reach the goal and if he is given enough time to accomplish it. This is, of course, another way of asserting that *equal results* are possible--and it completely neglects genetic factors. Such reasoning may be an important reason for the huge dropout problem in public schooling. Genetics are most surely a factor in learning, and there are limits to what children can learn, some more, some less. Those many young people who are forced to try to learn things they are not capable of achieving are surely disaffected with schooling, youth with negative self-concepts acquainted with failure. This is a major failing of schooling, one that is indeed foolish.

THE PSYCHOLOGY AND PHILOSOPHY OF THE AGE

In the current era, these two factors are inextricably intertwined, each influencing the other; and, surely, they are profound affectors of educational and school policies. It would be a serious error to underestimate the influence of these powerful societal forces that are affected by humanistic doctrines and a misreading of man's nature. Both, so dear to the halls of ivy and the bureaucratic mind, are terrible millstones weighing down the social order in general and the schools particularly.

It was Alan Bloom who, in his brilliant book *The Closing of the American Mind*, bewailed the German philosophical connection--that is to say the philosophy of lostness and meaninglessness of life. Quite correctly, Bloom pointed to the fact that historically Americans had been an optimistic people. The entrance of some German philosophers had a profound influence on American consciousness and judgment. Many such philosophies could be considered, but a brief consideration of two of them demonstrates the problem, these being nihilism and existentialism. Both absolutely deny and attempt to refute Christian truth, and thus breed lostness and hopelessness.

The first of these is based on the committed idea that values are baseless and that nothing can be communicated or known. There are no trustworthy moral values; all former theories of morality are to be distrusted. Certainly Christian theology and the *American Creed* are not trustworthy. It is a philosophy of dreadful lostness, of hopelessness that reaches even to the desire to destroy the social order. Perhaps the noun *nihility* describes it best: nothingness and nonexistence.

The second of these, existentialism, is as damaging. It presents humans as alone in an uncaring or hostile world with impersonal forces at work to destroy them one by one. There is neither God nor justice. People have the choice to lose with class, a certain bravado, as they exercise freedom of choice and are responsible for their own actions. It is a bleak, bleak view of man and his world and is in direct conflict with the *Word of God* and the *Creed*.

But someone is sure to assert that there are those claiming to be Christian, often schooled at the most prestigious universities, who claim either to be Christian existentialists or--and this is very, very rare--Christian nihilists. Be sure that nearly all claiming these titles are not evangelical believers--or for that matter truly believers at all. The terms are in conflict. Existentialism and nihilism are humanistic concepts and philosophies.

Particularly the intellectuals, unbelieving theologians, and faux intellectuals accepted these godless philosophies--which, of course, means they were presented as truth in liberal churches, the halls of ivy, and nearly all humanistic conclaves. This arrogant deifying of lostness invaded the American middle class and was a huge plaything of the upper classes wed to the arts.

The influence was (and is) immense. A self-fulfilling prophecy of lostness and failure replaced optimism and faith in God for many people. God, they said, was dead. But the negative philosophies profoundly affected all institutions, not the least of which was schooling. The horrible vacuum left by the philosophies bore bitter fruit in adolescent suicide, school dropouts, violence, and the mounting number of school problems that seem to many unsolvable. The two philosophies of lostness and hopelessness remain disastrous to the nation and its schools, but they are powerful Influencers of what happens in the education of a child. One thing is sure: many psychologists and psychiatrists rubbed their hands together with glee; business was going to get much, much better. And it did, growing beyond what many of these people could have imagined, but lost people going to lost psychiatrists and psychologists getting lost humanistic advice were and remain lost. The solution, the Gospel of Jesus Christ, was all but shut out of the schools, while the psychology of lostness became a humanistic religion.

The psychiatrists and psychologists joined other mental health workers in trying to bring humanistic philosophies and ideals to working with the young (and all) people who were in need. They meant well, but the damage was monstrous. Those buying into the humanistic theories, particularly the terribly misguided Rogerian psychotherapy procedures, (and many, many did,) accomplished substantial harm. They were wrong in their confidence in man's basic goodness and wisdom. In like manner, they were horribly incorrect in their belief that feelings of guilt were evil perpetrated on the young.

The claim, then, that the German philosophies of lostness, as exhibited particularly in existentialism and nihilism, were correct in describing the horrible condition of humankind and were everywhere part of schooling was so. The charges, too, that this mentality increased the feelings of lostness and alienation of moms, dads, and children cannot be denied. The psychology and philosophy of humanist mental health workers invaded all of the social order including the schools. The lost philosophers and the lost humanistic psychologists joined hands to perpetuate tremendous damage to both the nation and its youth. And during this rape of minds and values, the American Civil Liberties Union waited, stalking every effort to teach the only hope: salvation through Jesus Christ. A continuing question remains pertinent: What in the world could the schools have done better in a time that all the media, the unbelieving church, the humanistic legislators, and a huge number of other elites embraced these false ideas?

THE ERA IN HISTORY

To a substantial degree, we are children of our age. When times are good, when the money is rolling in, when all is going well, the mood of the electorate is optimistic. Because education is appreciated and lauded, money is everywhere available during these times. Schooling becomes more experimental and child-centered. Creativity and development of the imagination become far more important than learning facts and skills. However, more than just good financial times affect the mood. Peace or a great military victory leads to euphoria that results in good times for the schools. Anything, in fact, that raises the spirits of the citizens usually results in favorable times for the schools.

Already mentioned was the Johnson era. Times were good, save for the Viet Nam Conflict. Business was profitable. Money was spent in the noble but misguided effort to build the Great Society so longed for by President Johnson; and the public smiled on schooling, many perceiving it to be the hope of the era to build a great people and to abolish poverty. But, even in this, there is (and was) a pendulum swing, back and forth, back and forth, the schools dangling in the wind at the whim of public mood.

The 1970's were a terrible time for schooling. Bad financial times contributed to the worsening situation, joined by lack of faith in American institutions. Test scores went down. Japanese and German production and sales, like a gigantic tidal wave, eroded American pride and confidence. Unemployment often reached frightfully high percentages. College graduates, having substantial trouble finding jobs, were moving back home. Liberal churches were preaching the defunct humanism, thus, in the long run, breeding hopelessness. The television cameras focused on the homeless. Crime multiplied; so did the national debt. The bloom was off the rose.

Schools, of course, bore the brunt of the attack. There was no way they could please the indignant public; nothing could solve the problem. Thus, the schools were and remain hostages of the particular era in which they exist. It could hardly have been worse for the schools. But business got better. The good times rolled again. Other nations lagged behind America in the business realm. Jobs became plentiful, and the stock market soared. Schooling was/is once again in the good graces of taxpayers. Thinking people comprehend the positive influence public schooling has historically had on the nation. There is a broad base of success on which schooling can build, and this is hopeful indeed. But never forget; schooling, like all institutions, reflects the period in which it exists.

THE POWER IS REAL

The power of all these elite forces is very real. Indeed, the elite authorities determine what will happen in the nation's institutions, school being but one. The federal, state, and local governments, the elite professional organizations, the peer group, the heroes of a time, the tremendous authority and dominion of the media, the political party in power, the socioeconomic level, the genes, the psychology and philosophy of the era, and the particular era in history all conspire to exert an enormous power over all areas of the social order including the schools.

In a better time, the home and church would have offset the elite forces with the very character that made them such important institutions. Armed with *God's Word* and the *American Creed*, they formerly stood firm, willing to do battle with the powerful elite forces. These forces, primarily humanistic, were tempered by the church and home; and this, in turn, had much to do with what happened in education. It was and is primarily the ancient battle between the religion of humanism and God.

But what happened when the home fell apart because of the selfishness of the era and when so many of the historic mainline churches joined the humanists in promoting the religion of man by the hypocrisy of calling God's name while preaching humanism, the enemy of the Great God?

The very two forces that had neutralized humanism fell in line with the humanistic movement. The decaying church and home represented (represents) a most grave problem for the United States of America. They had formerly maintained a balance of sorts, acting as a mediator between the religions of Jesus Christ and man. In this, they had kept the *American Creed* alive in the schools. When they surrendered to the selfishness and humanism of the era, America was done very, very serious damage, and the schools---along with other American institutions--had lost the influences slowing the humanistic steamroller. Then humanism became the cardinal principle of the public schools, whether the schools knew it or not. The elite forces identified in this chapter were given *carte blanche,* and America's fatal infection

Other Elite Power Forces

became the schools' organizing principle. It is no wonder that Christians join others in lamenting what appears to be a hopeless situation. Humanism can destroy the nation and lead it into judgment. This being so, the elite forces that formulate school policy remain more dangerous to the common good than nearly anyone perceives.

Chapter Five

THE RESULTS: WATCHING A NATION DIE

Most of the powerful societal influences alluded to in the last chapter are educating the nation in precepts and ideals far removed from what the *Bible* and the Creed say--and, for now, these negative forces seem to be winning. Biblical scholars often consider why America is thought not to be mentioned in prophecy alluding to the end times. Could it be that the nation is, in fact, dying, rotting from within, having turned its back on the Great God? Could it be that this country, the political hope of mankind, the golden dream upon which the Creator, the great Jehovah, smiled, is perishing? Are we, in fact, watching a nation die? Have the powerful elite forces educating Americans, many of them proponents of humanism, won the day? Late in time, is America in its death throes? Must God look elsewhere for a people and a nation to pronounce His truth? Maybe so. But maybe not.

It is not too late to make amends. Yes, we certainly may be watching a great nation die, but there are miracles of God. Perhaps He is not yet through with the land of the free and the home of the brave. Perhaps, He will use this very book to drive home the truth that humanism has torn apart the nation, that the powerful elites formulating American educational policy, school being but a small part, may very well destroy the nation. It is, then, education, understood in its broadest sense that Americans must address with vigor and dedication. The time is past when believers can simply gather on Sunday morning and night, as well as Wednesday night, and worship and pray. Now they must rise up to do honorable battle against humanism, the powerful educator.

Happily, it is not too late. It is late, very late, but not too late if Christians are willing to shoulder their crosses. If they do not, the cause is lost, save intervention by God. We are at the crossroads and must take the high road else humanistic education may very well win in the United States. We stand on the edge of the abyss in the shadow of the Cross and the empty tomb. We teeter, balancing ourselves while we honor man, not God, as humanism issues the siren song, calling, calling. Dear reader, very, very, very much is at stake in the sunset of America's greatness.

MAN MUST CHANGE

Any discussion of the results of humanistic education at every level must focus on the nature of humankind. The forces of humanistic education analyzed in the preceding chapter are based on a particular philosophy of what are the essential characteristics of human beings. It is here, of course, that the focus of the entire problem analyzed in this book must be directed.

The humanists conclude that man is basically good. He is perfectible, and he is, by nature of his intelligence, improving steadily. If he falters, it is environment that brings him down. The evil, then, is in the social environment--not his own soul. It is true, they believe, that if basically good man can improve his social surroundings and environments a better and better nation and world can be built. He is perfectible--and he is ever improving. And this very social progress will continue because he is intelligent enough to continue to amass increasing knowledge as research builds on knowledge edging him ever higher and higher. The nation, the world, will get better and better only if the social environment is improved step by step. There is no limit, given his innate and beautiful character, to the humane world that he can and will build. The great danger to the flawed belief, of course, is Christianity, which teaches exactly the opposite.

The believer understands that all of this is incorrect. Because man is desperately wicked by God's rules, he needs changing. He requires a Savior. He needs to come to the foot of the Cross. He needs to ask for forgiveness and to be saved. He needs to be changed. Without this experience, the Christian understands, there is no lasting problem solution; it is here that humanistic efforts stumble and fall. Infected by sin, man, no matter the nobleness of intention, cannot author the solutions America requires. The analyzation of the humanistic teachings results in our proposal, made later in this book, to overcome, or help to overcome, the problems. The suggestions will assist in evening the playing field in the war between Christianity and humanism, and this is crucial.

The schools and the homes must join the church in this quest. The first two of these help prepare the youth to accept Christ and the *Creed*; their responsibilities in this regard are of paramount importance. Unfortunately, it can well be argued that they are failing American institutions that have joined the armies of humanistic education. They must, in fact, return to the historic calling of inculcating the *American Creed* in the youth who are to be educated for membership in America and to participate in its dream of hope and dignity. Even more important, the church absolutely must return to its historic goal of bringing sinful man to the saving knowledge of Jesus Christ.

MORAL RELATIVISM

Few, if any, social movements are more deadly than humanism's dedication to moral relativism. Truth, the philosophy indicates, is what a particular group or person believes it to be. There are, then, no absolutes; right becomes what a social group or person defines it to be. Because the enemy of this philosophy is any ideal that there are universal rights and wrongs, the *American Creed* and the *Ten Commandments* are thus disparaged and attacked. In fact, the insanity of this misguided, convoluted philosophy boggles the mind. It can lead, finally, to chaos and anarchy. If successful, it will severely damage the *Creed* and biblical truth. This horribly misplaced faith in man's reason and sense of justice, his basic goodness, looms as a major influence to destroy America and the religion of Jesus Christ; yet many humanistic elite educators, in one way or another, educate to this end, whether it be in school or elsewhere. Imagine, the moral relativists have profoundly convinced many, including numerous decision-makers in the schools, and, all too often, the churches, that there is really neither right nor wrong.

What should the public schools do in such a time? Involved as they surely are in politics, they have no choice but to reflect the community. In the give and take of political pressure, they must take the pulse of the taxpayers who own the schools. At the same time, they must not let a minority point of view convince them that it is a majority, and they must reflect the admirable values of the community rather than the base ones.

But do a majority, in fact, accept moral relativism? If they do not, it would confound the forces of the elite humanistic educators who know very well how to influence. Schooling, then, bowing to what these educators perceived to be consensus thinking (and it probably was), became nervous about teaching anything whatsoever concerning what was perceived as right or wrong.

About this time a *situation ethics* appeared on the scene, fitting the relativistic philosophy nicely. Since there are no *a priori* values that are right and wrong, the environmental situation sets acceptable behavior. What is right in one situation may very well be wrong in another. It would be quite impossible to overestimate the damage done to America and its *Creed* as a result of this perverse movement.

But the time was ripe. Under the onslaught of the elites, it appeared that value-free schooling was a majority view; the schools fell in line, an ideal that the National Education Association had also attempted to orchestrate. Consider this: The schools were to be value free; teachers were to remain neutral on values. Indeed, and this should cause a chill in thinking people, the American Civil Liberty Union (ACLU) waited in the wings to bully schools and to bring suit against those holding certain values to be true. The *American Creed* was under direct attack, for this group promised to sue (and did) because any teaching of values was, they said, instruction in religion---and thus illegal under the *First Amendment* to the *U.S. Constitution*. How very low the ACLU had sunk in its efforts to obliterate the very value system authored by the *Constitution* which they claim to represent.

The teachers (who were supposed to be morally neutral) were often involved in a curriculum featuring situation ethics. All around the nation, students were taught that certain behaviors were right in one situation and wrong in another. One is reminded of the urging that neither murder, nor rape, nor denial of one's god, nor any act of itself, is automatically wrong. When the situation is right, any one of these may be acceptable. God help us all as such poison is spread to the youth.

Add to this the development of moral dilemmas, and the terrible failure of public schooling is better understood. A story that involved moral choices was shared with the students, after which each of them was to rate, on a scale from worst to best, the rank order of good or evil of each character. All of this was discussed in class with--and this was absolutely demanded--the teacher remaining neutral. The youth were not to be taught values at all; they were simply to discover what they already believed and to feel well about these beliefs. Any change in these values could, really, come only from other students convincing them of their errors, the ultimate in silly peer influence. It is hard to conceive that even the humanists could accept the preposterous belief that adolescents could have any logical basis upon which to build life values. Their values are in the process of being discovered and made. Values do not come innately from one's inner self. Such reasoning fuels the societal crisis of the excessive narcissistic love the youth have for themselves that many thinking sociologists and theologians believe is the tragedy of the era. The youth must be *taught* values.

Another result, of course, is the damage done to the needed sense of responsibility for one's own actions, the lack of which defines much of the trauma of the current time. If humans are not responsible for their actions (and humanists, as explained earlier, think mankind is basically good), social institutions must be, they claim. This dangerous thinking results in a theory of social causation of human behavior in which no one is personally responsible for anything.

Any thinking American would surely correctly view this as an act of intellectual war against America and its *Creed*. A sworn enemy of America and its hallowed dream could hardly inflict as much damage as the humanists

The Results: Watching A Nation Die

do. In many ways, the public schools, hands tied, understood the danger of value-free schooling. Some courageous teachers willing to lose their jobs pursuing righteousness and working against the value-free schooling were genuine American heroes and heroines. They did make a difference.

But in the final analysis, the public schools are operating against powerful elite educators. They are, to a degree, locked into the humanistic mentality. But private schools--as long as they operate within the law--can and must teach what the people owning them want. If the school is Christian, for instance, the values and ideals would reflect the *Bible* and Christian truth. The religion of Jesus Christ could/would be taught as a fact. Everything Christian could and would be taught, and, in all probability, the *American Creed* and patriotism would be cardinal objectives. This truth, no doubt, explains the amazing growth of private Christian schools. In such private schools, children of believing Christians study values and theology acceptable to the parents.

At about this time, the serious reader may be wondering about the comments we made that Americans continue to accept and honor the *American Creed*. Why, then, did we claim that the taxpayers probably accepted much of the humanistic drivel in the schools? The answer is very important, for it has much to do with what is proposed later in the book. A hierarchy of values exists in all people. There is some reason to believe that the *Creed* was more influential on values and behaviors before the disastrous late 60's and early 70's. It is probably so, then, that the *Creed* is less important than it earlier was and that the education of narcissistic schooling in the last three decades and more has unfortunately been successful. But still the consensus *Creed* exists--and it remains the political hope of the schools and the nation.

OPENNESS

In his landmark book *The Closing of the American Mind*, Professor Alan Bloom explained that the one value displayed for sure by students is openness. They have surely been instructed, trained really, by nearly all the humanistic elite sources, including schooling, to be open about everything. Not only are students to be open to all things but so, too, are faculty. A popular evaluative instrument, claiming quite incorrectly to measure teaching ability, looks carefully at perceived teacher openness.

This is all predictable given the absurdity of humanistic mentality. If man is good, if he is what the humanists believe and teach him to be, it follows that he is going to accomplish good as he perceives it. Since man is godly and moral, they believe, humankind will direct itself toward the good. This being so, people must be accepting of all behaviors in every area of life. If a person is *politically correct*, he is to be utterly open about everything. Since many of these people stand firmly against the *Creed*, Christianity, and historic values, they must, by the very nature of their beliefs about people and their motivations, shun being judgmental. In order to achieve this goal, openness is a high-level virtue to them.

It sounds wonderful to adolescents who, by the very nature of the glands directing them, are delighted to accept everything as normal--even the hedonistic, narcissistic base thoughts humans share. Openness signifies acceptance. If nothing is wrong, if there are no consensus admirable values, then people should be open to ideas that are far different from those they hold. This makes substantial sense to the elite humanists who persuade in educational matters.

But this is abominable to many thinking people. To insist on open-mindedness in all things is to be closed-minded to the *American Creed* and Christianity. Behaviors attacking the *Creed* or Christian faith should not be viewed with an open-minded attitude, for to do so involves willingness to be won over to the beliefs repugnant to the individual's very sense of right and wrong. The tenets of Christianity as well as the *Creed* present some things as right, some as wrong.

Still, though, many public schools join the elite forces in this openness error. How are those who believe firmly in the *Creed* and, more importantly, the religion of Jesus Christ to react to their children being taught openness as a major societal behavior and value?

A few examples are useful. If the youth are free to make their own decisions concerning all claims by others, hence, open-mindedness, what should they do in the following situations?

A human, really hating his parents, plans to murder them. A young man, testosterone flooding his adolescent system, decides to rape a female classmate. A friend is selling *crack* to elementary students. A man is committing incest with his daughter. A homosexual asserts that his sexual behavior is normal and acceptable. A teacher tells his class that no lifestyle is better than another, that, in this regard, homosexual families are as moral as the historic American family.

These few examples make the point. No Christian, no person accepting the *Creed*, could possibly be open-minded to these situations, nor should he be. Rather, he should be closed-minded to such deplorable behavior and open--minded to the truth of the *Bible* and the verity of the *American Creed*. In this openness movement, the humanities are, in a very real manner, teaching closed-mindedness to very high-level values that make America such a great nation.

This open-minded business is a direct affront to believers who well perceive that closed-mindedness must sometimes be taught. In all of this, a very interesting question may be raised: Is a public school curricula featuring the misguided teaching of open-mindedness in direct disregard of *First Amendment* rights? In this regard, are children being forced by the states to study ideas in direct disregard of their religious tenets?

This is yet another way to assert that this sensing of good where it is nowhere in sight actually is a force that bids fair to make evil, which surely exists, no matter the claims of the humanists, appear good. This, of course, is the type reasoning that the liberal humanists love. If they can open the sweet human heart and soul to understanding, if they can allow the student to walk in the other man's shoes, love and goodness and beauty and everything nice will transpire. Humankind will flower and the world will be a very, very magical place.

Nonsense. Exactly the opposite is more likely to obtain. But the humanistic forces, school being profoundly influenced, stand firmly for this horrible agenda. Surely, the *openness* philosophy represents a terrible threat.

GENDER, FEMINISM, AND ANDROGYNY

The situation between men and women turned bleak as the civil rights movement, fanned by the educational elites, gained power, influence, and judicial justification. When feminism gained huge successes as a result of the mass media, the courts, the universities, and other sources, the biblical views of the sexes as absolutely and clearly expressed in the *Holy Scriptures* became blurred and confused, and this very societal confusion and anti--Christian philosophy influenced public school curriculum planners. The sorry result was the inclusion of radical feminism, androgyny, and sex education, all of which should not have been there, in the schools financed and owned by the taxpayers. Permit us to wonder how the home and church let their obligations pass to the state.

Again, however, the movement in schools follows the social order. If the schools are wrong, and they are in this case, what about the liberal churches and the crumbling homes? Everywhere at once in America, the war had begun. Unhappy, unfulfilled women seeking power identified the Civil Rights Movement as the vehicle to gain fairness (and this was praiseworthy) as well as to move into mortal conflict with men in all areas (and this was not).

The leadership of the feminist movement came largely from disaffected women whose rage was motivated and highlighted by the media. They often exceeded good taste, truth, and judgment as they attacked males primarily for being men. It was, of course, expected of a humanistic endeavor disregarding

God's Word. In fact the movement, if moderated to ease the insane left of the group, would seem to make considerable sense to someone who did not accept the religion of Jesus Christ. But believers, being bound by the truth of the *Scriptures,* well understand that the *Bible* makes very clear the roles of men and women in their relationships, the church, and the family. Once again, what seems right and fair to the nonbeliever is sometimes unacceptable to God. Humanists, of course, ridicule this type statement, muttering something about men writing the *Scriptures* to maintain their paternalistic authority and the accompanying male-dominated social order.

This is not to assert that the feminist movement was all wrong. Beyond a doubt, the *Scriptures* speak of equal dignity for men and women--and this surely allows equal opportunities for success in the marketplace and the social order, as well. To the degree the feminist movement labored to this end, it was correct. The tactical error was to trash the female and male sex roles. Even many women who aligned themselves with feminism balked at this point. Moreover, the media turned its lenses and presses in the direction of the insane perimeter of the movement. The shrill claims of lesbians who were not content to leave their sexual preferences in private where they belonged discredited the crusade.

In the colleges and universities, many professors and students, loving causes, bought into the feminist campaign. Given the depth of their humanistic sentiments and their *politically correct* loathing of the middle class (about whose success they were very jealous), they rushed into women's studies in *politically correct* schools. It was enough to make veteran faculty, having chewed anti-acid tablets and gulped tranquilizers as they saw the terrible damage the black and Hispanic studies had done to the required societal consensus, start belching again and rushing to their physicians for further relief.

The absurdity flowed like free scotch whiskey at a university faculty picnic. The totality of literature, history, and social studies was attacked, and, all too often, women's studies became vicious and self-seeking. Anything projecting from anywhere, above, below, or sideways, became, in the most profound Freudian sense, the hated phallic symbol. In one program, a female professor asserted that any woman sleeping with a man was a traitor to the movement; she should lie, the professor said, with a woman. Another said that every time a woman slept with her husband, she was being raped. Still another recommended that women, in their epic war with the evil gender identified as men, should cultivate their hateful nature, what she identified as their *bitch.*

The universities were the most effective locations of the feminist movement. Academic freedom allowed a forum for the very most foolish and

The Results: Watching A Nation Die 115

dangerous claims. The liberal surroundings allowed and produced the most strange ideas as if insanity had become epidemic. Sexual harassment became a topic of the first order, and it affected the entire nation. Professor Anita Hill accused Clarence Thomas of sexual harassment, and university females were in ecstasy, even though there was no proof whatsoever that she had any case at all. But the feminist mood of the time was that a man was surely guilty if a woman accused him unless the person was politically correct. President Clinton, who supported abortion and other feminist positions and was proven to have used a young female employee for sex, was supported by many feminists who sold out their sense of justice for selfish personal gain.

Though true harassment should be stopped, the interplay between the sexes, which is healthy, suffers dramatically. And if a man who was the supervisor of a young lady with whom he fell in love asked her out, he was subject to harassment charges. Males became the hated enemy, the evil rapists who lived to debase women. The harassment issue is, indeed, a pivotal plank of the *political correctness* that has so embarrassed universities and that has become a laughing stock all over the globe.

The dedicated effort in the schools is to produce androgynous human beings, that is to say, males and females who are alike. Because the historic sex roles are to be obliterated, schooling is to be gender free. Girls would not play with dolls, nor would boys play with guns. Girls would not watch boys play sports, and boys would never rescue girls. Educate them to be exactly the same. Teach the boys to cry and the girls to be self-reliant. Schools should destroy, for once and all, the evil sexual stereotyping that has produced the *evil* rapists and that has made virtual slaves of females.

The goal was a complete remaking of the American culture. Believers surely cringe at this corrupt view of the sexes. The *Scriptures* have made utterly clear the considerable differences between the sexes that far transcend their physical differences or the ridiculous claim that environment alone fosters their behavior. What a comforting fact it is to understand that in *God's Word* both sexes are equal but distinctly different.

Janet Parshall explained the problem well in *USA Today*:

> There is a simple, historically proven way to eradicate sexual harassment: teach our children there are differences between the sexes, differences that make us unique and must be respected. Remember when we were taught to be "ladylike" and to act like "gentlemen?" But the very mention of traditional roles of girls as ladies and boys as gentlemen is enough to send any radical feminist back to her local support group.

Oh, yes, the feminist elite educating sources are very successful. Just consider the horrible damage they have wrought in confusing the sex roles as presented in *Holy Scriptures* and, along with other forces, in destroying the family.

It is no wonder the nation is in crisis, and, though most people have no sense whatsoever that this is true and would battle it vigorously, much of the affliction and grief of the time results from the confusion of men and women concerning their natures and roles in the family and social order in general. The Maker of the Universe and all things delineates the natures of men and women. It does not matter that many, thinking Him wrong, attack the biblical position.

They have been educated by the elites in the tenets of the humanistic faith. Not happy at being equal but different, the feminists march in rage. What they are not taught in school or by other humanistic forces is that, in a way, men and women are incomplete without each other. When they marry, there is one flesh, a total being, but each having different objectives and obligations. She complements him, and he her. Together, they are better than they would be alone. But they are very different, and God says they should be. The feminists disagree. It gets down, really, to whom should be believed: God or the feminists. They take absolutely incongruent paths. The public schools stand firmly for the feminist position, partially because of their humanistic focus, partly because of law.

This is surely a message of abject crisis to believers. In fact, the telling battle of the war of God's position versus humanism is very likely to be fought on sexual and gender battlefields. This could be America's secular and/or religious apocalypse. Hence, this problem will be considered carefully.

The Council on Biblical Manhood and Womanhood questions the uncertainty and confusion concerning the differences between males and females, even suggesting that the current assertions are damaging what God intended for both sexes in marriage. The radical, political efforts by disaffected feminists to deny the loving cooperation of husband and wife in a relationship where kind and loving Christian men provide leadership and loving Christian wives willingly support that leadership is decried, as are attacks of the merit of motherhood and homemaking. Nor should sexual relationships outside of marriage, scorned and attacked in the *Bible and the Creed*, be taught as acceptable alternative lifestyles. It boggles the mind, for instance, that homosexuality, clearly hated by God, would be presented to the youth as an alternative lifestyle. This is clearly teaching that sin is an acceptable lifestyle. Also, physical and emotional abuse occur as each member tries to get her/his own way in the vicious gender competition recommended by the wrathful feminists. It is the spirit fostered by the humanist elites of the era that has so confused the situation between men and women. And, surely, the very nature God gave to each of these sexes is subverted. This is very, very good for psychologists and psychiatrists. But God, not influenced by *political correctness* or disaffected women's groups, ordained men and women to be distinctively different in many ways. And this is good, very good indeed.

SEX EDUCATION

Sex education and the efforts to abolish the historic sex roles between men and women are to be considered together, for they are inextricably linked. In both cases, the family, America's most important social institution, is in deep jeopardy. No secular problem is more serious to the continuance of the hallowed American endeavor. Anything, anything at all, that attacks the family and family values, both under direct siege in the social and political arenas, must be strongly resisted. And schooling, owned by the citizens, must resist every effort to undermine the historic family and the values that have prepared the youth to maintain and to continue to build man's greatest social order. Make no mistake; much that is being taught in the schools is a direct attack on the family, a sign that the humanistic elites are hard at work.

Many of the programs, particularly in the efforts in New York City and much of California, are in direct rebellion to the *Word of God,* the *Creed, and the "Beatitudes."* The religion of radical humanism is the very reason for the curricula, and the truth is that many, many folk who claim to be Christian support the humanistic positions, many out of ignorance, many out of lack of genuine belief in the religion of Jesus Christ and/or the *American Creed.* Liberal churches too often fall in line with the humanistic views of family and sex. It may very well be, then, that the secular humanistic gender and sex programs accomplishing such harm do, in fact, represent the will of the people, a claim supported by many polls.

Arguments concerning the sex education programs rage and proliferate. Any intelligent discussion of this problem must include, also, the family, feminism, and an indepth consideration of the power held by parents versus that of the state.

Indeed, whose job is it to teach the youth about sex? Is it the job of the parents, the church, the mass media, the peer group, and/or the school? Christian parents should recall the humanistic nature of the schools. In the present era, however, the religion of humanism and its view of sex is the business of the schools, much to the abject consternation of Christians--and other peoples of conscience who do not subscribe to humanism. The humanists will be instructing the youth in homosexuality, abortion, and the families, areas in which Christians will very often be in abject disagreement.

Worrying deeply about their sons and daughters, many believing people view the problem as very serious. Most Christians believe that the task of teaching about these crucial problems belongs to the family first and the church second. They often do not want their children taught the humanistic beliefs.

Why? The *Bible* takes a very firm position on matters of family and sex, and Christians cannot allow humanists instructing their youth to be frivolous with biblical truth. The following items, usually included in sex education classes in the public schools, are all in disagreement with biblical values. Homosexuality is not an acceptable lifestyle, and often these people visit the classrooms, as schools try to teach happy acceptance of what is wrong. With an assumption that the youth are going to have sex no matter what they are taught or believe, the program-makers often turn to a judgment that premarital sex is acceptable. This being the situation, since the activity cannot be halted, they claim, the students must be taught to use contraceptives, particularly condoms, and they must not feel guilty when they err. Many humanistic psychologists and counselors strangely believe that no one should harbor guilt--which, incidentally, is needed so that conscience can deal with base behavior of those who sin. Some schools actually dispense condoms to the youth, really, no matter what they claim, sanctioning sex before marriage. Many schools actually teach the youth how to apply a condom. Girls are advised to carry condoms which, they are told, allow for safe sex--when, in fact, their failure rate is high. Abortion is sometimes taught as a birth control device, and most often is said not to be murder--which it surely is. Unfortunately, too, virginity in both boys and girls, is too often not held as the primary goal until one marries. And there are also claims about the roles of men and women in marriage that are in direct opposition to what the *Scriptures* teach. Indeed, the whole area of androgyny, considered earlier in the chapter, is a direct attack at biblical claims. God-made man works by the sweat of his brow to take care of his wife and children, and his wife tends his needs, with the understanding that, after God, he is head of the house. The wife, with no less worth than her husband, is in subjection to God and her husband, whose job it is to love his wife deeply-- as Christ loved the church. The sex education programs stand as a distinct threat to the education of the progeny of Christian parents and to those who honor the Creed. Sometimes, too, the morality of sex is not considered--that is that a human being is not to use another just for his/her pleasure and that there is responsibility in sex to care more about the partner than about one's self.

But not all, or perhaps most, of the school programs make the mistakes alluded to above. Indeed, there is wide difference in programs. Many of them do sometimes assume a Christian morality and teach the values of the *Creed*. As indicated earlier, what a teacher does when the class door closes often is

The Results: Watching A Nation Die

not to be found in the curriculum; and, make no mistake, many Christian instructors are at work.

Even when this occurs, there remains another very important question: What expertise and preparation does the sex education teacher bring to the classroom? After all teachers earn the right to instruct in the schools because of their preparation, knowledge, and expertise. And it is a fact, also, that this preparation should better enable them than the mothers and fathers of the youth. Unfortunately, however, most of sex education faculty cannot claim an indepth schooling in the subject. Very, very few hold as much as a minor in sex education, and most of them have had only one or two classes, hardly enough to allow them expertise. Even in the classes they took, there is reason to beware. Remember, most of these neophyte faculty have studied at the feet of humanists who work diligently to spread the humanistic philosophy. Perhaps it is an overstatement, but there is abundant reason to assert that, for a believing Christian, nothing good can come from sex education in the schools.

Clearly, the home rather than the school must teach the youth about sex. Liberals, believing in their hearts that the state, not the home, should be responsible for the youth, argue that the home has failed; hence, the federal government has the responsibility. Such thinking submits that America's most important social institution, the family, has failed--and it completely bypasses the church. It is interesting to consider that any *failure* of the family may well be laid at the door of humanism and liberal doctrine. Moreover, be sure that the schools and government have not solved the problems of sex; conditions have grown increasingly more desperate.

Sex education is a function of the home, and, if it does not succeed in given families, the failure does not even approximate the governmental boondoggle as it has influenced the schools and the mentality surrounding all of education beyond the schools. Secondly, sex education is a function of the church, and every church, no matter the size or wealth, has the utter responsibility for instructing the boys and girls in this matter that the *Bible* speaks of in such detail. Churches must take this very seriously.

Dr. James Dobson has quite rightly written, "The kind of sex education program now operating in America's schools is designed as a crash course in relativism, in immorality, and in anti-Christian philosophy." But if a teacher bases his instruction on the *Creed* or Christianity, the ACLU waits in the wings, like some avenging monster, to destroy the effort. And what is the typical charge of teaching historic morality, the *American Creed*? The liberal group brings suit on the basis of teaching religion, a travesty to the framers' intentions in the *First Amendment* to the *Constitution*.

As always, though, the nation is being influenced by the humanistic elites.

There is every reason to claim that, even if the schools were teaching what Christian believers wanted, the power of the other elite educators would far surpass their efforts. The media, the thousands of liberal churches, the peer group, and other powerful forces too often educate in matters of sex, marriage, and feminism in a way that is antithetical to the *Bible* and the *American Creed*. If the homes and churches have largely failed and if the schools continue to follow the dictates of the humanistic elite forces, marriage may be doomed, as sexual perversity and violence win the day. Who, then, will be left to speak out for the family and the *Bible's* strict orders for the crucial institution? Likewise, who will speak out for the Scripture's carefully delineated demands concerning sex? What, indeed, can believing parents do, as the very institutions of family, church, and school teach humanistic ideals? And are the schools really to blame, as many claim, for the sexual immorality and experimentation of the youth? For these horrible developments, blame, first, the humanistic elites whose every action draws the nation nearer the dusk.

THE FAMILY

The portrait of the dissolving family has earlier been examined in the book, but the explanation of the development surely belongs in this chapter, as well. The environment making a generation of narcissists and hedonists, each more selfish than the other, has come home to roost. The baby boomers, so many devoid of civilizing values, too often expect all things to go their respective ways. Many are all but incapable of love and commitment, as they watch *nannies* or nursery school people raise their children. It is no wonder whatsoever that they speak glibly and ignorantly of a village raising their children. The feminist steamroller has, some believe, profited women. Even if that is so, it has decimated the lives of children who had the utter misfortune to be born when their mothers and fathers made revolution against the historic expectations for the family. The psychology of the self and of the *feel good* humanistic charade has reached tragic fruition. Too often gone is the desire, in love, to sacrifice for a wife, husband, or child. And the media, both reflecting and mandating change, has massaged the unreal expectations toward sex and marriage, in general. It has further played and pandered to the selfishness of the time. The modernist church has blessed the ideal of divorce and, God help us all, of adultery. The children of the 60s, many now grown into real life functioning narcissists, fed full of humanistic ideals by philosophy and psychology of the time, poisoned by adolescent music, are so often self-focused that they could never stay married. And those who believe the claims of Hollywood and pornography concerning sex in marriage have, all too often, been forced to jump from bed to bed, joyously, they thought, seeking what they would not find--except, had they only known it, at home. Fed full of humanism's folly, they live/lived horrible lives, and they too often sired children who will live with increased alienation and disappointment. The horrible damage of the late 60's and early 70's continues in sons, daughters, and grandchildren. The sins of the fathers loom too large.

This decimated home was the most important single institution in America. It was the home, before any other societal entity, that made America greater than any nation and better than all. But now the many forces of education have conspired to put the home far beyond risk to ruin.

It is these sterile, selfish homes that send the youth off to school with too little love, too little socialization, too little character, and too little decency. Too much of the failure of schooling is that the homes are sending untutored little hedonists and narcissists who could have been so dear, who could have built such a wonderful world, had the humanistic elites been less successful in their influences concerning families.

But this very humanism that has fathered the evils weakening the family has also redefined what a family is, and this has resulted in a terrible social problem: confusion as to what a family should be. Certainly, this suggests a serious crisis--and it is. Christians should desire that a family be viewed as a man and a woman and their children. To be added are the grandparents, aunts, uncles, and other blood relatives. Most Americans, many polls indicate, would cast their vote for this definition--and so, too, should believers. Unfortunately, though, part of the trauma of the age is that the definition of family has been much expanded. In fact, a judge ruled that the Christian definition was religious; and the schools, based on *First Amendment* rights, could not teach it as the *model*. So what has happened? Many schools' sex education programs, certainly the *politically correct* varieties, teach alternative lifestyles. That satisfies the courts, themselves too often enemies of the American family. Desiring to feed the egos and self-concepts of the youth, they want very badly to make them feel well about whatever family situation they are in. And so, amazing to say, they broaden the definition of the family to include any group living together. Hence, they often bring two cohabiting homosexuals and present them to the children as a family in the best sense of the word. This is really *politically correct*, but it is sin to the Christian. This is typical of the experiences the sons and daughters of Christians receive in the schools. But, again, even if the schools taught God's truth in the matter, the power of the elite humanists to influence the media and other sources they control would have a far more dramatic influence in the overall education concerning the family. The problem should perplex parents day and night.

SUNSET OF AMERICA

CENSORSHIP AND THE RIGHT TO READ

In considering the problem of controlling precisely what books the youth read in the public schools and all areas of education, Christians often turn to a particular Scripture, *Philippians 4:10:*

> Finally, brethren, whatever is true, whatever is honorable, whatever is just, whatever is pure, whatever is lovely, whatever is gracious, if there is any excellence, if there is anything worthy of praise, think about these things.

America would be a far better nation if all the elite educators took seriously this admonition. MTV would be off the air; all of television would be transformed. The music would change utterly, while the vile "gangsta" rap music promoting violence and all sorts of evil acts would be heard no more. *Playboy, Penthouse,* and the other sex-promoting magazines would be out of business. Everything would change for the better. This, of course, the humanistic educational elite could not allow to happen, for they would be wounded in the worst of all possible places: their pocketbooks.

Moreover, there is considerable concern about censorship in the United States. As a young teacher, it seemed right for one of the authors to stand firmly against censorship, for he felt that whoever had the authority to preclude anything from his reading and seeing would have the power to censor the *Bible*, as well. And proud Americans, wanting the government out of their lives, often feel strongly enraged by any effort to censor anything in their lives, a position that does, in fact, seem compelling given the creeping attempt of the bureaucrats in Washington to control more and more of their lives. But in a world gone mad when every day, in every way, the morality of the nation sinks lower, and in an era when the restraining hands of the *Scriptures* are removed from the public forum and institutions, something needs fixing.

Many people have said that they cannot and will not support any efforts to curtail the right to read and to see whatever a person wants. Suppose there is a book in a junior high library telling of the sheer joy in killing a first grader after a protracted period of torture. Do you feel that junior high age youth should be able to check this book out of school? Should the school refrain from ordering and making available the publication to the youth? If you answer the first question *no* and the second *yes*, you do, in fact, favor censorship in the schools--and this is as it should be. The discussion should center on precisely where the line should be drawn.

Parents will and should fight every source poisoning their children, whether it be food at the lunch program, what they read at school and

The Results: Watching A Nation Die   123

elsewhere, or anything that threatens to infect them. One can be poisoned by what he reads as well as by what is eaten. And the elite humanistic educators have flooded the nation with those writings that make money, pandering to the lowest instincts and the humanistic doctrines understood by Christians as sinful and many other Americans as wrong. Such publications are often not published to offend. In fact, and this makes them more dangerous, many are sins rationalized over time by humanists so that the values seem to them to have become acceptable, even moral.

This is a serious problem in the schools where there is dedication to the students' right to read. This sentiment is shared all too often by the courts, which, time after time in decisions, have found in favor of severely limiting censorship of any type in the schools. At the same time, part of the humanistic movement in the schools, authored and carried on by the educational elites, is that adolescents should not be limited in what they read. The National Council of Teachers of English (NCTE), as one would expect, tenaciously works for the abolition of all censorship and the right of students to read what they desire. But many believers look at what is being read in school or in outside assignments and shake their heads in amazement and disappointment--even rage. Nearly everything that they believe in is trampled in the readings. In fact, it seems to many of these people that their progeny are being schooled in such a manner as to destroy what they have been taught at home and in their respective churches. This should not surprise. It is the battle they should expect: humanism versus Christianity. And given the humanistic power elites, this schooling procedure is quite understandable.

Comprehending well what they perceived as the danger of Christian demands, the humanists worked day and night to limit their influence. These people cleverly identified the believers as radical, and they were presented by the media (owned by the humanistic elites) as a reactionary minority of people who were unschooled and ignorant. Recall also, that the humanists see truth as being relative; anyone teaching Christian absolute values is, in fact, dangerous to these people.

Christian parents, joining others who perceive the danger of relativism and the critical import of the *American Creed*, cringe at what children read in school concerning sex, murder, evil, collectivism, liberalism, and other humanistic convictions. These loom large as attackers of the faith and the American dream.

So what about censorship? Let the humanists disagree, and let the courts support their position. This should not deter people of conscience who must contest the quite incorrect assertion of the educational elites that students have the right to read whatever they desire. Those of conscience must understand the difficulty in fighting the forces of the humanistic elites. Given their power, these elites appear to be winning. Nonetheless, the youth do not have the right to read whatever they desire in schools. They are children, needing to be guided and taught by adults. There is precedence to limit their behaviors. For instance, underage youth are allowed to purchase neither alcohol nor tobacco--and this is good. Reading can do as much damage as either of these, and probably more. Why is it that the humanists are perfectly willing to act against the use of these two damaging drugs and then give their blessings to the unrestrained right to read? It makes sense only if one understands the depth of the problem: the mortal combat between the religion of Jesus Christ and the religion of man.

COUNSELING

A significant amount of the counseling that children receive in school and that adults receive in private practice is humanistic. The beliefs about man's nature held by humanists have already been analyzed in depth. Be sure that this view is the theme and thesis of the counseling most people receive in public schooling and private practice. The entire package is too often predicated on an entirely false view of human nature. Though the humanist elites have sold the program well, many thoughtful Americans are in disagreement. For instance, Christians believe man to be sinful, needing change. He does not have the knowledge of all things. He needs help and lacks the resources to answer his questions. It is, again, the difference between Christianity and humanism, common sense and foolishness.

Relativism rears its ugly head again. For Christians, there are rights and wrongs as defined, first, in the *Scriptures* and, second, in the *American Creed*. The humanistic elites typically refuse this view. Here, really, is the breaking point in the counseling and guidance programs. The educating elites, believing in relativism, want no feelings of shame. Their efforts are, in fact, to get rid of all such emotion, for people are perceived as basically good. Why should good and worthy people be made to feel shame? This would damage seriously their egos and self-concepts, the greatest hurt that could be done to them. Though the elites will deny it, everything is to make people feel well about themselves. If your child went to a counselor and said that she felt suicidal, the helper might say to her, "I hear you saying you feel that you want to take your life." In essence, the counselor is holding up to the youth a mirror telling the child that she has within herself the ability, by the use of rational methods, to solve her own problems.

Nonsense. Most people know better. It is the very height of foolishness to believe that the youth should always feel well about themselves. In this misguided principle, there is neither improvement nor building of character, far from it. The youths--and anyone--should be made to feel well about themselves when they do right and badly when they do wrong. The latter feeling is the conscience telling them, insisting, that they improve. Without shame, without disliking the wrong one does, there is no improved character. It is the height of tragedy for one to like himself when he is behaving badly.

Just as concerning is the insistence by the humanist psychologists that a helper must be accepting of any and nearly all behavior. A student in a master's degree program was made to witness films of stag movies which included countless sexual deviations and cruelty. She turned aside, not watching. She was told in no uncertain terms that she should reconsider her major, that she would have to work with such sexual deviates and should not be judgmental. Can the reader believe the audacity of this?

CIVIC EDUCATION

Information concerning the civic knowledge of students (and Americans in general) is frightening. What happens when tomorrow's citizens are know-nothings about the present and past of their government? How can representative democracy work? In 1996, a *Washington Post* survey found that forty percent of Americans do not know the name of the Vice President of the United States; forty-six percent do not know the name of the Speaker of the House of Representatives; and only fifty-two percent said that the Republican Party is "more conservative than the Democratic Party." The schools and homes are failing miserably in this respect, and, as a result, the terrible implications for American democracy are staggering.

SELF-CONCEPT, SCHOOL, AND LIFE

There is no more difficult problem to face than the effort of the schools to build a favorable self-concept in the youth. Many conservatives perceive this as a major failing of the schools. Quite rightly, they point to the fact that excellence may have suffered seriously as the schools fell into line with societal demands in teaching and acting upon claims that a favorable self-concept was prerequisite to happiness and productivity in the American social order. Also correctly, they see this as a predictable goal of humanism, and many of these people understand the development as schooling's greatest failure.

But many of them have never taught a day in the public schools. If they had, and if they took seriously the teaching of Jesus Christ and the Creed, they would not be as sure as they are. Far too often, they speak from noble principles without knowing the facts--and thus do harm.

They are, however, quite right in arguing that the work ethic was seriously eroded in the effort. This loss in the American social order cannot be overestimated. No western nation can survive when the work ethic succumbs to indolence, and the United States has come very close to self-destructing because of the rush to leisure. In the self-concept movement, the schools remain culpable, but they are not alone. Most often, they simply reflect what they have been taught by the social order in general. It is, in fact, the social order itself that is to blame. Witness the results of the union movement in the nation. Witness the psychology that captured the allegiance of so many people in the nation. Dr. Spock and his humanistic colleagues had a profound effect in the business. It was common in the late 1960's and early 1970's to hear professors decrying the Puritan work ethic as evil incarnate. Almost all of the elite forces forging school policy approbated the self-concept curriculum.

The critics are also perceptive in insisting that the schools seriously erred in allowing students success without earning it. In this the schools were terribly wrong, for, even with public demand for self-concept schooling, the parents did not insist that the youth be rewarded without meeting fair and professionally set objectives. But meaning well, and tuned to the mood of the taxpayers, many, perhaps most, public schools elected to produce what they thought were healthy students who could face the real world because of the favorable images they had of themselves. School leaders were on the mark in insisting that school is not life. This being so, it is crucial that the home and church be dedicated to the mental health of the youth.

There was a mood abroad in the institutions of school, church, and family that self-concept was crucial. The schools were persuaded that this was perhaps the most important objective in public education, and many moved quickly to structure a situation that would, indeed, prepare healthy youth who were well mentally and who, as a result, would contribute substantially to building a better nation and world. They were partially correct, but they too often failed to recall that the pupils also had the demand to produce excellence in performance, as they were capable of accomplishing it. Also, they should have felt well about themselves when they made every effort to meet their schooling objectives. At the same time, they should have felt badly about themselves when they did not perform to this level. The failure to understand this was the capital error of many schools, one they should not have made in their dedicated and noble zeal to help the youth.

This claim is supported by an important research study accomplished by Roy Baumeister, Joseph Boden, and Laura Smart. Reported on in the *Journal of the American Psychological Association,* the researchers found that high self-esteem, rather than low self-esteem, is more likely to result in violence.

The Results: Watching A Nation Die

If, in fact, one has high self-esteem and receives feedback that calls to doubt the favorable self-image, he/she may very well become violent.

Indeed, high self-esteem may become arrogance, antithetical to both the Creed and Christianity, and low self-esteem may result in withdrawal. A fine balance must be reached: a humble glow of success when hard work and character have allowed the youth to achieve as inherited traits allow and a feeling of disappointment when reachable goals and/or adequate behavior are not attained.

In the admirable rush to help build favorable self-images, as demanded by the humanistic psychology of the era, too many students were awarded for non-production, success not earned nor justified, and this was/is a grave error. How very tragic it is that the self-esteem movement was mismanaged, for it remains true that a favorable self-concept, humbly integrated and displayed, remains crucial in the healthy development of a youth when behavior and learning conform to attainable goals demanded by schools, family and church.

But it all went too far; the ramifications of feel-good objectives did profound damage, as it reflected a pervading mood in the halls of academia. The humanists wanted to help these students and others from disadvantaged backgrounds. And there, in the late 1960's and early 1970's, a malignancy, built of well-meaning but incorrect emotions, grew rapidly. Many, many professors in colleges and universities set the tone for the public school trauma associated with the self-concept movement. Two dreadful developments were severely to damage higher education in a serious manner: a double standard in evaluation of student performance and, as a result, dramatically lowered standards. Only *political correctness* has done more damage to the image and function of higher education.

The double standard in university education did damage almost as serious. Caring humanistic faculty truly wanted to help minority students, in this time primarily black. Though professors will roundly denounce and deny this, many of them demanded far less of the minority students than of others. A double track was established that did no favor to anyone. The problem was made worse during the Viet Nam Conflict, when many professors refused to fail male students who, upon flunking out of school, were subject to the draft. Leading the attacks at U.S. participation in the conflict, liberal faculty were often dedicated to passing every male student, and standards tumbled. Higher education's innocence was forever lost.

The problem was made even worse by the *student power* movement. The radical humanists in higher education lost all good judgment in allowing students authority that they had not earned, could not handle, and were too inexperienced to comprehend. For the public, there was the academic liberal cant about integrity; but, in faculty minds, there was desperation. The power had been transferred to the students, and, amazing to note, student evaluations were perhaps the foremost hurdle tied to tenure and positive evaluations for faculty. More than most people comprehend, the students were morally blackmailing faculty. One of the authors accomplished a study concerning what factors were significant for instructors of writing to be evaluated highly by students. Two factors headed the list: giving high grades and taking classes with young faculty.

Too many faculty discovered that easing the difficulty of their courses, teaching like television comics, and awarding high grades allowed them to stay alive in the system. The resulting grade deflation called to question the very worthiness of secular education which had descended to a position of shame.

The negative elite forces formulating educational policy had found the professors easy. That thinking people wonder how they can, in good faith, send their progeny to study with these professors is certainly understandable. But their sons and daughters need a diploma as a ticket into the successful financial world; hence, confused parents, facing a Hobson's choice, continue to send their offspring, often fearing that the diploma will come at a dreadful price: the very souls of those they so love. Most of these have forgotten the excellent Christian institutions of higher education located throughout the nation. Bear in mind, too, that the public schools to which the parents send their children are filled with faculty who did, in fact, sit at the feet of liberal, humanistic professors.

Beyond this, the student success movement needs to be analyzed further. Conservatives must join other believers in understanding that there is a genetic limit to what a child can learn. And what about what he learns in school? Is it a good predictor of success for later life? It surprises some people to comprehend that schooling is actually a poor indicator of success in the business community and later life. Many things, including socioeconomic level, family, geographical location in which schooling transpires, and other factors are better predictors of future success. Many of the learnings in school do not translate to the real world. The very temperament of students, particularly of impatient boys, both brings them down in school and allows them to succeed in life. Moreover, grades are a poor predictor. Any evaluation must understand that absolute grading, that is to say the same objectives for all children, is both unprofessional and, really, anti-Christian. A child can only achieve as far as his inborn talents allow; the calling of the schools is to make sure that each child achieves to the limit of his ability. If that were truly accomplished, the schools would write a far greater success story than by measuring each child by the same standards--that is to say, by

The Results: Watching A Nation Die

largely rewarding the inherited traits. Recall, too, the point made earlier: Grades are a poor predictor of success; school is not life--far, far, far from it, a truth that disturbs many conservatives, particularly those who have not been teachers and who have not observed the terrible effect on humans who have labored to the limit of their abilities and were made to feel that they were losers.

Schools are surely correct in rewarding what a child is able to do, particularly, as has been analyzed, since the institutional learnings are not absolute goals for success in the outside world. In this, the negative elite forces were right. It is absolutely necessary to recompense those who achieve as they are able, but the schools exceeded their boundaries in their rush to build favorable self-images in the youth. Indeed, they fell, too often, into the humanistic foolishness of rewarding non-production in a frenzied effort to instill these favorable self-concepts. This tragic result has been one of schooling's most grievous errors. Born of good intentions, fueled by the elite forces, the schools went too far, thus damaging the noble intent of schooling students to work at the limit of their inborn abilities and to be rewarded rightfully for such effort. One of schooling's most noble objectives was severely damaged because it went too far--losing really, the defensible objectives it had. But mark this well: The angry voices against differing objectives for children, based on what they are able to do, are wrong.

Dr. William Glasser has well explained that for any person to function well he must feel that what is being accomplished is worthwhile and that someone cares for him. In any situation where people work and live together, this is critical. Think, for instance, how many fewer divorces would occur if both partners felt that what they were doing was worthwhile and if their mate demonstrated deep, enduring affection. But even here there are two factors to consider: The person must be doing the very best to succeed, and the person loving him/her must be worthy and part of the real world. In other words, the person must feel well about himself when doing his very best and must feel well when loved by a person of quality. Schools can and must meet these two objectives no matter the angry attacks by fellow Christians who know far too little about the classrooms. What seems right to them is too often wrong.

But the absolute equality demanded by the liberals, the media, and the psychologist elites has no place in this problem. Students are not equal; the uniform results that the liberal educators and politicians expect will never occur. They simply cannot, given ability differences in the students. It is not surprising that the liberals demand such schooling. But is it not very strange that, in the demand for absolute grades, conservatives also share the same expectations?

Such people demand competition, asserting its primacy. In part, they are correct. Competition is absolutely critical. But don't forget; in schooling the competition is unlike that in the real world. It is far better that the school (and the churches and parents) prepare the youth to compete in the marketplace. This is accomplished not by producing losers but by educating healthy people to compete in the social order. Losers will lose. And what a shame for an institution that has such a poor record in predicting success to produce losers. Yes, there must be competition; but, given the genetic differences, each child must compete with himself, reaching objectives that he can attain. Then, feeling well about these efforts and successes, he is healthy enough to face the marketplace. Failing to reach objectives of which he is capable, he should surely fail. He must not be lied to about his work and achievements. The schools must be his helper, but, finally, they must not lie to him. Without the work ethic and responsibility, he is ill-equipped to succeed in the marketplace. To the degree the schools have had a hand in this, particularly as they have allowed him to succeed without proper effort and accomplishment, they have failed him--and deserve the rage of parents and taxpayers.

TEACHING EVOLUTION

Few practices are more disconcerting to believing Christian parents than the teaching of evolution as a scientific, believable truth. These believers accept the biblical explanation of creation--which, to them, is the beginning of truth. Scientists argue that this belief is based only on faith, yet current-day biblical scholars are willing to argue the case on the basis of scientific knowledge.

The biblical position nettles the humanistic scientists, along with non--believers who attend liberal churches. These people simply cannot and will not entertain any thought that the *Bible* does, in fact, expound the truth about creation and the development of humankind. Humanists are utterly committed to battling the biblical claims, railing at attempts by public school programs to teach the verity of *God's Word* on the subject.

In recent years, the U.S. Supreme Court refused Louisiana's attempt to mandate that both views, the biblical and the evolutionary, be presented to the youth in the public schools. As explained earlier, the High Court has found that humanism is, in fact, a religion; but it is teachable because it is part of the consensus *American Creed*. Hence, evolution cannot be attacked at the point of its greatest weakness--that it is, indeed, humanism which is surely a religion. Wringing their hands in despair, believers rightly wonder if there is an answer to the humanistic indoctrination of their progeny concerning the origins of mankind.

Far too often, students are forced to accept the evolutionary interpretation

The Results: Watching A Nation Die

of creation as the truth. This, of course, is an area that is ripe for attack; for, no matter the claims to the contrary, evolution, when related to the origin of man, is no more than a theory. This fact is crucial. If, indeed, theory is taught as truth, science is being desecrated. Schools must not, absolutely must not, teach theories as truth. And since evolution, as an explanation of man's origin, is theory, it is required that other theories be taught as well. The biblical truth cannot be taught as the truth in the schools, nor can it even be taught as another theory. But the science teacher has no right whatsoever to claim the truth of one of the views at the cost of the other. This the public has a right to demand.

The schools are foolish to demand and teach as truth the evolutionary explanation of the origin of life. To cause strife over a theory is ill-advised. Why wave a red flag at taxpayers in a time when the schools are under fire?

Strangely--and in an entirely different manner--the indoctrination of evolution in the schools may well be vulnerable for *First Amendment* reasons. Indeed, it may well be teaching a religion. The doctrine of biblical creation is accepted by monotheistic faiths like Christianity, Islam, and Orthodox Judaism. Given the history of Supreme Court decisions, this view cannot be taught as truth. But what about evolution? Assuredly, this doctrine is crucial to New Age and Hinduism, both surely religions. How, then, if called to explain, can schooling teach as truth a theory accepted by these two religions? Indeed, this is a legal area deserving much consideration. Even non-believing parents might join hands with Christians in a battle against instruction in a tenet of, say, Hinduism.

Evolutionists often claim that Christians are incorrect in arguing about origins of human life. It is common for these people to deny interest in origins, but such claims are no more than subterfuge. Any scholarly examination of the scientific views pertaining to evolution supports the fact that they are vitally interested in the beginnings of human life. Such an interest is central to evolutionary theory.

Creation scientists must continue to focus on the practice of letting the issue be decided on the basis of scientific evidence. This they are willing to do. Among the areas are embryology, paleontology, genetics, and many other subsections of the humanistic evolutionary position. Schooling, if fairness exists, should look at the facts of both positions, but, given the law, they cannot.

The elite educational forces have strongly affected the building of an evolutionary agenda in the schools. Obviously, the humanistic view supports the theory as truth. Seldom, if ever, do television, law, or social pressures support the biblical position. And what are Christian parents to do?

ALCOHOL, OTHER DRUGS, AND TOBACCO

These three horrible curses loom as some of America's (and the world's) most serious plagues. Sad to say, certain of the elite forces school the youth, in one way or another, to use these killers. Note that even in the national legislature the tobacco interests are so influential that an inordinate number of favors have been awarded them. It is bad business, indeed, for a congressman to challenge them. And note how the mass media, particularly in magazines, films, records, and television, not so subtly support the use of liquor and, though this has improved some, tobacco.

The situation is much worse as alcohol usage is heralded by television and radio. Any sports fan is overwhelmed by the beautifully made beer commercials. In the evening programs, liquor is most often a prop, indicating that the use of alcohol is required in social situations. Without end, there is the terrible romantization of alcohol use. It does not redeem the media when it offers programs against liquor, for the terrible damage has already occurred. The powerful peer influence to use alcohol has been a result of media brainwashing. But the home has added to the tragic education. Father and mother too often use alcohol and, God help us all, too often think that drinking is quite normal. Their children are lured with Shirley Temples to prepare them to quaff the deadly narcotic. We have heard parents encourage their sons and daughters to drink at home if they must use liquor. Pray tell, what effectiveness can school programs have against such damaging education?

And so what do the schools do? Far, far too often, they assume that the youth will use alcohol and begin with the ideal that responsible usage is the best that can be achieved. Most programs teach the dangers, and they may mention abstinence. But refraining from any use whatsoever of the killer and ruiner of lives must, absolutely must, be the goal. In this, many schools have failed, and their lack of success is ensured by the elite forces educating for liquor use. The problem will not be solved in the schools, but it could be helped.

The situation is different with drugs. Of the elite forces, adolescent music is the champion, far too often, of drug usage. Rap music is the enemy in this regard. So, too, are the peer group and many of the magazines. Paperback books also must share the blame. Seldom, though, are television and radio guilty. Again, how can schools successfully answer these forces?

Parents join the public at large in assuming that the innocent youth are ignorant about controlled substances, an assumption that does not pass scrutiny. The taxpayers assume that if the schools provide their progeny with the facts about drug usage that the problem will be aided enormously. Some believe, also, that frightening the students will help, although this approach

The Results: Watching A Nation Die

is an affront to the humanists who believe that the youth are far better, more intelligent, and more worthy than they really are. Unfortunately, there is scant evidence that either of the approaches works well, although there is mounting proof that fright may have a measure of success.

The fact is that junior and senior high school students are typically well-informed concerning drugs. The problem far transcends what they know; it extends to what they are. Those who claim that today's adolescents are often selfish hedonists and dedicated narcissists are not far from the mark. Pleasure is a cardinal objective for many, perhaps most, of them. They have unwittingly been well taught by their baby-boom parents, many of whom raised their fists a few years ago and exclaimed, "If it feels good, do it." The damage of the late 60's and early 70's is endless. The hurt to the nation did not cease with their selfish excesses. It lives in their children, and it exists like a black cloud of doom over the land they worked to destroy.

When confronted with a new pleasure, a new vice, the youth often assert, "I'll do anything once." But it does not stop with once, and, goaded by the forces mentioned above, the terrible education excites the youth's glands and the frightful problem proliferates. The fact is that the adolescent years are a time of experimentation, particularly with those behaviors attacked by the very adult world standing in their way.

This serious problem is made worse by easy access to drugs. In every hamlet, town, and city, the youth know where to secure the narcotics. Exciting new pleasures, the siren call of pleasure many times multiplied, lure them; and close friends, the very peer group that is their most important influence, far, far too often approbate the situation.

The school, of course, will not, cannot, solve the problems of controlled substances. If the public expects such a solution, it is sadly misinformed. As indicated, all the school can accomplish is to give information and to frighten; the latter of these must be resurrected in public education. Narcotics are not romantic and wonderful. This the youth must learn from people who have suffered because of the tragic use of controlled substances. Take them to the prisons, invite to school the broken, and have them work with those who gloriously have overcome the addictions. Take them to the courtrooms where dope sellers are given long sentences. Bring in families who have suffered so horribly because of loved ones who threw away their lives on drugs. Speak often to and of the broken and ruined. Scare them. Terrorize them. Then give them the facts--which they already know.

But the schools should do more in fighting this war. There must be no patience with drug users and sellers who have been caught. It is society's job to redeem them, not school's. It does not matter that they may be nice kids. The administrators must immediately disassociate the youth from the school situation, so that other students will understand that they are indeed responsible for their own actions. If laws are broken, the schools must prosecute. A slap on the hand may well be the worst possible procedure for the offender, and it most surely is for those eager to become parts of the drug culture. This is war, and half-measures are not acceptable. The humanistic fable that people are basically good and will behave correctly and responsibly if given the proper and correct information is simply not true nor acceptable in fighting the terrible battles with controlled substances.

At the same time, the faculties and administration must be held to the same procedures. If a teacher does anything at all to approbate drug usage, he or she must be punished as are the students. Faculty and administrators must surely be exemplars for the youth.

Still, though, these recommendations (and any others that may be made) will not, cannot, solve the terrible problem foisted upon the schools by the social order. The solution far transcends schooling. An example works well. Recently, a father discovered that his son had used marijuana. Enraged, the father shouted, "I'm going to the school and attack the principal!" Someone said to him, "Why not go to church, instead, and attack the preacher? It would make as much sense." And so it would. Why in the world is the school responsible? Why not a liberal Supreme Court that has toyed capriciously and irresponsibly with constitutional intent? What about the mass media? What about the peer group? What about the parents themselves? Are they not all responsible?

This is another way of saying once again that the problem is the social order. Certainly home, church, and school must join hands in the war. The Supreme Court must stand firm, thumbing its nose at the American Civil Liberties Union. Local law enforcers must be vigilant--and they must believe in punishment first. The mass media sources must redirect their focus. Different heroes, eschewing the vile rock and roll and rap ingrates, must be discovered. Churches must forego the social gospel and teach about sin and forgiveness--and that *thou shall not* is a huge part of both the faith and living it.

In the final analysis, then, what should Christian parents expect of public schooling in educating their progeny about controlled substances? The facts should be taught, and fear should be an important adjunct. Rules must be made and adhered to, and punishment, fairly administered, is crucial. Policing the youth in school and the surrounding grounds is, too.

But this all pales before what the home must do--and, to a lesser degree, the church. Indeed, perhaps the most important job the school could accomplish is to teach the parents the facts attendant to controlled substances. If the schools do not accomplish this, the churches should most certainly turn their attention in this direction.

Alone, the schools will surely fail. They must not be viewed as the primary evil in the problem. They operate against principalities that far outreach their efforts and capabilities. The elite educators are accomplishing very, very great damage. The school can share facts and it can frighten, but this is a good bit like spitting into a whirlwind.

ATTACKS AT CHRISTIAN SCHOOLING

Believing Christians must seek a far different schooling for their progeny, and this the humanists deride. The cardinal principle would be schooling leading to the foot of the cross and salvation for each child. Obviously, these are primary callings for the family and church; but effective preparation in the many avenues of schooling must be a cooperative venture between these two institutions and schooling. This is far more likely to occur in Christian schools where there is much consensus.

Schooling, the believers would urge, should be based on the tenets of Christianity, not only the verity of the *Scriptures* but the values representing the faith. Indeed, the spiritual, moral, and intellectual truths of Christianity are the business of private Christian schools. Earlier, we wrote that schooling should prepare the young in the knowledge and skills preparing them to compete successfully in the social order. Also, the schools were to shape the youth to share the aspirations, abilities, and the beliefs needed for full membership in the majority culture and the marketplace.

The first of these would please believing parents; knowledge and skills attendant to success are surely worthy goals. But the second could be construed as a way of conforming the youth to a non-Christian environment. Such a feeling is partially so, but recall that the *American Creed*, in its high-level consensus values, is highly influenced by the *Ten Commandments* and other crucial Christian values. Lacking, however, is what is most important: the truth of Christianity. Without Christ, the values will never be reached. Without salvation through grace, there is no lasting hope. Without Christian values and an understanding of them, the trip to the cross is a long, long journey in a land where the home, and too often the church, fail in their Christian teachings.

In the overall consideration of the value of Christian schools, however, there is a momentous factor seldom considered. The level of maturity of the student is a determining factor in making any decision about whether or not he or she should be shielded from the mass culture and public schools. The old tale of the preacher's daughter going wild after she leaves home is a common stereotype. Supposedly, she was so protected from the excitement and pleasures of the existent world that she turned to riotous behavior.

The reasoning, then, is that in order to cope with a sinful environment, the youth should be brought up with the hope that the Christian home and church background will (or, more precisely, might) allow him or her to prevail over the sinful environment. The same rationale often alludes to the fact that Christian schools and parents structuring the life of the youth to exclude the *real world* are dubious remedies. Such people decry Christians hiding their proverbial heads in the sand.

Such reasoning might seem compelling. How can one overcome a problem by hiding from it? Indeed, it is a world filled with sin in which a person will live. At some point in time, certainly in adulthood, Christians must adequately deal with the problem. But what succeeds with one child may fail with another, and part of the reason has to do with maturity, both in age and maturity in faith.

The unspeakably glittering lure of sin is a (perhaps the) major stumbling block of all people, Christians notwithstanding. Indeed, this is a matter of most serious import, focusing on the very salvation of one's soul. Nothing, not anything, is as important, not self-concept, wealth, popularity, marriage, comfort, or anything else. During the adolescent years, and even before, the things of the world, the romantic, appealing lure of sin, bewitches the youth. Put simply, a huge percentage of adolescents will yield to the temptations of this world, just as their seniors do; and this is surely true of the sons and daughters of Christian parents, as well.

Should they, then, be insulated, as much as possible, from the temptations as they mature and become knowledgeable in doctrine and Christian truth--and surely until they accept Jesus Christ as their Savior and grow in their strengthening faith?

The argument can move in either direction; hence, there should be no arrogance in arguing either viewpoint. Nonetheless, some, perhaps many or all, young people will profit spiritually from being isolated, as much as possible, from evil until they are mature enough, both in age and in faith, to face the siren songs with confidence and the indwelling of the Holy Spirit. Sanctuary for people can be very positive, indeed.

It is true that many youth would profit hugely from attending evangelical Christian schools that work day and night to forge the *whole armor of God*. Likewise, they would benefit from parents who control their friendships closely, approbating only those who come from Christian families, and who control the television set and the CD player.

Bear in mind that immature youth can be easily drawn into strange behaviors and values. And so it can well be argued that the youth would better be prepared to answer evil if they have been imbued with the faith day

The Results: Watching A Nation Die 137

and night and if their environments are a controlled Christianity. Then, if all goes well, healthy Christians, mature enough to make sound judgments, can more adequately answer Satan's claim for their souls.

But the pressure brought to bear on the parents is almost more than they can bear. Coveting freedom and what friends are allowed to do, their children demand license to taste the appealing fruit of a corrupt world. How many parents yield to the attacks, reasoning that the youth must be popular, liked by their peers, and generally enjoy the existent world? Obviously, many parents, to a lesser or a greater degree, yield to the angry taunts of the adolescents. And, rationalizing, they believe that the home and church background will win the day. They are, in fact, the ones who hide their heads in the sand. Not to be underestimated is the power of the peer group, the mass media, and other more than powerful societal influences. Indeed, it is quite possible that many of these youth, having seriously damaged their lives following the adolescent, romantic inclinations, might have prospered by the type of controlled environment that delays, to a degree, at least, their full participation in the contemporaneous social order. Healthy people, the saved and mature, are more likely than others to prevail over evil. Christian schools are very important, indeed--perhaps utterly crucial.

This enrages the humanists, the ACLU, the courts, the media, and other societal forces, as they labor to attack Christian schooling and certainly the funding of it through the use of any public funds.

POVERTY AND HUMANISM

Any discussion of the problems of public schooling meeting the needs of the students must revolve around the problem of poverty. Far too many Americans are being raised in poverty-stricken homes, the causes being the very social problems typically mentioned. The inner city, what some sociologists identify as an area populated by a permanent underclass, is a brooding storm of failure and defeat replete with the expected poverty. One-parent homes, most often headed by women who are shamefully paid less than men, abound. Rural areas join the inner cities in the plight of poverty. Some, not all, of the problems attendant to poverty are made worse by the humanist movement.

The terrible blight of poverty must, if America is serious about its highest-level values, be lessened dramatically. This is, of course, the moral objective, but there is also a practical problem: Spreading poverty is a social problem of the first order. It is, in fact, social dynamite that threatens to destroy the social fabric of America. Letting the problem continue to develop and proliferate is to send the nation into societal crisis; and, in this, the humanist elites will have done much harm.

Some progress has been made; there have been notable efforts from the federal and state governments to help. A few did; most didn't. Many liberal actions, in fact, exacerbated the situation and added dramatically to the plight of the poor, a failure that was no small factor for the rebirth of Reaganism in the 1994 elections.

What can schools do to help? They cannot produce the same environment in which people will work. Instead, all the schools can do is understand the environment and do their best to prepare people for it. The best that can be hoped for, though, is that moral character based on the *Creed* and mind set based on the work ethic be achieved as the youth learn the skills to succeed. This is the hope that schooling can contribute to a solution of the plight of poverty.

The school, then, can help with preparation for the job market as a child's ability will allow, the morality to build a better, more successful world, and a favorable, earned self-concept. Together, these can be useful to the battle against poverty, along with the immediate dismantling of the multicultural instruction that is so disastrous in factionalizing the youth and thus sealing them into poverty.

These will not, however, solve the problem of poverty. They simply provide the youth with the skills, mind set, and morality to work successfully and honorably in the battle to overcome poverty--or at least to make huge inroads toward the goal.

And all of this must happen as people are taught that success results from hard work and preparation. They must not be tied to the dole--at least those who can do for themselves. Never again can the government drive the fathers out the back door as it has tragically done to black families. It is true that many programs, some well-intentioned, accomplished the terrible result of killing enterprise, self-concept, and the work ethic by the dole. Sometimes it is needed, and when it is, it should be provided--but only as a last resort for the very, very few who cannot, for one reason or another, work to succeed in the marketplace. The whole ideal of the dole must be reexamined. The state has no right to rob one of his self-concept and sense of accomplishment unless, in rare, rare cases, there is no other choice. Otherwise, one is to be paid only for working. In this educators, laboring hand in hand with business, could be of enormous help. They must, in one way or another, exert pressure to stop the failed giveaway programs.

Since slave days, many black families have experienced little or no success. There is, among many of them, no span of accomplishment to build bridges between the generations. Much hope resides in the churches, particularly among black youth. Men like E.V. Hill, great Los Angeles

The Results: Watching A Nation Die 139

pastor, stand as giants, preaching the gospel of Jesus Christ first and political action far second. Many other Christian leaders have joined Hill in making the church the single most important social institution helping the black youth. Other pastors have too often turned merely to social action. As notable as Dr. King was and Jesse Jackson and Al Sharpton are, they turned to this social gospel. How much better they would have performed if they were ministers of Jesus Christ first and social action leaders second.

At the feet of great men like Rev. E.V. Hill, black young people come to understand that they are precious in God's eyes and have infinite worth. They learn what salvation means and experience it. They learn to love and forgive. They learn the *thou shall nots* of the *Ten Commandments*. Any social action preached to them that does not concern itself with these precepts will surely fail, and, from those failures, flames and violence will be repeated again and again.

But schooling, too, has a monumental calling. Indeed, the schools must work day and night (and this will result in a firestorm of criticism by some humanists) to educate the youth in such a manner as to abolish ethnic and racial dependence locating the youth in the ghetto or barrio. An important objective of the schools, in this regard, is to prepare youth to become Americans who have been accepted as a part of the majority and who have the skills and demeanor to join the majority in the marketplace and neighborhoods.

The liberal-humanistic demand for multicultural schooling, as analyzed in depth earlier, must be eliminated from the schools, for it fuels the failure of minority youth and, even more importantly, of the nation itself. If the multicultural misadventure is not defeated, the angry, confrontational groups, each dedicated to getting more than others, will make problem-solution of poverty all but impossible. The war of extermination that may very well be fought in the streets will be disastrous. Pluralism must not be rhapsodized; American consensus must be.

Properly handling the situation, schools can help diffuse the serious situation leading to poverty for so many poor people in the nation. The schools must work day and night to meld all peoples into the dream of the put-upon of the world: to become Americans. In this regard, two important objectives become clear: to produce Americans who share a committed belief in the *American Creed* and to bring the youth out of the ghetto and their allegiance to racial and/or ethnic groups of their national origins.

These, coupled with the work ethic and responsibility, will help dramatically. Add the learning of salable skills, allow laws demanding an equal opportunity and a level playing field to be enforced, and there is some hope positively to affect the problem of poverty.

GLOBAL EDUCATION

As America has faced declining markets and watched other nations succeed in the marketplace, as some have shouted that the nation is no longer a major producer of goods but an information society, as the media has endeavored to trash man's greatest nation, there has developed the sense of a global village. Liberal humanists, many hating capitalism's unparalleled success, demand schooling that emphasizes global education. This demand far too often identifies a person as a leftist-leaning humanist who also champions the misadventure of multiculturalism.

This is not to say that American youth should refrain from studying and being aware of the realities of world trade. They surely should not, but this is just a section of geography courses. And such study must not attack America--which is precisely what happens far too often. A huge problem in any indepth study of these factors is time. A cursory examination of global trends and actions is acceptable. However, making such study a cardinal objective is quite wrong.

Moreover, such study can do substantial wrong. Too often global education is used by the multicultural crowd to attack the nation. Instead, the youth must be taught that the United States is special--unique, really, in the family of man, the golden culmination of man's long, lonely walk through time. Patriotism toward the nation has been earned and must be displayed, for the nation shines with the hope of freedom and dignity.

The liberals often snicker at such claims. The magnificent republic of freedom and opportunity is debased by this crowd who do not understand human nature--and thus all too often look toward socialism and communism. These people absolutely must not go uncontested in their desire to use global education to attack the United States and to foster socialism and communism. Their very efforts to do so are everywhere apparent in the schools. Make no mistake, though; many universities and colleges are burning the midnight oil educating the students to accept global education and thus negate America. Indeed, this is a problem that should be monitored diligently by Americans.

NEW AGE

The bitter fruits of the humanistic philosophy are nowhere more graphically evidenced than in New Age philosophy/religion. It refuses the existence of the God of the *Bible* and his son Jesus Christ; rather, it worships science, human progress, and potential, the primary goal being to glorify man who is said to be neither sinful nor evil. Everyone, save believing Christians, is welcome in the faith. A new world order and religion is to be formed, and will come when the Messiah of the New Age and the Antichrist with Number 666 lead the New World Order. Spirit guides will help in this regard and promise peace and love. All institutions will propagate the faith, and Christian ideals will be attacked--though Christians will be included into the faith. Man will be seen as godly and science will be a part of the godhead.

Some of the religious practices and rituals include karma, reincarnation, levitation, goddess worship, palmistry, occult visualization, sexual licentiousness, and altered states of consciousness.

Many will claim that the preceding paragraphs are overstated, that the New Age Movement is not nearly so dangerous nor comprehensive as claimed, but, at its worst, it will birth the Antichrist and lead the nations toward Armageddon; at its best, it is a developing world faith contesting Christianity in every way. Whichever, it is the same unbridled humanism that has already wounded America.

Few people making policy and teaching in the public schools are dead set on teaching the truth of the New Age Movement. Most don't even know what it is. Nonetheless, many New Age procedures and values are taught in the schools. Among others, faculty teach and textbooks print school work in karma, self-love, astral travel, occult visualization, divination, occult meditation, and occult symbolism.

Some texts and some faculty members use some of these approaches. Meditation is frequent, as is the use of the Ouija Board. Visualization is not uncommon, and witchcraft is studied, now and then. Halloween is celebrated. Eastern religions influence curricula. At least one text teaches the use of spirit guides.

How disconcerting should these practices be to believers? There is, after all, Christian meditation, and certainly not all of this practice is New Age. Yet most of it is humanism. Thus, believers should, in fact, be very concerned at any New Age procedure, whether it is perceived to be New Age or not.

This being so, what can believers do? They can calmly explain to the school board their concern, asking that the practice be removed from the schools, that their children be excused from such school assignments, or, if all else fails, bring suit against the schools on the basis of *Amendment One* to the *Constitution*. The schools would be teaching the youth a religion. It is well worth trying in the courts.

VIOLENCE

From the time of man's second generation, violence has been a very real matter of fact. When his interests are at stake, when living spaces are invaded, when groups gather, even sometimes for perverse rage or pleasure, violence is a real and terrible matter of fact. To suppose, as some humanists do, that this behavior is typically the result of environmental factors is to miss the lesson of both the *Scriptures* and history: By nature, man is sinful; part of this is evidenced in violence and cruelty.

It is not, then, surprising to comprehend the existence of violence in the nation and its schools. In a very real sense, there is less violence than in some other nations; however, this offers no solace, given the astounding expansion of inflamed cruelty in America.

And if the social order and the schools are to combat this curse, the problem must be analyzed in some depth. Nonetheless, though, the solution lies far beyond changing social structures or schooling the youth. It comes only, if at all, from changing man's nature, that is to say, as a result of accepting Jesus Christ as Savior. There are actions to be taken by both the social order and schools: They can help much, but the terrible scourge will continue. Of this, the reader may be sure.

In America, the situation turned from bad to grave. Murders accelerated in the great cities and in rural areas, earlier thought to be relatively safe. What had been a terrible disease has become an epidemic of slaughter and pillage. Youthful gangs in the urban areas leave a trail of blood, and then they bring the disease to smaller towns. The battle is over territory, race, ethnicity, failure, and a host of social and personal problems. Perhaps the greatest tragedy was that pre-adolescents became murderers. The involvement of children in the most horrendous crimes is more than Americans can take. As bad, no one is safe anywhere. America is indeed under siege by its own people--and few believe there are solutions that will work.

In 1995 and 1998 there appeared to be hope, for some serious crimes lessened, but some research attributed the numbers to the fact that there were fewer youth in the groups typically committing the crimes. The percentages may go down from time to time, but the graph will continue upward.

The schools have not been left out. Violence, unimagined even twenty years ago, is an everyday occurrence. Could it have seemed possible that the schools would erupt into violence so serious as to threaten the very future of the institution? And what does this portend for the next decade and more?

Consider the existent world. Values have given way in a large measure to self-gratification. For many youth, everything and anything go. Gangs breed violence; so, too, does the mass media. Influenced by these, the peer groups, particularly in the great urban areas, fight in gangs for turf. One-parent families profoundly influence violence, and multiculturalism breeds warfare between the races. Class warfare makes worse the terrible problem. And what about those who carry their soap-boxes to save the spotted owl, yet champion the worst of all violence: the butchery of babes in their mothers' wombs?

The Results: Watching A Nation Die

Poverty is a huge factor, as is the chipping away by the Supreme Court of rights that were held by policemen in protecting people from the crimes leading to violence. All of these factors, and others, combine to foster the violence that bids to destroy the nation and its schools. Indeed, if this violence is not abated and contained, America's future, particularly given the polarization caused by the multiculturalists, is dim.

In the meantime, Christians send their children into schools that are a microcosm of the very real and violent world. They are in enemy territory but still in America, the dear land, which is under mortal attack and, God help us all, may be dying. We must not allow this great nation to expire. It is God's work to save it. America must not fall to humanism without a battle.

AND SO?

Several times in this book, we have argued that the children may be in enemy territory when they attend the public schools. The point has now been made, and it surely paints a dismal picture.

A brief review is useful to make very clear this terrible fact. Moral relativism, the idea that there is neither right nor wrong and that all is relative, is in direct opposition to what the *Scriptures* and Creed claim. Not only that, but the teaching of openness to all means being closed to the *Scriptures* and the *American Creed*. The whole business of sex roles and marriage is in conflict with the *Bible* and with the *Creed*, as is most sex education. Imagine, a child being given a condom, an act absolutely indicating that premarital sex is acceptable. Imagine, in such classes, a child being told that homosexuality is an acceptable alternative to marriage. The family is trashed, and its values are ridiculed.

Anything can be read; children should enjoy the right to read what they want, no matter what poison it is. In counseling, they learn that guilt is their enemy, although it is surely required for improved behavior. The self-concept programs are built to make students feel well about themselves, no matter their values or efforts. The teaching of evolution is an affront to believers. Programs teaching wise use of liquor and foregoing abstinence must concern parents. The liberal humanist schooling teaching the power of government to control and help the poor is in opposition to the self-reliance of the *Creed* as well as the *Bible* and the responsibility of families for their own. New Age practices are plentiful, and children are living in fear of being killed or maimed in school. But all of this is not true in all schools. Numerous teachers mean well and work with dedication to prepare good people who have learned the skills, behaviors, and values to become producing members of the nation. In spite of huge failures of some schools, many continue to distinguish themselves.

Christian teachers are often missionaries as they stand against these horrible school procedures, and they do moderate the problem. Moreover, some schools are better than others--particularly in areas away from urban areas.

But the problem remains. Are there answers--procedures we should utilize--things we should do? What, indeed, can Americans do?

Chapter Six

FOUR CARDINAL PRINCIPLES OF HOPE

The deep problems which characterize education in the United States have been investigated and analyzed in some detail. If what we have indicated in this book is correct, America is in grave jeopardy as it contends for its very soul. It is clear, too, that the essential features of the crisis far transcend the institution of schooling, reaching to every nook and cranny of the social order. To be remembered, also, is that the triad of home, church, and school are, beyond a doubt, critical; for they are the mediating institutions that should, if they are operating as they must and in close accord, neutralize the huge and dangerous might of the humanistic power elite.

It becomes very worrisome, then, when the evidence gathers that these institutions have all too often lost their bearings, thus increasing dramatically the enormous educative power of liberal humanistic elites. Because of this, the United States teeters on the edge of the precipice, its golden dream at stake.

There are, however, four cardinal principles of education that offer hope. These are the first and most important objectives for the schools, but--and this is required for their success--of the homes and churches, as well. The cardinal principles include the following instruction and learning:

(1) a through knowledge and appreciation of the *American Creed*
(2) a decision-making reasoning process with the *Creed's* values used to arrive at judgments (the churches and homes should teach the *Ten Commandments* and the *Creed* as the values)
(3) the skills and mind set to become a society, a people, who perceive of themselves as Americans
(4) the societal and work skills that prepare the youth to become contributing, successful members of the nation.

In this chapter, then, the battle lines are drawn for the contest between the religions of Jesus Christ and humanistic man. At the same time, it should be clear that the home, church, and school must carry the brunt of the operation, joined by the very person reading this book. Can these four forces emerge as the healer and preserver of the golden dream? Is it possible that these forces can overcome their own shortcomings and the overwhelming power of the liberal humanistic elites to carry the banner in this very holy war? We are compelled to inform you that we think so.

We tell you that the very future of America as the shining light upon the hill, as humankind's last and best political hope, is under mortal siege; and, as we wrote earlier, this war must not be lost before the battles are fought. No time can be wasted. The home, church, school, and person reading this book must enter the fray now.

SCHOOLING AND THE *CREED*

The crux of intelligent attacks levied at the public schools typically focuses on one or a combination of the following: Schools do not teach a way of life that is acceptable to those embracing the *American Creed*; they fail to teach the Christian history and background of America; instruction does not represent any consistent system of moral and intellectual values; schools do not educate students in a trustworthy social and personal philosophy that unites them with other Americans into an integrated society; they do not adequately prepare them for the world of work; they meander from one fad to another; they have become the tabernacle of man's worship of himself; and they have not made progress in solving the nation's most concerning social problems.

Forty years ago, W. O. Stanley, in his landmark *Education and Social Integration*, wrote this:

> Unquestionably the clarification of the foundations of order and coherence in American education is the paramount problem facing the educational profession today.

That this problems has deepened dramatically in the four decades since Stanley completed his historic book reaffirming the claim that schooling (and more precisely the social order itself) is deep in mortal crisis, particularly as humanism has gained control.

About this, Stanley reflected:

> The educator is first of all the vicar of society charged not only with imparting to the young the knowledge and skills necessary for participation in the activities of their society, but also with developing them into persons who share the aspirations, the abilities and the beliefs required for full participation in it.

In these matters, schooling reflecting humanistic and multiculturalistic ideals, has moved far afield.

A result is the claim that schooling offers a patchwork of subjects, a humanistic organizing principle, and few or no binding ideals--save the lost claims of humanism. To Christian and many other thinking people, these developments are intolerable. If the situation does not change, Christians and multitudes of others will have no choice but to send their children to private schools or to home school them, a development that looms as a serious threat to the public schools--particularly if a voucher system or tax relief for educating the youth is acceptable to the courts and legislatures.

There is still some time, however, for the public schools to offer education that would be minimally acceptable (as long as the church and home achieve as they should) to many Christians, as well as to other disaffected taxpayers. Such an achievement would be far from perfect for these people; this is true, at least partially, because the legalities will not allow the type schooling desired and because the humanistic faith, probably representing the majority belief of Americans, is so firmly ingrained as schooling's organizing principle.

The recommendations made here will not only partially satisfy Christians, but they will also result in far better schools, no matter the ravings of those who have a huge stake in the current failures in the schools. All the problems will not be solved; however, momentous improvement will occur--but here, too, the home and church must accomplish what we recommend, or the schools will improve only nominally. Huge changes will be demanded of the schools, the first of which is to look back, to "ask for the old paths where the good way was" and to update as well as to reinvigorate the institutions.

The recommendations begin with the forementioned organizing principles of the schools: to teach students in such a manner that the *American Creed* becomes their very foundation of judging right and wrong and, after this is accomplished, to use the *Creed* to solve problems where there is not agreement. All of this will occur in a melting pot environment, and a major objective will be to socialize (prepare the youth to fit well into the majority society) and to acculturate them (prepare them to accept and assume the beliefs, skills, arts, social forms, and material traits of the majority). This, of course, eliminates multiculturalism and raging pluralism. Instead, the proposal insists that all youth be schooled to become upright, moral Americans taught to accommodate themselves to middle-class membership and to identify themselves as Americans.

Recall that a society is correctly defined as a social grouping of people held together and institutionalized by common behaviors, beliefs, and values. Already addressed is the compelling question of whether or not such social accord continues to exist in the nation. We have asserted that it does and remains America's great and abiding political hope--much to the utter chagrin of the multiculturalists and other humanists who disrespect America.

Since there is a magnificent consensus *American Creed* and since its high-level values offer the political hope of humankind, the imparting of this *Creed* is prerequisite to improvement in the schools. This must be accomplished! But the courts have not been so charitable, often insisting that any instruction in values is, in fact, teaching religion. These same courts insist that the consensus values must be taught, that they are part of schooling. They must represent wide accord, truly representing the values of the people. This necessitates, and this is absolutely crucial, the conducting of a value survey in each community, else values taught may very well be identified as religious instruction. The value survey that we authored and propose here must be accomplished, and it is to be done right.

If there is a statistician in your district, or if there is a university nearby, sophisticated statistics could be utilized if truly random samples are collected. This approach might make the results more meaningful for scholars; however, the reporting of percentages alone would be more useful for the public at large--and this is the group to whom the results should be addressed.

If there are other values that you wish to test, include them; however, the list included in the questionnaire represents extensive research. We are confident that the list represents the *American Creed*, but we do not desire that you automatically accept these values as American consensus. Use the *American Creed Questionnaire* and find out for yourself the validity of our claims in your community. Should you want to test other attitudes, though, two statements are needed for each value: one to measure the value and, two, to see if the value should be taught in the school.

Following is the questionnaire:

THE AMERICAN CREED QUESTIONNAIRE

Following is a group of statements for your reaction. Because there is a plan to share with the school district and the community the values shared by the people living in the school district, it is important that you fill out this questionnaire. You will remain completely anonymous. No scores will be reported for any single person; it is what the entire community believes that is important and that will be reported.

Thank you very much for your time in filling out the questionnaire. The results will surely be shared with you.

You will note there are five choices. Survey question 1 is this:"I believe in recognizing the moral worth and dignity of people." If you strongly agree, answer 1; if you agree, answer 2; if you have no opinion, answer 3; if you

Four Cardinal Principles of Hope

disagree, answer 4, or if you strongly disagree, answer 5. Do this for every statement on the questionnaire.

Answer each of the statements by using only one choice.

1. I believe in recognizing the moral worth and dignity of people.
2. I believe that the schools should teach as truth the moral worth and dignity of people.
3. I believe in freedom as well as the restraints necessary to maintain it.
4. I believe that the schools should teach as truth the belief in freedom coupled with the restraints necessary to maintain it.
5. I believe in equality that means worth and dignity for people.
6. I believe schools should teach as truth equality that means worth and dignity for people.
7. I believe that America should reflect a social order so conceived and so operated that every person can grow to the fullest level of his/her capabilities.
8. I believe that the schools should teach as truth a social order that is so conceived and so operated so that each person can grow to the fullest level of his/her capabilities.
9. I believe that America should be a perfect union, one and inseparable.
10. I believe schools should teach as truth that America should be a perfect union, one and inseparable.
11. I believe that America should have a representative government operated as a republic and a congress representing the will of the people.
12. I believe that the schools should teach that America should have a representative government operated as a republic and with a congress representing the will of the people.
13. I believe that government is for the expressed purpose of serving the people.
14. I believe that the schools should teach that government is for the expressed purpose of serving the people.
15. I believe that government's power comes only from the consent of the governed.
16. I believe that the schools should teach as truth that government's power should come only from the consent of the governed.
17. I believe that there should be protection of the electorate from governmental excess and inequity.
18. I believe that the schools should teach protection of the electorate from governmental excess and inequity.

19. I believe that the power of all branches of the government should be limited to the *Constitution*.
20. I believe that the schools should teach as truth that the power of all branches of the government should be limited to the *Constitution*.
21. I believe in the innate right of all citizens to life, liberty, and the pursuit of happiness within the law.
22. I believe that the schools should teach as truth the innate right of all citizens to life, liberty, and the pursuit of happiness within the law.
23. I believe in freedom of religion.
24. I believe that the schools should teach as truth the freedom of religion.
25. I believe in the dedicated belief in the sanctity of the historic family with the belief that it is the nation's most important institution and the understanding that traditional marriage vows are sacred.
26. I believe that the schools should teach as truth the dedicated belief in the historic family with the belief that it is the nation's most important institution and the understanding that traditional marriage vows are sacred.
27. I respect practical wisdom.
28. I believe the schools should teach as truth a respect for practical wisdom.
29. I believe in the crucial importance of honesty and integrity.
30. I believe the schools should teach as truth the crucial importance of honesty and integrity.
31. I believe in the work ethic with the understanding that success comes from work, study, and application.
32. I believe the schools should teach as truth the work ethic with the understanding that success comes from work, study, and application.
33. I believe in an equitable system of law protecting the populace from crime and dishonored contracts.
34. I believe the schools should teach as truth the importance of an equitable system of law protecting the populace from crime and dishonored contracts.
35. I believe in the existence of adequate armed forces to protect the citizens and nation from threat to the *American Creed*.
36. I believe the schools should teach as truth the importance of adequate armed forces to protect the citizens and nation from threat to the *American Creed*.
37. I believe in laws that allow an accused person every right to prove his innocence.
38. I believe the schools should teach as truth the importance of laws that allow an accused person every right to prove his innocence.

Four Cardinal Principles of Hope

39. I believe in the personal responsibility of each person for his actions.
40. I believe the schools should teach as truth the responsibility of each person for his actions.
41. I believe in due process under the law for all people.
42. I believe the schools should teach as truth the importance of due process under the law for all people.
43. I believe in the dedicated belief in the preeminence of the American republic with the willingness to become one with the majority and to participate in the democratic process for improving it.
44. I believe the schools should teach as truth a dedicated belief in the preeminence of the American republic with the willingness to become one with the majority and to participate in the democratic process for improving it.
45. I believe in free economic enterprise within the bounds of fair play.
46. I believe the schools should teach as truth a belief in free economic enterprise within the bounds of fair play.
47. I believe in assistance for those absolutely unable to help themselves.
48. I believe the schools should teach as truth to believe in assistance for those absolutely unable to help themselves.
49. I believe that murder is wrong.
50. I believe the schools should teach that murder is wrong.
51. I believe in honoring mother, father, and family.
52. I believe the schools should teach as truth the honoring of mother, father, and family.
53. I believe in fairness in dealing with people.
54. I believe the schools should teach as truth fairness in dealing with people.
55. I believe cruelty is unacceptable behavior.
56. I believe the schools should teach as truth that cruelty is unacceptable behavior.
57. I believe that undue coveting is unacceptable behavior.
58. I believe the schools should teach as truth that undue coveting is unacceptable behavior.
59. I believe in the dramatic limitation of government in lives of Americans.
60. I believe the schools should teach as truth the dramatic limitation of government in the lives of Americans.
61. I believe that one's behavior should reflect courage in meeting life's problems.
62. I believe the schools should teach as truth that one's behavior should reflect courage in meeting life's problems.

63. I believe in the willingness to forgive.
64. I believe the schools should teach as truth the willingness to forgive.
65. I believe in a disdain for arrogance.
66. I believe the schools should teach as truth a disdain for arrogance.
67. I believe in loyalty to family, friends, church, and nation.
68. I believe the schools should teach as truth loyalty to family, friends, church, and nation.

It is necessary that you administer the *American Creed Questionnaire* correctly, particularly in the selection of a random sample. Ideally, it would be best if you could administer the *Questionnaire* to everyone in a given school district, but this is almost always impossible--except, perhaps, in some very small communities. In random sampling, a sample is drawn which should be as much like the entire population of the district as possible. That being so, you can speak with considerable confidence about the entire group from which the sample is drawn.

Probably the best plan in this situation is to pick a simple random sample. Assume that you are living in a community of 10,000 people. Obviously, you would not choose to test all of them. Instead, you might select a sample of, say, 500 people to represent the whole. The sample must be chosen by random selection procedures; and in the process, each person must have an equal opportunity to be chosen with every selection.

All ten thousand names could be listed separately on sheets of paper the same size. They could then be put together, mixed well, and 500 names selected. It is crucial, however, that each time a person's name is drawn, the slip should be placed again in the 10,000 grouping of slips; for each draw, every person must have one chance in 10,000 to have his name selected. This is required for random selection. This process would be terribly time-consuming, hence, not very practical. The easiest way would be to assign each of the 10,000 people a number, from one to 10,000. Consult the math teacher for a table of random numbers. Have him explain how to use it to select the sample which will approximate the entire population.

One can then speak with some certainty about what the people in the community feel about the *Creed* and about the degree to which they believe it should be taught in the schools. You will have discovered which of the high-level values are shared by a majority of school district members and the strength of feeling about each of these valuations as well as which of them they want taught. You will also have attended to legal problems, for if, indeed, you locate the consensus values, and if they are not the *Ten Commandments*, it becomes legal to teach the system. There is every reason to believe that the NEA and ACLU cannot, then, justify attacks at the teaching

Four Cardinal Principles of Hope

of the consensus *American Creed* as teaching religion. The shared values, as long as they are within the law, can be taught. This will be the start of schools meeting public expectations and returning schooling to its former place of admiration by the taxpayers who own the institutions. This principle can again result in schooling with order and clarity.

But all of this will come to nothing if the results are not effectively shared with school district taxpayers. The newspaper, television, radio, clubs, churches, all parents, and other organizations in the community must be informed. The results must be professionally sold to the public, and they should, as a result, agree that the primary principle in all of schooling is to teach the verity of each plank of the *Creed*.

Another example is useful. Assume that you are living in a town populated by 60,000 people. Suppose you decide to select a simple random sample of 3,000 people, and you are successful in achieving a sample somewhere near that number. Then consider *Statement One* in the *Questionnaire*: "I believe in recognizing the moral worth and dignity of people." Suppose 800 strongly agreed; 1500 agreed; 250 had no opinion; 250 disagreed, and 200 strongly disagreed. The findings might well be reported like this:

TABLE ONE

Statement Number One: I believe in recognizing the moral worth and dignity of people. N=3,000

	Strongly Agree	Agree	No Opinion	Dis-Agree	Strongly Disagree
Number of Respondents	800	1500	250	250	200
Percent of Respondents	26.7	50.0	8.3	8.3	6.7

The written discussion of *Statement One* (and each of the statements would be analyzed in a similar manner) would approximate this: *Questionnaire Statement One* was supported by 76.7 percent, with nearly 27 percent strongly agreeing, and 50 percent agreeing. Just 8.3 percent disagreed, while 6.7 percent strongly disagreed. Only 8.3 percent had no opinion. There is substantial consensus that the sample strongly supports *Statement One*.

But at what point can one understand the values to represent consensus? In matters as crucial as this is, any judgments should reflect caution. We think that the *strongly agree* and *agree* should total at least 75 percent. Even with this demanding percentage, there would be some concern if a block of 25 percent strongly disagreed.

Should more sophisticated statistical work be desired to address a professional audience, parametric statistics might be considered. If there are statisticians in a given school, such an approach would be possible. Also, a nearby university could help set up such an evaluation of the questionnaire, and it would, from a scholarly point of view, be more significant. The audience being addressed, however, must be considered in announcing results of the *American Creed Questionnaire*. Do not forget, that for the dialogue to be effective in the school district the reporting of numbers and percentages is probably far more useful.

It may be, that you will feel that a simple random sample is not as useful in your school district as proportional random sample. If there are particular groups (tiers) of people in your district who should be examined separately, the proportional evaluation might well be used. Perhaps in your particular evaluation three groups are politically strong and often do battle with each other. Suppose these groups are professionals (of which there are 400 in the district); factory workers (of which there are 1200); and retirees (of which there are 200 people). Assume that you desire to select a random sample of 360 of the population of 1800 in the three groupings. Of this 360 person sample, the percentages of each group must be considered. If the total of the three groups is 1800, then the 400 professional people represent 22.2 percent of the total (400/1800); the factory workers are 66.7 percent of the total (1200/1800); and the retired people are 11.1 percent of the total (200/1800).

The sample, then, would be chosen in this fashion: Three hundred sixty persons are to be randomly selected from the 1800 population. Since professional people total 22.2 percent of the population, obviously that percentage must obtain in the sample. Hence, 22.2 percent of the sample of 360 would be 79.92 persons, rounded out to 80 persons. In like manner, the factory people represent 66.7 percent of the sample of 360 people, the total being 240.12, rounded to 240 persons; the retired people should total 11.1 percent of the population, the total accruing to 39.96 persons, a number rounded to 40.

There is to be a proportional random sample of 360, a 20 percent sample. All of the professional people would be assigned a number, and, using a table of random numbers (see the math teacher), 80 names would be drawn. Following the same procedure for factory workers, 240 names would be selected, while 40 retired persons' names would be chosen. Add the three numbers and the sample of 360 people is in place. Unlike simple random sampling, this group represents the percentage numbers in the sample that are

Four Cardinal Principles of Hope

to be considered from the population.

The results for each question would approximate the reporting on *Statement One*, "I believe in recognizing the moral worth and dignity of people."

TABLE TWO

Statement Number One: I believe in recognizing the moral worth and dignity of people. <u>N = 3 Groups: 80 professionals; 240 factory workers; 40 retired people</u>
<u>Total sample: 360</u>

<u>Percentage Responses</u>

	Strongly Agree	Agree	No Opinion	Disagree	Strongly Disagree
Professional People	79.0	11.4	5.0	2.0	2.6
Factory Workers	60.0	23.4	10.0	4.6	2.0
Retirees	90.0	5.0	3.0	1.8	1.8
Overall	76.3	13.3	6.0	2.5	1.9

The discussion of *Statement One* might look like this: Concerning the reactions of a proportional random sample of 240 factory workers, 80 professionals, and 40 retirees, there was a huge consensus. Overall, 89.6 percent reacted favorably, with 76.3 percent strongly agreeing. Just 4.4 percent answered *disagreed* or *strongly disagreed*. In further analyzing the percentages, it is clear that the retired people most strongly approbated the statement with 90 percent, while the factory workers totaled 60 percent. Still, though, the percentage results overwhelmingly support *Statement One* as a consensus value among the three groups tested. You may be surprised to discover, as you will after completing the data gained from the *Questionnaire*, that there are admirable consensus values in your district You should not be, for all over the nation the results are very much alike; they are surprisingly similar. It is just not true that the *American Creed* is dead. It remains alive, and that is very, very, very good news. It is a profound social and political hope for America and, indeed, for humankind. America has not yet seen its best days, no matter the rantings and ravings of the naysayers.

The *Creed* is alive--and hope hangs like a halo over the beloved nation.

Do not yield to people who assert that the values comprising the *Creed* are mere words and that American behavior does not reflect them. To understand the serious error of such assertions, read Gunnar Myrdal's *An American Dilemma*. He well explained that the abiding problem of people in the United States is the refusal to live up to the high values they truly accept. These behaviors, the low-level values, must be adjusted upward, toward what they truly believe as evidenced in the high-level values comprising the *American Creed*. Perhaps the very most important goal of American institutions is to restore us to the consensus values that so distinguish this hallowed nation.

Having completed evaluating the *American Creed Questionnaire*, the schools will have in hand the consensus values shared by the school district; this is the beginning of a magnificent revolution for your school. There is, indeed, a bright day coming.

No longer must you refrain from teaching what should be the primary goal of schooling: building good and decent people who share in the *Creed* that represents the political hope of mankind. Out of confusion, you may very well have been reflecting the tenets of the humanists' agendum, teaching a lie as if it were the truth. Now you can take the high road, rediscovering the old paths that made this land the oasis for man.

The first calling of schooling, then, the First Cardinal Principle of the schools, is to teach the *Creed* as the truth, as the foundation on which to make practical and moral judgments. To the believer, this demand still sounds like humanism--and, in a way, it is, until one understands the genesis of the *Creed*. And consider what is now transpiring. What about the teaching of moral relativism, existentialism, nihilism, and the plethora of other humanistic abominations?

The faculty, from kindergarten through secondary school, should be assembled and told that the *Creed*, the consensus values they helped identify in the district by being involved in the *American Creed Questionnaire*, is the very first objective of the schools. The *Creed* must be indoctrinated as the value foundation on which to make all judgments and the rudder to guide behavior (although the *Ten Commandments* will continue to be taught as the primary value system in the homes and churches). Gone forever, it is hoped, will be the idea that good values come from the very souls of untutored youth.

The faculty should be directed to use their creativity to overhaul the curriculum. In the literature selected, in teacher presentation, in the redirection of courses, in the school rules, in every aspect of schooling, the genius of the faculty should lead to a birthing of the *American Creed* as the first business of the schools. Teachers must comprehend that there is really no other choice, as they socialize and acculturate the youth in the *melting pot* of

THE NEXT STEP

But it will be clear to any thinking person that, even if the *Creed* is imbued in the minds of the students, they will be sent into a nation that too often lives the low-level values, a social order in which the bitter seeds of man's nature, the tragic instruction in moral relativism and the humanism of the era, have brought America low. Where there is not agreement among Americans, there must be a process of problem-solving that will use the *Creed* as the measuring device and that will use a method of inquiry that will utilize the *Creed* to solve problems. Such a method of inquiry and decision-making is the Second Cardinal Objective of schooling.

But the decision-making procedure must gain precedence only after the planks of the *Creed* are firmly affixed in the students. The use of the procedure is not for younger students, although the steps and moods must be mastered from the very beginning of schooling. The values inherent in the *Creed* are requisite, but so, too, is a method for using the values to solve problems where there is no agreement.

This humanistic liberals understood several decades ago. Many embraced Dewey's theory of experimentalism. Scientific knowledge builds on such information so that, over time, man's decision-making, based on such knowledge, will get better and better. Increasingly, Dewey wrote, decisions will be better and more informed. Man will get wiser and yet wiser. Increasingly, decisions will be made on fact and not fancy. Believers, of course, knew that it would fail because it misread human nature and did not consider carefully enough human emotions. An answer was Professor Charles Raup and colleagues' book *The Theory of Practical Judgment*. Raup and his associates, humanistic admirers of Dewey, added dealing with emotions in the decision-making process to Dewey's experimentalism. Reduced to its essentials and changed in important ways, practical judgment becomes very useful to the Christian conservative. Raup was committed to the idea that, in a nation like America, decisions are made in groups, and they must be built on consensus of good values among the decision-makers. In many ways this was acceptable, but it failed grievously in two areas of concern: first, people are not necessarily imbued with admirable consensus values and, second, the single human voice is all but stilled. The first is solved by indoctrination in the students of the consensus high-level values comprising the *American Creed*. Second, and we shall explain this in the following pages, the single human voice, so important in history's movements, must be written into the decision-making process. One person can, and has, changed society for better or worse. Recall Martin Luther, the apostles Peter and Paul, Adolph Hitler, Billy Graham, James Kennedy, and thousands of others. Sometimes the single human voice far transcends group decisions. That is precisely the reason why both group and single-person decisions must be central to the process of decision-making and deliberation, and both reason and emotion must be involved in any concept of decision authority.

As indicated earlier, the decision-making procedure comes only when youth become mature and when the *Creed* has been mastered. But the preparation in the moods and steps is prerequisite to the procedure.

A further glimpse at practical judgment allows an understanding of its strengths and fatal flaws. The theory itself is expounded by Raup and his colleagues in the book *The Improvement of Practical Intelligence*, published in 1951 by Harper and Brothers. Taken quite seriously over forty years ago, it eventually waned as an important influence in the schools; however, it remains, with the additions we shall add, a very important tool in building a concept of authority in using the *Creed* for decision-making, particularly where there is little or no agreement among the decision-makers.

Raup and colleagues were particularly interested in decisions concerning what people should do in groups to make decisions when accord is lacking. In this, four steps are crucial. The first step, then, is the decision concerning what should be done under a certain set of circumstances in a particular situation. In a search for the answer, both the scientific approach and moral and ethical ideals are necessary. The final group decision, though, must focus on the particular facts and problems of the case being considered. The result of the decision-making process is a type of general policy formulation that is useful in future similar situations, and it is, indeed, Raup claimed, the product of morality and factual data.

Part of this was so; practical judgment provides well for using facts in the group decision-making process. It does not in matters of moral judgment. Just as there must be a methodological concept of authority in decision-making that is based on a protracted study in which one masters the steps and moods, there must also be, and in this Raup's procedure is lacking, a foundation of values taught which includes the planks of the *American Creed*.

Every child must know the planks of the *Creed* better than anything else he will study in school. He must *master* the *American Creed*. He must hold in his pocket or billfold a card listing the planks of the *Creed*, and when decisions are made in school he should have the card in hand, and, until the list is absolutely memorized, read the valuations on which the judgment is based. As he develops his value system based on the world's most salutary system of values, his opinion may have some value; the *Creed* has far more.

Another of schooling's most important objectives is to socialize and acculturate the pupils. This must focus in the schools on the teaching as truth the consensus value system; on this the whole objective depends.

It is more than ironic that such an approach could possibly result in schools reconstructing the social order, the fond goal of the humanists. But to their utter disgust, the reconstruction is not the liberal, huge government, socialistic model they have championed for decades now. Rather--and this is cause for celebration and hope--it is reconstructing what earlier offered the political hope of humankind: the *Creed* and its magnificent dream. It is reconstructing for the old paths that alone can answer the nation's manifest social problems.

Raup was correct in listing four moods prerequisite to practical judgment's success. We added another, and the resulting five moods are indeed worthy of careful consideration. They are, in fact, so important that they become a major goal during the first eight years of schooling and must be the first business of all classes taught. The students must absolutely master the moods to make operational the reasoning process we shall recommend.

Mood One (Indicative)

This mood involves the use of facts to solve problems; it mirrors the experimentalism of John Dewey and the scientific method. The learner must do his homework to the degree he is able, given his grade level and maturity. He is required to know as much as he can about the subject at hand, comprehending the problem, potentialities, and, based on these, possible solutions--all based on the *Creed*.

Such an approach allows the student to submit the ideas to be tested with logic and factual investigation--but, even more important, by the validity of the planks of the *Creed* used as the foundation on which to base problem solution. Even at an early age, students can be asked to deal with simple facts rather than mere feelings, and this is very good.

Mood Two (Optative)

Mood One should result, more or less, with the student having the facts of the situation. Then, he must work well with the decision-making group, an action perceived by Raup as absolutely crucial in a democracy. Also, and this may be impossible for many, he must suspend his unbelief as he listens to other group members. He must be willing to be convinced that the speakers in the group are potentially correct. This necessitates, too, that each person in the group faithfully represent his thinking, based on the facts and the values inherent in the *Creed*. If any person in the group fails to express himself, practical judgment will not work. The result of all this is to bring the group together in consensus concerning the problem and its possible solutions--at least the plan of action to attack it. If the first and second moods are reached, a useful course of action is in sight.

But Raup and colleagues do not adequately consider the single human voice in the Optative Mood. Each student should, during the discussions alluded to above, hold a card listing the parts of the *Creed* (The Christian youth should also have such a list of the *Commandments* for church and Sunday school), and the group should be contested whenever the presentation or solution fails to meet the *Creed*. The group may, in fact, even after following the two moods, be wrong. Where there is a truth, it may very well be bartered away in the procedure of practical judgment--and this is to be much feared.

If so, it can be stopped only by the single voice contesting it in the name of the *Creed*, the *Scriptures*, or faulty research. Such a development would most assuredly not please Raup, who would very likely announce at this point that the moods had been inadequately learned. The system, he might very well claim, has broken down at this point. But the youth, with the courage and determination of firm and right values, will explain his position calmly and clearly to the group members. He should invite them to join him and reconstruct the judgment with the *Creed*, the *Commandments*, and research.

This single human voice can and frequently has changed the very course of history; thus, any concept of authority in decision-making must consider this possibility.

Mood Three (Contemplative)

In this mood, the student withdraws from the group to reason carefully and thoughtfully concerning what has happened. Each person has considered what have been identified as the facts and the group feelings. That being so, it is time to reflect. Time, relaxation, and further consideration are important. Perhaps one's own value system and personal feelings most come to bear in the contemplative mood. Are the facts correct? Are the planks of the *Creed* used for decision-making?

Mood Four (Moral Individualism)

Following the suggestions at the end of the preceding paragraph, the student, after suspending his unbelief and listening to the group carefully, will stand alone when the *Creed*, the *Commandments*, or the research are inade-

Four Cardinal Principles of Hope

quately or incorrectly understood and utilized. This is our mood, not Raup's.

Mood Five (Imperative)

This is the action mood and encompasses two primary ideas. First, every member of the group must represent his feelings completely and well, as mentioned earlier, else the entire process will fail. Secondly, the ideals of the group must result in consensus which satisfies the entire group, and this consensus must result in a program of action to deal with the problem at hand. Without the program of action, the entire process is a waste of time. As indicated in Mood Four, the person representing the single human voice, splintering from the group at large, must also draft a program of action and endeavor to convince the entire group of his position. If this is impossible, he must start his own program of action.

Having mastered the *Creed* (and in Sunday School the *Commandments*), as well as the moods, the student is ready during his more mature years in school to utilize practical judgment along with our variations in solving problems in which there is not accord.

But will this work? Can students, beginning in the early grades, learn this completely? Of course, they can, but the planks of the *Creed* must be the Cardinal Principle in the schools. Can the students master the moods of the process of inquiry building on practical judgment? Again, yes, they can if the school teaches it as the Second Cardinal Principle of the schools. If this process is successful, the stage is set for the needed conservative revolution in schooling.

The next step, though, must be added: making decisions where there is not agreement or when confusion and emotion rule the decision-making process. Schooling can indoctrinate the *Creed* (as it should and must), and it can probably be successful in teaching the decision-making process to most students. It is time, then, to allot huge blocks of time in the later years of high school to making such decisions. In this regard, Raup lists four steps--and it should be no surprise to note that they parallel the moods. The group assembles to make its decision concerning what to do about some problem where there is not general accord, and the procedure would approximate the following:

(1) Clarify the common purpose of the group and identify the desired state of affairs concerning the problem at hand.
(2) Survey and assess the existing state of affairs--get the facts.
(3) Adapt the ideas of the group to the claims of the situation as a whole.

(4) Join the group ideal in planning a program for action.

Our addendum, as indicated in the moods, would also affect the steps. If the *Creed* and/or the *Ten Commandments* are being misrepresented in the group decision, those in disagreement should endeavor to convince the group of its error. Failing that, they should withdraw from the larger group and forge their own program of action based on the moods and steps.

The first two cardinal principles are absolutely necessary for this to occur; otherwise, the needed improvement will not happen. The schools must determine the consensus values and educate people exactly to what these values are. Then the genius of faculty, taxpayers, and administrators should conspire in planning how precisely, in every course throughout the school, kindergarten through high school, to teach the moods of the *Creed* along with the planks comprising the *Creed*. After these teachings have taken root, sometime in the last three years of high school, the great (and small) conflicts on which there are disagreements will be subjected to the decision-making process explained in this chapter. These behaviors and mentality represent the glorious rebirth for schooling; they are surely absolutely required. Then the other changes begin, and the healing can become splendid and hugely successful.

THE MELTING POT

Schooling is for the expressed purpose of housebreaking the youth into the majority society and culture. This is simply another way to say that the schools must become, as they were when the institutions were accomplishing miracles, a melting pot. The first demand is that faculty, administrators, and school board members comprehend that America is the highest, most glorious social order in man's walk through history, that this dear land is, indeed, the shining light on the hill, the golden dream, man's most fervent political dream. Faculty and administrators who feel otherwise should not be hired.

Radical humanists attack the teaching of western culture, and they too often growl about *dead white men* who have set policy, an argument that is utterly spurious. America is, thankfully, a western nation, and the culture, arts, wisdom, and political realities are unmatched. Of course, the schools teach western culture; they could do no less. And to let disaffected groups representing other parts of the globe demand that the American culture not be the goal of schooling is to abdicate America's greatness.

The objective, in this regard, is to structure schooling so that the Third Cardinal Objective is realized: Every student will be educated to become an American who shares in the golden dream and who has the mind set and skills

Four Cardinal Principles of Hope

to become a happy, productive member of middle-class America. Every child, then, should be instructed, in each course, in each activity, to be an American who shares the *Creed*. Critics incorrectly argue that this approach is dehumanizing to new Americans. Exactly the opposite is true, as the youth are prepared for full membership in humankind's greatest social and political order. It is true, too, that minority people also influence the majority as they join the group. Witness the quite amazing influence of blacks in music, sports, religion, and politics. What about the Latin influence in dining, music, and dance? Indeed, as the minorities become one with the majority, they influence it as evolving occurs.

This means, of course, that nearly anything separating people will be stripped from the schools. The death knoll will peal for the entire multicultural misadventure. This will require much effort, for the approach is everywhere extolled by some faculty and professional organizations. Multicultural objectives must disappear from the schools. Instead, the cultures are to be lovingly absorbed into the majority.

Indeed, the formation of the *melting pot* cardinal principle in schooling requires huge changes in educational institutions; but they must, absolutely must, be made. There will be no minority clubs or activities. All is American. The stories selected to be read will typically feature both truths of the *Creed* and the greatness of America. The importance of myth will be considered in teaching both. The halls will be filled with pictures of American heroes. The presidents, along with great Americans of every ethnic, race, and minority group, will be included, not because of their minority background but because they are worthy Americans. Democracy will be extolled; Marxianism and fascism will be taught as evil. The pupils will be taught in such a way as to make them proud to be Americans. The tired, the poor masses, yearning to be free, have found a home in America. The institutions, including schooling, must surely educate them to become one with the golden dream, to become Americans, to fulfill the fervent hopes of their fathers and mothers, to hold their heads high as Americans, and to enjoy the fruits thereof.

SOCIETAL SKILLS

It is no secret that the declining skills of public school students reflect a major weakness of schooling. The schools still do not do well in this area, and part of this is a result of too little time to accomplish the needed goals. Presently, school is asked to do far more than it can. This means, then, that as long as the schools are asked to do all things, including what the home and church have failed to accomplish, more time is needed.

But there has been improvement as indicated in *U.S. Schools Can't*

Teach? Don't Believe the Myths, published in *USA Today,* March 13, 1996. SAT scores rose fourteen points from 1990 to 1995. Students are also taking more demanding academic courses, and they are competing far better on tests with students from other nations than they formerly did. Beyond a doubt, there is some improvement, but much more is needed.

Also, it would be well if the school day were lengthened and the school year increased. These would help in the implementation of the recommendations made in this book. In each skill area, i.e., reading, writing, speaking, listening, math, high level thought processes, computer use, typing, and other applicable areas, each attending department and specialty area could formulate and operate a clinic, a lab where every child needing help in one or more of these skill areas could get help: evaluation of particular weaknesses, a professional diagnosis, therapy after prescription of just what the youth needs, and cure to the degree each child can achieve.

Someone will surely argue that such an idea has merit but that, in all practicality, such a procedure is too expensive. Nonetheless, it is within the realm of possibility. One could argue, for instance, that class size be increased substantially. The sum of research concerning class size does not dramatically submit that class size makes a difference. In fact, quite the opposite is so. If there is some loss of identity in larger classes, it would be more than rectified in the improved skills the students will achieve either alone or in small groups. Cardinal Principle Four, the teaching of needed societal skills, is crucial to America's future--and that of the youth.

These Cardinal Principles are a foundation on which to educate Americans, in the schools, homes, and churches, but they are only a beginning. The church and home must focus on Christianity and salvation. Together, the three great institutions can rebirth America and its dream.

Chapter Seven

WHAT THE SCHOOLS MUST DO

With the four Cardinal Principles in place, the public schools have the social and moral ammunition to join the home and church in contesting for the very soul of the United States. These three institutions can neutralize the tremendous power of the liberal education elite, but this will not occur if any of the three fail--and all are doing so now. In the schools, the Four Cardinal Principles are the foundation of the entire program.

RELATIVISM, OPENNESS, GERMAN PSYCHOLOGY AND PHILOSOPHY

The relativistic view of morality permeates the public schools, as it does all of the social order. There is no room whatsoever for relativism in educating young Americans. The *Creed* is right. Where there is not agreement on the moral absolutes, the decision-making procedure will be utilized.

In like manner, the terrible humanistic demand that the youth should be open-minded in all things will fall before successful teaching of the *Creed* and the process of inquiry and decision-making. The planks of the *Creed* are absolutes, thus precluding the notion that one should be open-minded to all sorts of foolishness, even if it is in direct opposition to the *Creed*. Students will not be taught to accept behaviors and thoughts antithetic to the *Creed*. Adultery is wrong, as is homosexuality. Cruelty is wrong, as is murder. Hundreds of other behaviors are not to be accepted according to the *Creed*. Many liberal humanists will disagree with this position. Nonetheless, students will be instructed that they should surely not be receptive to all things, that sometimes openness is in direct disagreement with the *Creed* and with Christian values shared by those who penned the *Constitution*.

The negativism of Freudianism, nihilism, and existentialism is based on the premise that there is no God save humanism. This, students must comprehend, and they must surely not be taught that life is hopeless. The psychology of Freud has increasingly been proven false; nihilism and existentialism are beliefs derived from the hopelessness of non-belief--all the natural consequence of man honoring his own feeble efforts rather than God's.

The schools must teach that there is hope based on the *Creed*, the decision-making procedure; and, it might be suggested, in what they learn in church--and this will demand huge changes in how the schools approach the use of the *Creed*, the decision-making process,
and the books and materials chosen for the curriculum.

BUSINESS AND THE SCHOOLS

For years in the institutions of higher education, a smoldering hate of business has been passed on to students by faculty. Many of these educators are collectivists, socialists, Marxists, or, at the very least, liberal humanists. Understanding the commitment to collectivism, the sworn enemy of the American Republic which is based on the profit motif, the reader can understand the misguided effect of the university influence on beginning teachers and, indeed, hundreds of thousands of students so influenced by liberal humanistic faculty. It would be difficult to overestimate the damage done by these professors. Many of the answers do, in fact, rest with business leaders who must expand their influence on the schools. Their assistance is at least as important as that of the universities. They should make equipment available to the schools, advise on curricular matters, help set policy, be active on school boards, and generally help the schools produce the skills necessary to allow students success and to prepare them to lead the nation in a technological age of excellence. The claims of university professors that the nation is now an information society and not a leading manufacturer must be contested and changed. America is both.

Local businesses should hire youth and help train them for success, and they should, when possible, help finance students less likely to distinguish themselves in an academic setting. This means also that the universities should have a diminished influence in public schools. Business can bring more breadth than higher education to its helping the schools. For instance, it can focus more clearly on industrial education, both for those who do not excel in school and for those who can be leaders in industry. Business people know far more than humanistic professors about the skills needed for the youth, both now and in the foreseeable future; hence, they should be in leadership roles in advising the schools. And it is more than ironic, as well, that these persons may even be of more use than liberal, humanistic faculty in preparing the youth for the information society that many professors love.

This inclusion of business will arouse the ire of many in higher education, but it is necessary. Business can help immensely, and the schools would be wise to tap this important source.

ONE-ISSUE LEADERS

Problems also exist in the leadership of the schools, particularly in middle-management, especially in those decision-making positions that deal with minority groups and multicultural education. One of the most damaging blunders of multiculturalism and other special interest areas of schooling is the focus on the ethnic or other special interest group instead of complex of subcultures. In this regard, many programs are led by ethnic persons who, the reasoning of the time asserts, are uniquely qualified to comprehend the problems of their people, or who are led by one-issue romantics dedicated or trained to serve a particular minority group. In his noteworthy classic *The Road to Serfdom*, Friedrich Hayek explained:

> Planning . . . unites almost all of the single-minded idealists who have devoted their lives to a single task . . . the result not of a comprehensive view of society, but rather of a very limited view and often a great exaggeration of the importance of the ends they place foremost . . . . It would make the very men who are most anxious to plan society the most dangerous if they were allowed to do so--and the most intolerant of the planning of others.

Transferred to ethnic (or any minority or special interest) schooling, Hayek's observations are compelling. Romantic policy-makers, fired with a fervor from their respective cultures or ideologically wed to the welfare of one minority at the cost of others, become addicted to spending tax monies to focus on the one subculture. The results tend toward separatism. These people exaggerate the importance of their particular goals and forego the comprehensive view of the social order required to educate both minority and majority pupils to succeed in the marketplace and to attain a lasting dignity. This narrow, myopic view has hurt schooling badly.

The one-issue people must not be located in leadership roles in the schools. Administrators at every level must comprehend that the schools are for the expressed purpose of socializing and acculturating the youth to join middle-class America and to become Americans, to help remove the barriers between the youthful human beings who are to be the nation's future citizens. They do so by preparing them to be one with the majority American culture. This means that all persons who set policy in any manner see the broad picture. This is crucial in a curricular process meeting the needs analyzed in this chapter. One-issue people are not acceptable.

At the same time, the entire public residing in the school district must have increased input in school planning. In every area of such planning, the local citizens should surely be involved, as they represent the varying and various groups comprising the community. They should not represent a majority on any committee, but their stamp should be everywhere apparent in all school matters.

DISCIPLINE AND VIOLENCE

The efforts of the negative humanistic elites has, to a very large degree, fostered this problem in the nation, and it is surely society's dilemma. As is true with all such insoluble problems, they pass to the schools, institutions that obviously cannot author any solutions whatsoever. But the schools can act to minimize violence in school and, perhaps, to help somewhat in dealing with the problem outside school.

Self-concept is a crucial factor. People who like themselves display less aggression than those who do not. Therefore, an important goal of schooling is to foster a favorable self-concept in each youth who deserves it. Nonetheless, a student should not be made to feel well about himself or his actions when effort or character is lacking.

The schools should surely work toward producing an environment in which pupils are afforded every effort by faculty and by program to reach two objectives: to feel both worthwhile and cared for at least in some aspects of schooling. Each pupil should feel that he has worked hard to achieve and thus has earned the right to feel well about himself in the situation. Also, he should, by dint of his tenacious effort, know that the teacher cares for him. He should feel very well about himself in these situations, but the emotion should not be the same when he fails to give his best, is dishonest, or hateful. Obviously, no matter the anguished claims of the humanists, he should not feel well about himself when he does not try or when he behaves badly. Much to the utter disgust of humanist psychologists, he should dislike his behavior and his conscience should trouble him. School must surely not be planned so that each student feels well about himself no matter what he does or says.

As indicated in the preceding paragraphs, caring teachers should work diligently to teach students the skills to feel well about their school performance. This is the reason we recommend a clinic and workshop situation for students needing help. As indicated, the problems should be diagnosed, and therapy should lead to cure to the degree the child is able. This, of course, necessitates a listing of the behavioral steps to learning the skill, from simplest to most complex. It must then include the teaching strategies for each step and the instruments to measure performance. The result is professional diagnosis, prescription, and therapy resulting in cure. Obviously, everyone will not start at the same place nor achieve at the same level. Hence, grades should not be absolute; seventy five percent should not be the passing grade for all students. The huge genetic differences between students must be considered as students are allowed success within their ability levels.

The problems surrounding gangs and other potentially violent student groupings, long apparent in the great cities, have spread like some horrible cancer to the hinterlands. What happens on the streets is not trouble in the schools, but the terrible problem must be controlled in these institutions--and, perhaps, helped.

Any success is tied to the school rules on discipline and crime. Nothing related to the gangs is suitable in the schools--not certain colors, dress, or demeanor. The rules must quash such incendiary harbingers of trouble, and they must accomplish it harshly, perhaps with suspension and legal charges. School discipline rules must be printed and in the hands of each student. As in all areas of the schools, the code of behavior must follow the *Creed*; it is to be impartial and harsh. It is quite possible to have a school motto of *A Friendly School for Friendly People* and make it well known to the youth that the school means business in all matters of behavior; punishment must be fair, legal, quick, and severe.

It is clear to many school officials, police officers, and judges that easy punishment and second chances may not be useful for schools or students. Moreover, if the behavior is criminal, the schools should prosecute fully. Every student must comprehend that the school is, indeed, a friendly, loving place when he behaves acceptably but that it moves quickly and firmly when rules are not followed. All offenses are serious even though they may seem not to be. Second chances should seldom be allowed as the faculty, with loving emotions, teach the youth a huge truth: Everyone is responsible for his actions and he must face punishment, reward or even neglect for these actions.

Faculty and administrators must live by the same rules as the students. They are, no matter the rantings of the teacher unions, to be moral exemplars, and they are bound by the same moral rules as the youth. In hiring policies, the first objective should be to employ moral faculty, those who share in a deep commitment to the *American Creed* and those who believe that the first concern in schooling is to produce good people who share in a dedicated commitment to live the *Creed*. Legalities make getting this information difficult, since legal procedures preclude, all too often, asking questions in interviews that concern morality. Once the school has researched the value system of the district by administrating the *American Creed Questionnaire*, it is a sound idea to ask prospective school employees to study the planks of the *Creed* and then explain to them, since the list reflects the values of the district, that the First Cardinal Principle of the district is to teach the *Creed*.

The prospective employee would then be asked if he/she could accommodate him/herself to such an objective. The answer very well may indicate a great deal about the person.

Also, every effort must be made to find something in the schools at which a student can succeed grandly. Perhaps it is a club, athletics, drama, weight-lifting, dancing, subject matter clubs, a particular class in school, a teacher who cares, or something else in the program. Such success is essential for many youth now disaffected with the schools. In cases where such success is reachable for the very youth who would be disruptive, violence would lessen; and the schools would work day and night to provide such success early in the schooling process, before students become discouraged and defeated.

To be remembered in all of this is that adults run the schools. Even when the pendulum swings, as it will continue to do lest the suggestions we shall make in this chapter are implemented, to the worst of the liberal, humanistic child-centered schooling, the adults should still make the rules, enforce them, and the students do what they are told. They must comprehend that the only thing they can control in the schools is themselves. They will be taught the rules, and they will study at the feet of caring, loving teachers who demand right action.

But faculty members can go too far. If they go beyond what the law allows, if they are cruel, if they are unfair, they are wrong. Still, they absolutely must maintain control. Above all, violence will not be tolerated; nor will weapons of any type. The weighty arm of retribution will fall swiftly on such criminal behavior, particularly for possession of weapons. For this crime, the student should be legally charged and dismissed from school.

If required, armed policemen should be located at every door to the school and metal detectors should be utilized. In love, the schools must become tough. It will help some of those who disrupt the schools and who behave criminally. More important, it will help those youth who, more or less, behave and who are in school to learn.

Finally, the study of violence as a human behavior must be introduced in school, as tragedy and loss accompanying the behavior are to be studied in literature and history, and as the social psychology concerning violence is considered in depth. After all of this, Cardinal Principle Two, the decision-making process, will be utilized in the secondary school to formulate a plan for each youth and each group to deal with the terrible problem of violence. At the same time, the faculty, joined by citizens and the school board, should use the same process in decision-making based on the *Creed* to project and implement procedures to limit violence, both in school behavior and in the overall lives of their students.

THE MASS MEDIA

In the goal to build better people, that is to say those who have successfully been taught to use the *Creed* (and for the sons and daughters of Christians, the *Commandments*), there is a consuming need to study the mass media in such a manner as to both comprehend how they appeal and to answer their immorality with the moral principles of the *American Creed*. Such curricular work and study should occupy an important and honored position in the school program from kindergarten through high school. Such endeavors should lead to study of television and newspaper advertising, political and moral bias in all areas of the media, values and the lack thereof presented, and the danger of MTV. The handling of the news should be carefully monitored. The list goes on and on, but always the examination should be made in light of the *American Creed* as the measuring device.

All of the media should be evaluated and understood. Radio and newspapers should be examined in depth. So, too, should CDs, tapes, magazines, and books--always from the standpoint of their failure to follow morality as defined in the *Creed*.

SEPARATISM

Nearly anything recommending political or social separatism between groups of people, save for men and women to maintain their considerable God-given differences, is unacceptable in the schools. The *melting pot* organizing principle has already been recommended as one of schooling's cardinal objectives and is, of itself, an institutional procedure denying separatism as political and social goals. This, of course, dooms the horribly damaging multicultural movement in the schools. Gone would be such courses and programs as black studies, female studies, Hispanic studies, and other polarizing school efforts.

Anything the schools do to subvert, in any way, the consensus that must unite Americans in this confused age that seeks to disunite them is to be resisted absolutely. In all areas of school planning, one question should remain: *Am I, in any manner, teaching separatism, the sure enemy of the American Dream? If so, there must be absolute change, for I am employed to educate the youth to be Americans who can and will share bountifully in the American Dream and Creed.*

EQUAL OPPORTUNITY

Of grave import to curricular planning is the ideal that every student be awarded an equal opportunity to succeed both in school and later the marketplace. It is no surprise to anyone that this requires herculean efforts by the schools. It means, more than anything else, in the skill areas of a course, particularly in the practices requisite to success in the marketplace, that teachers be able to identify precisely what a student can do in this area at any given time--and this is too often lacking in the schools. As explained earlier, this means that the steps of a learning objective, from most elemental to most complex, must be identified. Then testing to locate where each child is performing in this continuum of learning is required, followed by instruction so that each child, can in the skill areas, work at his own level. A student is to begin at the level where he is performing at a given time, and the evaluation should focus on how far he has come--on what has been learned. This will, of course, vary from student to student, most often subject to the genetic wealth of the pupil as well as his environmental background. The calling of schooling is to maximize the learning within each student's capability.

In all of this, the schools must disabuse themselves of the notion that learning is simply a function of effort and time, a belief shared by a huge number of liberal humanist critics of the schools. These people, somehow claiming that schooling should yield equal results rather than equal opportunity, are dead wrong, absurd really, a fact attested to by career teachers and a plethora of research. Indeed, native ability is far, far more important in school success (and everything else) than most liberal humanists believe.

But equal opportunity is both morally and legally demanded of schooling--and this is as it should be. And it means, perhaps first of all, that the profession work diligently in order to diagnose at every level a student's performance on the continuum of skills that are defined and measurable. Few schools, indeed, have such a capability to diagnose and offer therapy leading to cure (learning). It also means that students of special needs, both superior and below average, have such particular help planned for their respective needs, and this necessitates a gigantic amount of preparation time for teachers as well as a different way of delivering the learning. The labs utilized for instruction mentioned earlier may very well result in larger classes and in some situations team instruction. It very well may entail the use of well-trained aides in the labs as well as the utilization of parents who elect to give time to the equalization of opportunity and professional programs for all students.

But the same teaching for all students neglects the very fact that there are important inherent differences in what a pupil can and will learn. For the gifted, good, and average students there must be a sophisticated, demanding academic program constantly attuned to the newest data for which there is certain knowledge. For those who cannot do well in such a situation, the last three years of secondary school should surely focus upon vocational preparation based on advice and leadership from business. Claims by the ACLU that this represents an act against minorities should be resisted. Everyone must be provided an equal opportunity to succeed in school. This also means that the youth must finally have the opportunity to succeed at his ability level, and this surely signifies that the vocational job preparation is crucial for true equal opportunity. It also asserts that liberal humanists demanding equal results are dangerous to a genuine equal opportunity for all students. The humanistic, liberal philosophy concerning the matter is, too often, misdirected, for schools should produce excellent programs. They cannot, however, guarantee equal results.

Unfortunately, what we have called for here, particularly the lab situation, is more difficult to plan and implement than it seems at first hearing, and this primarily is the fault of the institutions that prepare the neophyte faculty. Indeed, in many areas, the university and college faculties, far more interested in preparing MAs and PhDs and too often hating the very thought of educating teachers, simply know far too little about academic preparation to teach in the first twelve grades.

Sadly, it probably is so that the universities and colleges based on the humanistic ideal are the greatest evil in causing the problems alluded to in this chapter. Of all the sources feeding the humanistic falsehood into schooling, those institutions predicated on the humanities and humanistic doctrine are both the most infamous and ineffective--and this many people do not comprehend. But some institutions of higher education are more culpable than others, and some academic departments are far worse than others. Public school administrators must study this with great care and hire conservative students from less liberal departments. Even better, conservative colleges like Hillsdale College, Hillsdale, Michigan, should be combed for prospective teachers. Christian colleges should be the first choice in the search for potential faculty. But public school administrators must study in great depth how students are being prepared for teaching in the various institutions of higher education and their many and varying departments. Then, as indicated, the schools must bring substantial and firm pressure on the state boards of education to demand professional preparation while at the same time insisting that more of the education be located in the public schools themselves.

Moreover, the patient must help heal himself. A broad program of dedicated inservice education must be financed and instigated by the schools and perhaps the state. If the universities have failed--and they largely have--then the public schools must, until the problem improves, reeducate their own teachers.

There can truly be no equal opportunity for students unless teachers are prepared in the skill steps attendant to learning. There must, absolutely must, be professional diagnosis and therapy. Short of these, teachers are guessing--and there is far, far too much of that today.

GENDER

Before more serious damage is done, the separatist movement between men and women, stoked and fed by radical feminists, many of them in universities, must be reversed posthaste.

The feminist position that women should have equal access to the marketplace and equal pay should surely be taught and supported by the schools. But the movement toward teaching androgyny, which is the commitment to prove that men and women are essentially the same (environment and culture fuel the differences), is absolutely wrong and must be contested. By no means, these people teach, should the two sexes be viewed as different, save in their plumbing. This belief is a serious error, indeed; and this very dedication to confounding the historic sex roles is built on quicksand. Men and women are hugely different, and this is good. The differences should be celebrated, and the historic sex roles are to be taught in the public schools. Women must be given equal opportunity for jobs and advancement, but males should be taught that to be masculine and a man is good. Likewise, women are to be taught that to be feminine is a desired trait and that being a female is good. This business of making the sexes one surely fuels the war between them and the resulting dissolution of the family. All the current attempts authored by the radical feminists and the liberal, liberal university faculty to change the very nature of males and females must be removed from public schooling. The outraged cries of the humanistic liberals, homosexuals, and radical feminists are loud; but these shrill outcries very likely do not represent the majority and, rightfully, must be resisted with dedication and vigor. The high-level value statement in the *American Creed Questionnaire* that concerns the family will afford a basis to reassert the differing and wonderful natures of the sexes and the critical importance of maintaining the differences.

SEX EDUCATION

The values comprising the *Creed* also apply to sex education, which is

What the Schools Must Do

another way of asserting that the teaching of consensus morality is of higher moment than the teaching of biology or openness. No student should have to take sex education in the schools if the parents are in disagreement with such study. Christians join other principled people who are very likely to believe firmly that such education belongs in the home and church. No parent should allow his son or daughter to take a sex education course authored by SIECUS or Planned Parenthood.

Sex education programs can do huge harm. To provide condoms is to condone sex between the youth, no matter humanistic claims to the contrary. To deny students the teaching that they can make moral choices and thus abstain from sex until marriage is teaching humanistic hedonism as acceptable. To make students feel well about sex outside of marriage is to call God a liar. The *American Creed* cries out against the humanistic, hedonistic philosophy of sex before marriage.

If such a program is instituted in the schools, it should be the product, first, of the values inherent in the *Creed*, and this eliminates the entirety of many current programs; secondly, it should involve the community as well as the faculty in accomplishing the planning. Nothing whatsoever that denigrates the historic family should ever be taught. Mom and Dad, children, and relatives are the family. Two homosexual parents are not. A commune is not. The hallowed and celebrated family remains the nation's most important institution; and in order to satisfy those living in one-parent homes should not be presented as just one of many choices. In this regard, homosexuals should never be brought into the classroom and presented as just another family choice.

More than anything else, students of all ages should be taught that, first, sexual relations are a moral problem. The biology and other aspects of the subject are far less important than the question of what is right and wrong. And it begins with the truth that people are not to be used just for another's pleasure. In this corrupt age, the baby-boomer generation has preached the psychology of self-gratification, using others for one's own gain. In any sexual situation between a man and woman, the partner's feelings must come first. Anything less is animalistic behavior and should surely result in any individual feeling shame and disdain for himself. The horrible tragedy attendant to the family breakup in the nation has surely taught that both sex before marriage and casual sex are, in fact, wrong. The organizing principles of the sex education program should be: just say no until marriage and mean it, and marriage is for a lifetime.

ALCOHOL AND DRUGS

In both drug and alcohol school programs, there are two primary principles: getting the sure knowledge about these controlled substances to the youth and frightening them. At the same time, every effort must be made to teach them abstinence, the only worthy goal. The current humanistic mentality concerning alcohol is most disturbing and dangerous: Since the students are going to drink, or are doing so already, they insist that it is incumbent upon the schools to help them do it with wisdom. Nonsense! The job of the schools (and all institutions) is to educate them not to drink at all. What, indeed, if the same mentality surrounded drugs--that the youth should be taught to use them wisely? The lesson is unimpeachable: No use of controlled substances is acceptable. It may be hip for counselors and other faculty to teach that moderate use is acceptable, but such action is wrong---lethally so.

Research does not really support the efficacy of fear or knowledge, yet they are the only weapons the school has. Thus, the program should very well focus on the terrifying aspects of drug and alcohol use, and it should provide all the knowledge that is and becomes available on the subject.

For those who are drinking or using drugs, well-trained counselors should be available; for alcoholics Alcohol Anonymous is available--as are treatment centers.

But responsibility is also critical, and certainly it is a wing of the *Creed*. Students must be held responsible for their actions concerning drug illegalities and errors in judgment. If they are caught selling drugs on school property, the force of law should immediately be brought against them, both in the schools and in the courts. If they are caught using drugs on school property, they should receive a substantial suspension. The second time, after being afforded all due process of the law, they should be dismissed. Students must surely comprehend that schools cannot and will not put up with drug or alcohol misadventures. The school must indeed mean business and the students must understand that in school (and life) there is punishment and pain for illegal behavior.

Any thinking person is likely to believe that this goes without saying, that nothing new is being stated here; however, an example is worthy of further consideration, although it refers to a college campus instead of a public secondary school. A retired campus policeman from a university campus explained that a few years ago he and his fellow officers were instructed to look the other way for alcohol and drug usage so that bad publicity would not occur. A serious error at the university level, it would be a grave mistake in the public schools. Instead, such criminal behavior by students should be headline news, as should the strict punishment that follows. Part of the solution results from fear, and this is good. Both the parents who own the schools and the students who attend must know that there is punishment, hard punishment, for drug infractions on school property or at school functions.

Perhaps the worst of all the controlled substances, tobacco, has not been discussed. Like liquor, cigarettes are legal to people who are of age; public school students are not. Again, there is only information and fear to be used in dealing with the problem. Such programs might very well turn more often to fear than they do. Let the youth see the terrible results of tobacco. Go into the hospitals where patients are willing and speak with them as they gasp for each breath. Let them visit with doctors and look at x-rays. Let them observe lung surgery for dying smokers. Have them study the empirical research concerning smoking and early death. Frighten them, even for what may seem to be small infractions, like getting caught smoking on school property. The first offense, the rules might well state, should result in a three or four day dismissal from the school; and it should, even the first time, be entered on the permanent record of the student. Students must know that there is a stiff punishment for such infractions.

HEROES AND MYTH

Earlier, we wrote at length about the importance of proper heroes and myth in the school program. The faculty should work with creativity and diligence to select such heroes and heroines whose achievements represent the high-level values comprising the *American Creed* and the historic and literary moments that highlight the heroes and their actions. The list, though updated, would look much like earlier ones, and its objective would be to foster behavior featuring loyalty, integrity, and patriotism.

Some or all of the following names could appear, and, when possible, pictures would adorn the halls of the school: Abraham Lincoln, Thomas Jefferson, Benjamin Franklin, Nathan Hale, Paul Revere, Ronald Reagan, Martin King, Dwight D. Eisenhower, Douglas MacArthur, Helen Keller, Billy Graham, Betsy Ross, Henry Ford, Joan of Arc, Corrie Ten Boom, Thomas Edison, Knute Rockne, Joni Erickson Tada, William Jennings Bryan, George Washington Carver, Joe Lewis, Cassius Clay, Winston Churchill, Red Skelton, Ernie Banks, Robert E. Lee, Andre Dawson, Jim Abbot, Dr. James Dobson, and hundreds of others.

The *Creed* will be reinforced by these lives. The students will hopefully thrill to integrity and character, and they will be building a foundation representing the *Creed*. Then, later in high school, they would study the very battles that some of these people waged with their dark sides. Discovered would be the bitter price paid when the *Creed* is forsaken, if only for a moment. Humans, including all the students, will have to do battle with evil in their lives. To comprehend that even the heroes who have achieved mythical status fought this battle, sometimes losing, may very well make the church's message clearer. All of this is part of the quest to educate students to become fine, moral adults who share in the *Creed* and the American social order.

CENSORSHIP

Even though there are many who believe that any efforts to choose certain books for the children to read rather than others is censorship, the students dare not have carte blanche in what is read and taught at school. Nonetheless, it is true that the courts have all too often refused to approbate any sort of censorship in schooling; and the National Council of Teachers of English has unfortunately affirmed "the student's right to read."

Crucial to making selections in ordering books is the *American Creed Questionnaire* included in this chapter. Concerning, for instance, pornography, the High Court rules that "community standards" are a pivotal item. With the school's results from the *American Creed questionnaire*, the consensus values, the "community standards," will largely be known, resulting in a satisfactory basis on which to make book selections within the law.

The *Creed* can thus be the major factor in ordering materials for the library and, indeed, in which books will be used in the classroom. In this regard, the committee involved in ordering the books and in deciding which will be used in the classroom should adequately represent the community or school district.

These local taxpayers, representing community interests, are invaluable, both legally and professionally, for their decisions gain a powerful legal prominence. Always, the key questions in the committee decision would be these: Does the book present favorably a plank or planks of the *Creed*? And, in later years of high school, does it well demonstrate the evil and heartbreak attendant to failure in living the *Creed*?

The same reasoning should follow in teaching the books, although other factors should be considered, as well. One of these is to teach the American cultural heritage to the students. But this very heritage also instructs that there were atrocities and other grievous failures in the nation. About these, there should be no lies. In the last three years of high school, after the *Creed* and the myth are in place, they should be carefully examined. It is time, then, to turn to Cardinal Objective Two, the use of authoritative decision-making policy to examine the shortcomings and make decisions about what the person might have done to live up to the *Creed* or about the tragedy inherent in the failure to live up to its tenets.

Ultimately, then, there must be a choice of books ordered and used in the classroom. If people choose to designate this as censorship, then so be it, but the choices still must be made concerning reading materials. The reason for defending the choices, both morally and judicially, is the *Creed*. Again, this is but one important reason why the *American Creed Questionnaire* is absolutely demanded of the schools.

CHRISTIANITY

Earlier in the book, the legality of what concerning Christianity can be included in the school curricula was explained. The schools, however, desiring no trouble, were quick to de-Christianize. Part of this was done because of overreaction to the new court decisions, part because humanistic institutions hardly want to teach about a supernatural deity. By so doing, however, many schools simply ripped Christianity from the schools. From an academic point of view, they made the most serious of errors: lying to their constituency about the quite remarkable effects of the Christian faith on the history and letters of the American political experiment. The schools must tell the truth as they socialize and acculturate the students for the American social order. Certainly the teaching of English, history, and geography should consider how the religion of Jesus Christ has so profoundly affected America.

As in all areas pertaining to schooling, school officials and faculty should surely study the law. For instance, prayers may be given on school property by students who have not planned to do so with faculty or administrators. Christian clubs can meet after hours if other such organizations are allowed to meet. The *Bible* can and should be taught as literature. Christian speakers and musicians are, likewise, allowed to use school facilities if other groups are permitted to do so. The schools would do well to allow these Christian influences in the schools. It builds good will among believers, and in classrooms it allows the history of the nation honestly to be taught.

EVOLUTION

The Christian view of creation cannot be taught as the truth, nor can it be required learning or subject matter. Given the liberal nature of the U.S. Supreme Court, such a ruling should unfortunately be expected. But of this be sure, no matter the arrogant and/or anguished cries of many scientists, both evolution and creationism are theories, no matter the claims of the humanists who teach the theory that evolution accurately explains life origins on the planet. Hence, the schools can hardly, in good faith, choose to teach the evolutionary theory as the truth--but they all too often do. This, of course, must be brought to the attention of the board of education and to the community, as well, perhaps in letters to the editor or in town hall meetings.

If the evolutionary theory of life's origins is to be taught at all, it must be presented as one theory of creation. An honest science teacher would tell this to his pupils, and he would suggest that their pastors might well have an entirely different view. Never must students be forced to lie to pass a test on the subject by affirming that evolutionary theory, though unproven, is true.

On this problem of the origins of life rests a considerable amount of the anger believers harbor for the schools. These institutions must handle this situation carefully, with kid gloves, in fact. It is in the school's interest not to anger Christian parents over an unproven theory. Over such confrontations, the efforts are redirected to vouchers financing the schools and to the tax breaks that parents of youths attending Christian and other private schools should receive. It hones the sabers of discontent.

NEW AGE PHILOSOPHY AND RELIGION

Schools using New Age procedures are courting trouble, and they should be legally challenged on *First Amendment* rights--but only after an open and kind discussion between the disaffected citizens and school officials. It is difficult to conceive of deep commitment by most faculty to the New Age movement. The best guess is that few faculty would not think it important enough to fight for. Most do not even perceive that they are, in fact, teaching the New Age religion.

But Christians must perceive that everything they believe to be a part of the ill-conceived religion is not--at least not always. For instance, meditation is an excellent procedure for many Christians; there surely is such a procedure as Christian meditation. It is when spirit guides are sought that believers should be concerned. There must not be paranoia, but the New Age procedures must be carefully monitored in the schools. Any overt effort to teach New Age procedures as the truth must be battled, as indicated earlier, and viewed as teaching religion in the schools. The courts would then have to decide.

EDUCATION FOR ACADEMIC EXCELLENCE

For those able to master the material--but only for them--there should surely be an academic mix of demanding courses in junior and senior high school that approximates the following: four years of English, three years of social studies, three years of science, three years of math, one year of geography, one year of civics, two years of a foreign language, one year of computer usage, one year of business, and a thorough knowledge of the *Creed* and the decision-making process that will start in kindergarten and never end.

Even these able students do not all operate at the same academic levels, and, as a result, absolute scores may be all but useless. It is, of course, ridiculous to make, say, seventy percent the passing grade for all students. Such imperception cheats both the genetically gifted and the genetically limited. It may be conditionally acceptable for the two-thirds of the students within a standard deviation of the mean. But what of the other third of the students? The most gifted of the students are hardly challenged by such standards. As earlier explained, the steps to any learning must be understood, and there must be measuring devices for knowing exactly where each child is in the continuum of learning objectives. Then students can be asked to grow hugely in the learning and, sometimes perhaps, ninety-five percent might not be acceptable. Very, very much must be demanded of these able students; however, their innate genes must never be the reason for a high (or low) grade. It is what they learn, based on professional diagnosis, that will determine the grades. For this reason, absolute grades are simply unacceptable. Hard, demanding work must be expected of each student--and this involves long hours of homework.

EDUCATION FOR THE WORK WORLD

In the current rush for academic excellence, at least twenty percent of the pupils are being short-changed, and this presents a serious problem for the social order. Those who learn from three-fourths to eighty-five percent as quickly as their peers are, in many ways, the forgotten students. Part of them are environmentally cheated; some of them are genetically limited. Most are both. School, of course, operates to help the youth overcome environmental factors and to maximize what a human's genetic blueprint will allow.

The problem is that no one knows what part of a student's learning is environmental and what part is genetic. For this reason, every effort must be made to overcome the environmental factors. To assume that any child will remain learning seventy-five to eighty five percent as fast as his fellows is to type the youth all too often to second-class status. But there eventually comes a time when it is apparent, in perhaps fifteen to twenty percent of the cases, that some students are going to remain in that group. These youths need special help, and they must get it.

They are not going to attend college; most of them will never read at more than the sixth-grade level. They surely should be prepared to make a living, and this means rapidly expanding vocational preparation. But there are factors militating against what seems to be this logical curricular ideal.

The first of these is political. Almost surely, a disproportionate number of these students will be from one minority group or another. To prepare these youth for the world of work rather than college will likely be perceived as segregation. The schools must not give in to these charges, even if they must adjudicate them in the courts. The children are to be helped, and part of the schools' job is to educate parents concerning the importance of such understanding.

The second is that powerful elite educational forces are demanding more preparation for excellence in college. As a result, the vocational courses are severely limited. The huge numbers of students who must be prepared for the world of work are being gravely shortchanged.

This must surely change. Business interests must become the advisors for such education. Every child not attending college must have preparation that will allow him to live with dignity as a contributing member of the social order. Hence, schools, with the help of business experts, must unleash their creative genius to define the teaching these people need and to deliver such help.

This approach will help the student, and it will also aid the schools. Problems of violence and aggression will lessen. It is commonly understood that, if he cannot do well in school, a youth may very well succeed in trouble-causing. If he is reading at the sixth-grade level, what happens when he must endeavor to study high-level courses and he cannot even read the assignments? How long can he withstand utter failure? How long can the dream be deferred before it explodes?

THE FEDERAL GOVERNMENT

The public schools must do everything possible to resist the siren call of governmental influences. The federal government has no constitutional right in the schools. But too many people are buying into the idea that a federally-mandated curriculum and testing should originate from the bureaucrats in Washington, D.C. Liberal presidents and Congress may, one day, lead to governmental control of public schooling resulting from a constitutional change, a development that should be avoided at all costs. The sure path to the ruin of public education is to put it in the hands of Washington bureaucrats.

Schooling is, as much as the state will allow, to be in the hands of the local school districts. The people and faculty in these areas know the particular students they serve and can identify their needs. Also, schooling must stay as far away from politics as it can. The Congress and the Department of Education is composed heavily of liberal humanists who must be diligently shunned. And what about the political influence the National Education Association would bring to the situation if the federal government had the power? The very possibility makes the blood run cold.

In every way possible, the schools must *disassociate* themselves from anything whatsoever financed by the federal government. If the government finances something, it will surely control. One must understand the mortal danger to the *American Creed* when the federal politicians control schooling. The nation will be in deep jeopardy as collectivism, proved defunct in Marxism's fall, winds its tentacles around the public schools.

This is challenging, indeed, when cost is considered. Numerous educational theorists have rightly written about the use of local property tax to finance the majority of the school costs. It has become so expensive that these experts feel a limit has been reached concerning what the public can pay. Moreover, state courts are questioning if it is acceptable for some school districts to have so much more money than others based on the valuation of real estate. The position taken by some current theorists is that both the state and federal government should pay more, thus easing local property tax as the primary source. After all, the state has the legal control of the school; the federal government, quite rightly, has none. The state, many believe, should probably be a source of increased funding.

But--and of this be utterly certain--the majority financing should come from the local school district. The people must bite the bullet as they secure from taxes slightly over half of the required monies to run the schools. Like death itself, the federal government's dole must be refused. Tremendous power must rest in the local schools, and the politicians inside the Washington, D.C., beltline must have no influence over the local schools. Surely, the march of events from the 1960s forward has proved that point once and for all, yet national testing for students appears acceptable to Americans.

SCHOOLS AND THE HOME

The schools, of course, belong to the taxpayers in the community. It follows that these people should be treated with respect and affection. Always, the schools should be open to them, and they should be represented on every committee in the school. Their advice should be sought, appreciated, and respected. In every manner, they should be involved in all decisions made.

But the school should endeavor to do more. In matters of teaching academic skills, the schools should arrange workshops to help parents learn how to help their progeny. Indeed, in many communities, particularly the inner cities and isolated rural areas, parents need to know how to help the youth with homework. In matters of morality (an area in which teachers have no more professional preparation than the parents), teachers have nothing to say to parents; however, in teaching skills, the teachers should have the professional knowledge to offer help to parents wanting to aid their children.

SOCIAL PROBLEMS

The school has not and will not solve the great social problems assigned it by a sick humanist social order. It simply cannot, as it now operates, solve these problems. Any solution must begin with Christians from the school, the home, and the church working as they should. Even then, the humanist elites enjoy such power as to make this very difficult.

The situation, however, can be far improved by the recommendations made earlier in the book: the sure teaching of the *Creed*, the mastery of the decision-making process, schools operated as melting pots, and the youth being taught the skills needed in their social order. If successful planning occurs, if the home cooperates, and if the church does its job, there is considerable hope that social problems might improve slowly over time.

In almost every case the answers in this chapter were *politically incorrect*, which should tell the reader they are right. If our suggestions are followed absolutely, the schools will improve dramatically, though they will not completely satisfy believers for whom, rightfully, the only worthy cardinal principle is salvation through Jesus Christ. But in all honesty, the recommended changes will make the schools acceptable to most, particularly since legalities limit what the schools can accomplish. The humanistic factors, so disturbing to Christians and to other thinking people, will have been tempered. The public schools will be as good as they can be given the pressures surrounding them.

Thus, schools can, should they heed the advice offered in this book, fulfill their societal obligations, no matter the claims of naysayers. Many believers are unbending in their negative attacks at public schools, and surely such emotions have often been earned by shoddy performance. There is no question that good Christian schools would be better for most youth. The clamor for tax breaks or vouchers is an understandable demand by Christian parents, thus making Christian schooling within the reach of most of their progeny. Unfortunately, this would result in problems that could be terribly damaging to the nation and the very youth they want to serve.

Remember, we have argued that any solution must result from efforts of home, church, and school. Each must do its job, and crucial to the first two of these institutions is the religions education offered by families. The public school, no matter its excellence, cannot be the primary source of teaching the Christian faith. What is demanded is that these institutions do nothing whatsoever to harm endeavors of home and church to bring youth to Jesus Christ. If, indeed, the schools accomplish what we have recommended in this work, they are acceptable, even if minimally so, to school the youth. There is no question that over the years huge victories have been won. There can be again.

If tax breaks or vouchers financing all or a huge part of a child's schooling in private schools were enacted, the resulting competition could portend the doom of public education, a development that would resonate positively with many believers until they consider the dilemma more comprehensively.

Based on the *First Amendment*, private schools are not bound by the same legal demands as are public schools. Very often, private schools would be highly selective of the students allowed to enroll. In many schools the poor, ethnic, low average, and mentally handicapped students would not be satisfactorily represented, nor would average students be accepted. Certainly, since the choice of selection belongs to private schools, mentally and environmentally challenged youth would often be disproportionally enrolled. The public schools would be filled with these students, and problem would multiply in geometric proportion. The death of the public schools, operating as we outline, would even to the most devout of those of us who are evangelical believers be a serious problem.

This is, in no manner, a lack of faith against Christian schools, nor is it a claim that tax breaks or vouchers should not be a worthy political goal of believers. But it is to say that the schools, operating as we demand, must not be ruined. There must still be a choice. Politically, believers would do well to work diligently for the financial aid to send their children, to Christian schools with some financial help from the state, but the sum must not decimate the public schools operating as we recommend.

Probably a tax break or voucher accounting for twenty five to forty percent of a child's tuition at a private school would be fair and useful. Many more youths would be able to afford a Christian education, and such schools, given the increasing number of students, would be able with the financial help of friends and businesses to offer many scholarships to the financially needy. Still, the public schools would survive.

Such an approach should be politically battled for by believers. It is worthy, for it would allow for the dramatic growth of Christian schooling, the continuation of proper public schooling, and the competitive tension between public and private schooling that may very well dramatically improve

America's schooling. However, it will all come to nothing, really, if the home and church fail. Nor can it succeed unless the very people reading this book follow the recommendations in the next chapter.

Chapter Eight

WHAT THE HOME MUST DO

We have indicated that schools are very important to the mortal battle with sensate America, but the homes are even more crucial. Any solution to the nation's educational, social, political, and religious crises begins in the home, where parents must comprehend that rearing sons and daughters wisely and lovingly is the triumph of their lives. It supercedes their own plans and dreams, their own pleasure and weaknesses. It is the single most important goal of their lives and should be understood as precisely that.

As repeatedly written in this book, the elite power educators joined other negative forces in accomplishing frightful damage to the values and behaviors that so distinguished America, the result being a developing sensate social order in which mere feelings are paramount and virtue dramatically recedes. Deviancy is thus defined downward and downward. The result is narcissism (an overwhelming and neurotic love of a person for himself) and hedonism (absolute pursuing of pleasure as life's major goal); and these are twin destroyers of sons and daughters, decency, and civilization itself. The family should snap to attention in the grave struggle to salvage the nation and those they love.

Parents must love their daughters and sons absolutely. In every situation, the youth are to come first. *The American Creed* is to be taught as the truth, a critical statement of the values and behavior defining what is right. As this is accomplished, Mom and Dad are to turn their attention and effort in the direction of *training* their offspring from the very beginning to overcome narcissism and hedonism as stage development allows. Infants are by nature narcissistic and hedonistic and this is as it should be. Unchecked as they get older, however, these character defects may very well destroy them.

But will the *Creed,* properly understood and taught, win the victory? It can come very close to doing so. Indeed, it can make a far better and more worthy social order. It is a magnificent effort to heal the land for a period of time, perhaps for an extended term–and it is thus gravely critical to the nation. The home, joined by all American institutions, is to teach and live the planks of *the American Creed.*

Unfortunately, the lesson of history asserts that eventually the quite wonderful humanistic consensus *Creed* will yield to a sensate order featuring narcissism and hedonism. This is not to indicate that the humanists who embraced the *Creed* are unworthy; exactly the opposite may be so. They may be noble people with admirable values and behaviors, but there is in human nature, the soul, a defect that should not be underestimated. Eventually, even in the most exemplary social orders, the humane and moral values that characterized the best of behavior and valuations yield to a sensate order based on feelings rather than virtue, the fruits of which are narcissism and hedonism. The noted scholar Pitirim A. Sorokin wrote in his classic book *The Crisis of Our Age* that every social order will eventually become sensate, thus authoring its doom. We believe that the march of events in history supports his claims, and we further believe that America is only a breath away from becoming sensate--even with the great *American Creed.*

This indicates that something additional is required. *The Creed* comes close, but more is needed. The additional step, the glorious answer, is Christianity. Humanists tethered to the here and now, to the few years of their lives, often do not (and cannot) look beyond their lives, and thus far too often share a myopia tied to the current time.

Believing Christians should have a far different mind set. For them there are higher stakes than for humanists, no matter the high level values shared by both groups. Humanists face death as the end, what novelist Nelson Algren identified as "the last dark wall of all." Their steps lead into the graveyard but not out. Christians, having trusted Christ alone for their eternal salvation from sin, understand that they will live forever. Death is but a beginning, a triumphant stairway to Glory. They understand what sin is and perceive that there is a terrible price for such behavior and thinking. This sense of God's Law coupled with forgiveness in Jesus affords these people insight and knowledge that will-- if they live up to the faith they proclaim-- turn the world upside-down. Though Christians join all people in sometimes behaving badly, they offer the last and best chance to build and sustain a great society. One's actions are profoundly affected if his behavior and thinking prepare him for a glorious forever. He understands that his steps lead out of the cemetery. As a result of this belief the sensate ideal can wither and die, and that is precisely why Christianity is to be added. Remember, though, that it is the home and church that must teach it. School breaks the law in so doing.

In this chapter we are adding the *Ten Commandments (the Mosaic Law)* and the *Beatitudes (the Sermon on the Mount)* to the *American Creed* as values to be taught to sons and daughters. Read carefully the valuations comprising *Red Flag Behaviors* that identify misbehaviors and *Combined*

Broken Values of the Commandments Beatitudes, and American Creed, both of which follow. After thinking about them, would you not be wise to take the step–if you have not–beyond the *Creed* to Christianity? Are these not the values and behaviors you would want your cherished daughters and sons to accept? Would you not be wise to parent in such a way as to give them an abiding hope in everlasting life? What greater gift could they ever receive?

The record-keeping forms that follow indicate the values we believe should be taught to each youth. A careful record should be kept of each youth's behavior. Being narcissistic and hedonistic by nature, children will often behave badly–and this is to be expected, but there should always be a price to pay for misbehavior. Punishment would most often begin with a discussion between parent and child, but it would escalate substantially when the behavior becomes habitual. From the very first, sons and daughters are to understand that there is punishment for bad behavior. Of such is responsibility learned, and without it there is no hope whatsoever to defeat narcissism and hedonism.

RED FLAG MISBEHAVIORS

OFFENSE	DATE	WHAT HAPPENED
Has lack of sense of guilt		
Shows lack of sense of conscience		
Sneaks		
Displays self-centeredness		
Is unkind		
Refuses to stay on task		
Refuses to work hard		
Complains of being a victim		
Refuses to take advice		
Displays continuing anger		
Must win no matter what		
Refuses to complete tasks		

Quits easily		
Demands success without effort		
Throws things in anger		
Steals		
Refuses to accept fault		
Displays antisocial behavior		
Uses alcohol		
Uses drugs		
Uses tobacco		
Behaves in uncivilized manner		
Denies wrongdoing		
Shows arrogance		
Has temper tantrums		
Misbehaves at school		
Is violent		
Plays one parent against the other		

COMBINED BROKEN VALUES OF *THE COMMANDMENTS, BEATITUDES, AND AMERICAN CREED*

OFFENSE	DATE	WHAT HAPPENED
Dishonorable behavior		
Dishonesty		
Disloyalty		
Failure to honor parents		

Lack of compassion		
Unkindness		
Lack of forgiveness		
Lack of courage		
Wanting things too badly		
Lack of responsibility		
Demand for instant gratification		
Violence		
Refusal to work hard		
Refusal to accept authority		
Foul language		
Lack of keeping the Sabbath (observing the Lord's Day)		
Accepting idea of killing others		
Stealing		
Desire to get what is not his/hers		
Lack of gentleness		
Lack of righteous behavior		
Lack of being pure at heart		
Failure to control anger		
Failure to be a peacemaker		
Lack of anger control		
Failure to fulfill promises		
Failure to love others		
Failure to help those in need		

Guilty of false judgements		
Displaying sexual lust		
Love of money and things too important		

All of these values and behaviors are not applicable to infants, but most of them are. Certainly by junior high they should all be in place. At this time, and surely in high school, the peer group looms as perhaps the youth's greatest influence, and proper values must have imbued in the daughters and sons before that time.

Use these two forms weekly, perhaps daily, to note the pattern of their misbehavior. Deal with most of the improprieties, but move vigorously when the actions become habitual. Then the punishment is to be substantial; the youth *must* comprehend that they are responsible for unacceptable behavior–that there is a price to pay. They surely are to understand that parents will never bail them out of problems attendant to misbehavior.

Sons and daughters should understand that they are deeply revered and loved. Then they should be blessed with parents who excel in modeling and teaching the values. Finally, they should have parents who set standards of punishment that enforce the values.

The last of these requires huge effort by parents, who must decide the punishments for each of the values of *the Creed, Beatitudes and Mosaic Law*. What about first offenses? Often, if the law is not being broken by the youth, a firm discussion will suffice; but then increasing penalties are in order, most often focused on taking away something the youth values. In young children no matter the claims of sensate mental workers, spanking is an encouraged option. During the teen years, the problems can become grim, and the youth's very future may lie in the balance. Make sure the punishments are substantial. When the law is broken, go to the police or sheriff and report the crime. The youth must be stopped. If they become unmanageable, contact the Tough Love organization and get involved. The address is Tough Love International; P.O. Box 1069; Doylestown, PA 18901; and the phone number is 1 800-333-1069.

The list of rules and punishments will be in the hands of each son and daughter, and it will be posted in the house, as well. Seldom will there be parental shouting. Usually it is far better to say something like this, "Jack, you have chosen to behave badly; it was an awful choice. You know that you must face responsibility for your choice. The posted list indicates that you

What the Home Must Do

will be grounded for three days beginning tomorrow."

The best way to teach the values comprising the *Red Flag Behaviors* and the *Combined Values of the Commandments, Beatitudes, and the American Creed* is by parental modeling followed by dedicated teaching. The two value forms can be joined and five categories emerge: *honorable behavior; responsibility; compassion and love; wisdom; and courage.*

Modeling Honorable Behavior
Following are the behaviors leading to honorable behavior:

1) Displaying integrity
2) Showing pureness of heart
3) Maintaining honesty
4) Displaying truthfulness
5) Not coveting what is not yours
6) Fulfilling vows made to man and God
7) Showing righteous behavior
8) Controlling sexual lust
9) Not acting out on sexual situations
10) Maintaining a clean mouth
11) Honoring parents
12) Behaving in such a manner that honors family as the nation's most significant institution.

It is well for parents and grandparents, particularly Mom and Dad, to meet on a regular basis, study the values, and decide precisely how they will model certain ones, Mom modeling some, Dad others, and grandparents still others.

Your behavior will demonstrate the level of honor to daughters and sons. This, of course, means that you must work on your own values and behaviors going far beyond dialogues to action. You must first accept the values and then have the character to demonstrate them and grow in them. Will your progeny witness your integrity? Your honesty, pureness of heart, and truthfulness? Your righteous behavior? Your refusal to covet what is not yours and the fulfilling of promises to God and man? Your controlling of sexual lust and not destroying the family by sexual betrayal?

Will they evidence you always telling the truth? Will they find you ever honest and trustworthy? Will you follow through on promises made to them? Will they observe you lying on income tax returns? Will they discover you lying for monetary gain or a job advancement? Will they see you wanting a new home or a certain auto so badly that you will lie, cheat, or steal to get them?

All of these queries make abundantly clear that you must become fathers and mothers who are worthy and who model acceptable values as defined in *The American Creed, the Beatitudes, and the Mosaic Law.*

Modeling Responsibility

Following are the values attendant to responsible behavior:

1) Maintaining accountable behavior
2) Understanding that everyone is responsible for his/her behavior
3) Delaying immediate gratification
4) Working hard
5) Accepting authority

In all ways, parents will demonstrate to their children that they are responsible. They will pay bills on time and go to meetings at the proper time. Mom will be responsible for keeping the house clean and fixing tasty nutritious meals, and father will go to work every day, save illness, responsibly taking care of those he loves, his family. Mother will show responsibility by not insisting that she *compete* with father in earning a living. Neither parent will lament that he or she is innocent of something for which there is responsibility. Never will they be heard attacking their employers or, for that matter, anyone in authority over them. Their children will see them work hard, both on the job and at home, as they demonstrate that hard, demanding labor is central to success in life. Nor should parents succumb to wanting things too badly; rank materialism is a poor example to sons and daughters.

Modeling Compassion and Love

Following are the consensus values pertaining to these important human emotions and values:

1) Sharing the pain of others with dedication to show mercy or aid
2) Demonstrating kindness
3) Demonstrating forgiveness
4) Practicing non-violence
5) Showing love for fellow man
6) Assisting those who cannot help themselves
7) Accepting the moral worth and dignity of others
8) Having a deep respect for life from conception to death

What the Home Must Do

9) Refraining from harsh, unfair judgments of others
10) Demonstrating that mental or physical cruelty is unacceptable
11) Assisting people to grow to their fullest potential
12) Believing that every person has the right to worship as he/she desires
13) Demonstrating the belief that every person is free within the law and acceptable behavior to pursue life, liberty, and happiness

Compassion and love are the fruits of a healthy, worthy social order and are crucial to the improvement of the nation. Modeling to loved ones the steps attendant to these wonderful ideals is very important. Never should children see their parents cruel or violent, nor should they see them threaten each other. In like manner, parents should never make threats to others within hearing range of their children. Every parental behavior should reflect a dedicated effort to make and maintain peace. At the same time, Mom and Dad should labor day and night always to be kind, and part of this effort should focus on modeling forgiveness in the family and to all others. Moreover, children should never see parents making unfair judgments about others–and this typically puts an end to gossiping.

There are other behaviors as important. Perhaps there are relatives who are in need or it could be friends, perhaps a down and out veteran of the Viet Nam conflict. It is essential that loved ones see parents helping those unable to help themselves. Sometimes protracted effort would be made to help people grow to the highest of their capabilities. At Christmas and Thanksgiving Mom and Dad may choose to work with groups like the Salvation Army to help the poor. Never will parents belittle a person because of the way he or she worships, and Mom and Dad are to be people of compassion and love.

Modeling Wisdom

The modeling of wisdom to a sensate social order is a balm to an era in which mere feeling unfortunately drives behavior. Mom and Dad should turn immediately from feelings as the final judgment of behavior to wisdom based on study and experience. Three high level values to accomplish this goal follow:

1) Achieving wisdom based equally on study of the facts and on personal experience concerning the topic at hand
2) Honoring such wisdom based on study and experience
3) Demonstrating the use of this wisdom in participating in the democratic and personal effort to solve problems

Daughters and sons should not see parents basing judgments primarily on emotions and feelings; instead they should observe careful decisions predicated on study of the situation and experience.

Parents will also read materials by and about the great wise men and women of history, and they will share the information with their children, doing everything possible to model both the quest for wisdom and the teaching of appreciation for it. The youth will note that the parents put the wisdom to use in problem-solving. Indeed, wisdom is a powerful enemy to sensate thinking and decisions based on mere feelings.

Modeling Courage

Great people are courageous, and the modeling of this value and behavior is to be taken quite seriously by parents. Following are four values concerning courage:

1) Facing danger or adversity with valor
2) Facing danger or adversity with confidence
3) Facing danger or adversity with resolution
4) Facing danger or adversity with faith

There are times in every family when Mom and Dad could cringe with fear. Maybe he is about to lose his job. Perhaps he has just discovered that he has a failing heart. Maybe she has found that she has cancer. Maybe Grandpa has serious physical troubles. Trouble courts us, and tragedy lurks. In such awful times we are obliged to show our loved ones courage. We must model bravery, and we should face the situation with a degree of confidence and resolution. If we are Christian, we know that "not one sparrow falls but what God knows–and we are worth more than many sparrows." We know that God makes no mistakes and that eventually "all things work together for good to those who love God, to those who are called according to His purpose." Moreover, we have utter confidence that sudden death is sudden joy–that we shall live forever in sublime happiness.

What a wonderful model we can present to our beloved–who will surely face similar tragedies and troubles. We will model valor and we will have confidence. We will demonstrate resolution. Why will we be able to do so? Because a glorious forever beckons us, romances us, thrills us. What a legacy this is to sons and daughters: parents who are courageous–and with good reason.

Modeling and Christian Parents

Because of the profound influence of the *Bible* on the high level values of the nation, we have already identified the *Commandments* of the Great God; but, again, the fact that the refusal to meet any of them is sin, not simply breaking a more or folkway, makes modeling to the youth far more critical and grave than merely illustrating the *American Creed*.

How then can parents best portray the Christian model? They can begin by taking the *Scriptures* seriously and, if they are not Christian, go immediately to see a pastor. Turning their backs on the sensate, they can come to Christ, not only for themselves but for the dear little ones. Then let them accompany the youth to every event in the church, and allow them to see the parents making many new friends who share the same faith. They may choose to set up an area of the home where they pray, read the *Bible,* and discuss Christian topics each and every day. Let the youth witness parents on their knees asking for forgiveness because they failed, as all do, to live up to one or more of the *Commandments*.

Let them see their parents accept the God defined in the *Apostle's Creed*. Let them observe the joy in Mom's and Dad's eyes and the smile on their lips when they worship a Holy God Who loved them enough to send His Son to take every sin they will ever commit to the Cross and by His blood to pay the price for it. Let them see the tears of joy because the doors to paradise have been flung aside. Daughters and sons will be blessed beyond measure, though they may not perceive it at the moment, to behold that there is something very special in the lives of Mom and Dad.

At the same time the parents are wise to turn particular attention to living up to God's laws. The kids must sense that about these ten laws there is something very special. The Sabbath (or in today's world, the Lord's Day, Sunday) is to be treated as a special day for worship, rest, and no business. Mom and Dad will honor their parents, in love getting together as much as possible and, with care, often phoning. Never will the youth have the shame and heartbreak to see adulterous behavior by the parents. No matter what, Mom and Dad will stay together. They will not be violent nor wish badly for people; they will work day and night to refrain from stealing and lying. They will not display covetousness, nor will they worship false deities. Finally, they will neither curse nor want things too badly.

But when they do fail, and every person does sometimes, the children will see the tears and hear the prayers. Then they will share with son and daughter that they sinned and will do everything in their power to refrain from committing that sin again.

The American Creed is quite rare and wonderful, but its power to salvage the nation from a sensate age built on narcissism and hedonism is not absolute. As we have earlier written, much good can be accomplished, but the next step is required: turning to God and to Christ. To model all of this to those who are loved is, beyond a doubt, the greatest gift they will ever receive. That very modeling may save America, but, more important, it may lead sons and daughters to the opening of the doors of Paradise.

As written earlier, the youth are more likely to learn from parents by watching precisely how they live, and it is about the grave importance of this that we have written in this chapter. The fact is, however, that sons and daughters must also be taught by their parents.

Parental Teaching

As we have indicated, parental modeling of the high level values is the very best way to teach them, but there must also be teaching of them in the family. Two very productive ways follow.

Telling Stories and Reading. Stories that are either told or read to them delight most children. Every Mom and Dad would do well to tell or read stories to their children daily. In the tales to be told, the parents would plan in depth, leaving nothing to chance, to teach the high level values and to spin delightful stories as they hug their sons and daughters. The happy announcement, "It's story time!" will delight the youth; and bonding, fun, and learning will transpire. It is the ideal time to begin a wel-planned and joyous teaching of right behavior and values. Books are as useful and even more so when the youth are in late elementary school to junior high. Select books teaching the high level values, read them to the child, have the child read them to you, and discuss the values.

After Dinner Time. Another useful approach is to structure a family time after dinner. Hopefully the family members will come together in a relaxed, approachable mood. From the earliest years of a child's life, this should be a wonderful time of sharing and compelling discussions, and every family member is expected to be in attendance. Family discussions and business will transpire as well as each member sharing what happened that day. It is a time for warmth and joking as well as dreams and wishes, but it is also time to consider (and thus to teach) morality and intelligent decision making based on *the Creed, the Mosaic Law, Beatitudes,* and pertinent facts.

Once a week, the moral considerations will be the primary concern. If the discussion is particularly meaningful on a given night, it might well be continue for a second evening, but it should not be overdone each week. Every family member is to be heard and every rational comment is seriously to be considered. However, the discussions will not be allowed to degenerate into mere feelings unless the emotions are based on the high level values. From the very beginning, at each family member is mature enough to handle it, both facts and high level values will be the center of the discussions.

Each person (until he or she knows them absolutely) will have a listing of the consensus values. Often the subject of the discussion will be announced in advance by a family member so that each person can be prepared with facts that bear on the situation. A second grader might ask a couple of teachers or call Grandpa or Grandma, while a sixth grader might go to the encyclopedia. A teenager could go to the library and look up three or four sources. Perhaps they might cite what they learned from one of the few television programs they are allowed to watch or from what they have learned from the Internet. Parents might recommend a specialist for the youth to interview. The effort of course, is to educate the child to refrain from uneducated feelings and turn to facts and the values parents have taught.

Other Parental Concerns

The parents will work toward modeling what a home should be. It will, of course, be loving. God will head the family, followed by father, who loves his wife as Christ loved the church. In a loving way, mother is submissive to her husband and God. She is, at least, equal to her husband as a worthy person and will provide warmth, love, and socialization for the family. The group is a team, very different persons, yet one; and they are not engaged in the terrible competition that is wrecking so many homes. Both liking and loving each other, Mom and Dad are warm and pleasant. They are joyful and eager lovers; they hug each other and the children--and they love their offspring enough to maintain strict and loving discipline. These behaviors and ideals, the children must grow up with, along with the confidence that their parents will stay together, no matter what happens.

Even so, there will be times of trouble between Mom and Dad, and they may become serious. In nearly any family, there are times when the group might be destroyed--and in this age of narcissism and self-aggrandizement, divorce is epidemic. The selfishness of the age must be overcome. Indeed, the nobler one is, the nobler he/she is to his/her mate and family; and this ideal must be ever before the progeny. It is time, once again, for the rebirth of character.

And from the earliest years, each youth is trained to be responsible for personal actions, a most crucial factor in raising children. The parent must never bail a son or daughter out of mistakes. One of the worst errors made by Mom and Dad--and it is most often made out of love--is to insulate their progeny from responsibility for their actions.

Never should the child feel the warmth of self-satisfaction when he behaves badly or fails to do his best. As indicated earlier, the youth should know that he is loved. He should understand, too, that one should feel well about himself when he behaves acceptably and badly when he does not, no matter the claims of humanist psychologists and psychiatrists. For positive behavioral change, the child should surely feel badly about poor behavior. Many humanists do not understand this, and the very misunderstanding has contributed enormously to the narcissism and gross selfishness of the era.

During the years preceding school attendance, there are other behaviors and learnings for which the parents are responsible. Toys must never be picked up by the parents; the child will be responsible. He must also have demanding chores. Sharing with others must be successfully taught. So, too, should cooperation and consideration. The youth must demonstrate in his behavior that he is learning the *Ten Commandments*, the *Creed*, and Christian behavior. In all of this, the parents should be dedicated to teaching that housebreaks the child to fit into the best of the majority American culture and social order. Television must surely not be utilized as a babysitter given the overt humanistic indoctrination and degradation it represents. As important as any demands on the parents is their success in locating their progeny in proper peer groups. Such friends should be found in the church with young people who are being reared in Christian homes.

Though this is impossible in some families, Mom should try to stay home, even if the standard of living is lower. She should be there for her toddlers. She should feel that raising her children is the greatest and most gratifying experience of her life--and her greatest satisfaction. The youth should not be reared by strangers financed by either the state or federal governments.

Both Mom and Dad would do well to speak highly of education and, more precisely, of the importance of schooling. Such an understanding must be added to the *Commandments*, the *Creed*, and a Christian home as prerequisites for an earned, healthy favorable self-image, for success in the marketplace, and for membership in the middle-class.

And there is yet another creed that might constantly be used as a model for the sons and daughters. Little children should be taught of it what they can understand. By late elementary school, they should know it all. It might very well be used in the same manner as the *Mosaic Law, 'Beatitudes,"* and the *Creed*.

The Make Yourself Creed

(1) Make yourself do and think what you have been taught is right.
(2) Make yourself work hard and do your best.
(3) Make yourself understand that there are consequences for your behavior for which you alone are responsible.
(4) Make yourself behave so that your parents, grandparents, and other family members will be proud of you.
(5) Make yourself understand that life is serious and demands your best.
(6) Make yourself understand that anything you do can affect others.

Some readers may very well feel that we are recommending ideals of an earlier age, that our assertions are impractical in the current age of selfishness and self-serving, when marriages melt like ice on a hot summer day. We are urging for a return to the *American Creed* and the behaviors representing it. Also, we are demanding that the nation's only political hope is to turn back the clock, to, in effect, rediscover America's greatest days. Yes, we are recommending the historic, traditional (liberals call it the nuclear) family, the *American Creed*, and Christian truth. Pundits join hip comics in ridiculing television programs like *Leave It to Beaver, The Andy Griffith Show, Father Knows Best*, and other wholesome family television shows. To the degree they ridicule what the family should and must be, they demonstrate their collective ignorance of what America is about and pave the way for the tragic destruction of the family. In answering, Americans must *ask for the old paths, for they will bring peace.*

Hence, we have written about the preeminence of healthy families where Mom and Dad live together in a loving Christian atmosphere. This, of course, must be the goal. Nothing less is acceptable. People must stay together in marriage and learn to forego their own pleasure for the good of the children, and such action will eventually be their greatest satisfaction if they are worthy people touched by God's hands and the values comprising the *Creed*.

But what about the one-parent homes? First, ask the question that those seeking divorce should pose: *Is it possible for my mate and me to forget our own selfishness, our own culpability in the dissolution of the marriage, and, for the good of the children, resume our marriage and behave the way we should?* If possible the family unit should be brought back together, husband and wife remembering the wedding *vows* made before God and man. If there is a marriage that cannot be healed and if a spouse loses his/her mate to death, the job becomes more difficult. America has been built on the ideal of families helping their own. It is time, then, for fathers, mothers, uncles, aunts, grandparents, and other relatives to step into the breach and to assist; we mean really help. Such assistance in America is not, and should almost never be, the responsibility of government; it should be family and church. This ideal leading to action is crucial as the nation's people turn from the federal dole to personal and kinship responsibilities. The lack of such behavior represents a serious problem and must, if America is to retain its very soul, balance in favor of the family and against the socialistic power and enchantment of the federal government.

If the marriage cannot be repaired, if there were never a marriage, if the spouse is deceased, if the family cannot or refuses to follow its historic mandate to help, the children will be raised by only one person. Such a situation should never be represented in the schools or churches as normal and acceptable, for it is surely second-best. At the same time, though, many parents in this situation are indeed heroes and heroines, as they bravely do battle to approximate the historic family in every way possible. Their efforts are often praiseworthy, and they are to be commended. Making a virtue of necessity and working to accomplish more than is really possible, many of these people do an excellent job; but, even then, a considerable amount is lacking. The one-parent family is not an agreeable alternative to its historic counterpart. Homosexual partners are absolutely not acceptable as a family; such a pairing of like-sex persons flies in the face of *God's Word*, the *Creed*, acceptable socialization, and successful acculturation of the youth.

Christian Schools

Should believing parents send their children to Christian schools? In the public schools, disaster lurks--even for those youth who have been effectively socialized as well as acculturated and who have been imbued with the values of the *Commandments, Creed and "Beatitudes."* One must wonder if the peril would lessen and if the education would improve in private Christian schools.

If the public schools followed all the recommendations that we have made, if the home and church did their jobs, the public schools would probably be minimally acceptable for many Christians. Unfortunately, it remains highly unlikely at this time that these three great institutions will work effectively together. But should these youths be sent to private Christian schools?

Two huge factors are to be considered: quality of the programs and teachers. In this regard, it is important to note that in some states, based on *First Amendment* rights, religious schools and faculty are neither subject to state scrutiny nor minimal teacher preparation standards. Indeed, sometimes the teachers are neither professionally trained nor adequately paid. Relying on workbooks, many well done, these poorly prepared teachers do what they can, but too often the expertise and professionalism are lacking. Parents want excellent instruction for their children. There is also the very genuine concern with the quality of the programs. What about labs? What about sophisticated and advanced curricula? What about teachers who are experts in a given area of learning? What about equipment?

The nagging problem is lack of money. Often Christian schools are too small and underfinanced. As a result, the program is sometimes too narrow and provincial. Students do learn the religion of Jesus Christ, the most important knowledge they can have; but, too often, they do not receive the academic preparation and the inspiration of a well-prepared master teacher who inspires their very best. Sometimes, also, the school provides a poor physical environment, often just a few rooms in a church that may not inspire a child to learn.

Another factor, of course, is the cost to the parents. Some small Christian schools charge from $1,500 to $2,000 per student. The larger schools have a stipend of from $3,000 to $5,000 per pupil--though many discount the tuition for more than one child in the family. Also, many have scholarships for those with financial need. The best of these schools can offer programs equal to or better than those in the public schools even in the most demanding academic specialties. But can families afford the huge expenditures? If funds are available, however, Mom and Dad must surely send their progeny to these *good* private Christian schools.

There are hundreds, perhaps thousands of excellent examples of Christian schools, and they are the academic equal of the best public schools. Visit the following: Peoria Christian School, Peoria, Illinois; Liberty Academy, Lynchburg, Virginia; Westminister Academy, Fort Lauderdale, Florida; or B. R. Christian School, Kansas City, Missouri. Two of these are arms of renowned evangelical churches and their famed pastors: Liberty is an extension of the ministry of Dr. Jerry Falwell, and Westminister is an extension of the ministry of Dr. D. James Kennedy, senior pastor of Coral Ridge Presbyterian Church in Ft. Lauderdale, Florida.

Dr. Ken Wackes, Headmaster at Westminister Academy, in a pamphlet entitled *Which School for Your Child,* wrote:

> What I want to stress...is that God gave us a biblical mandate to provide Christian schooling for our children, no matter how good the public school is perceived to be. *Proverbs 22:6* says, "Train a child in the way he should go." That doesn't give us permission to deliberately school our children in the way they shouldn't go. Similarly, *Deuteronomy 6* commands us to surround our children all day and night with

constant reminders of God's presence, while *Psalm 1* says, "Blessed is the man that does not walk in the counsel of the ungodly...." Only once in the history of the church have Christian parents deliberately placed their children in pagan schools in contradiction to the biblical mandate, and that has been the Twentieth Century....

The lesson is clear and compelling. If there are excellent Christian schools properly financed and firm in the faith, students would profit from the schooling. If, however, the schools are underfunded, are without well-prepared faculty and lack many of the amenities of the public schools, we are less sure. On balance, however, we continue to believe that many students should be sent to Christian schools.

But what about smaller communities? Away from the wealthy suburbs and huge evangelical churches, the problem remains of whether or not the middle and small-sized towns can produce good Christian schools in the only possible way that many of them really can: getting believing churches in a given community to cooperate in starting and maintaining such schools. There is an answer, and it may very well be the most important recommendation made in this book. We must tell you, though, that many people, pastors included, tell us that it is impossible. We refuse such thinking, for, without such cooperation, the cause of Jesus Christ is done huge damage.

Can fellow believers, those who are evangelical Christians, join hands in building Christian schools? Can the non-charismatic churches accept the charismatics? Can the latter of these softpeddle speaking in tongues and placing physical healing almost equal to salvation? Can high churches cooperate with low churches? Can the premillennialists work with the postmillennialists? Can black and white churches work in tandem? Could they agree, for instance, that the *Apostle's Creed* would be the organizing principal of the school, the theology that would bind them together. Let the various believing denominations take care of their own particular claims in their churches. It is what happened on the cross and the third day later that should bind believers with hoops of steel.

If this cooperation were attainable, the proper environment would be in place for the rapid development of excellent Christian schools to rival and excel the local public schools in middle-sized and small towns.

Home Schooling

Because of growing disaffection with the public schools, the home school movement is expanding rapidly. For many Christians the feeling is that the youth should not attend public schools, a claim compatible with what we have written in this book. It is also true that there are excellent books and workbooks available for such schooling, although it is fair to wonder about adequate machines and sophisticated equipment for junior and senior high schools.

We are not quite as excited about home schooling as some of our colleagues and fellow Christians, although we do believe that it could work well in the elementary grades if Mom and/or Dad are professionally prepared to teach and if they can, with no damage done to the family, spare the time. It is good to note that the balance of research concerning achievement indicates that home schooling is at least as effective as that in the public schools. Nor are we particularly concerned with the argument that home schools fail to provide socialization. This will happen in the church and the ensuing relationships gained from the youths invited into the home.

In many churches, the scenario involves a number of wonderful families deeply committed to Jesus Christ. The parents are exemplary people and wonderful Christians. Opting to home school their children, they offer these youths loving education based, first, on the validity of the *Scriptures*. The mothers skillfully and dedicatedly teaches their offspring, and they have refused outside employment. No finer mothers could be found. It is, of course, more than a full-time job to be such a parent. But what about the bone-weariness they must experience? Could the family in the long run suffer? The answer to this question is important, indeed.

Still, though, it is clear that for certain parents and their children home schooling is quite effective for the first few elementary years of schooling and, also, beyond. It is true that research indicates that even in high school there is no trustworthy evidence suggesting that the public schools do a better job. From available data, it is clear that home schooling works well even during the high school years. Still, though, it is fair to wonder if Christian schools might not be better if the schools are available and if parents can afford the tuition.

Parental Attitudes

The parents should surely speak well of schooling in general. They should stand with teachers on all matters that do not conflict with the *Creed* or *Commandments*, and, if the child gets disciplined at school, he should be punished at home, also. The authority of the school must almost never be questioned in front of the youth. Remember that almost all children and adolescents lie on occasion when their interests are at stake. Parents must not be taken in by such behavior. They should be very careful not to support these lies, for, in the long run, such conduct by parents can be seriously damaging to their progeny.

It is common for well-meaning parents and grandparents to act on the presumption that misbehavior is a lack of maturity that will disappear when the youth matures–that when the child or teenager gets older inappropriate and evil behavior will disappear. Such reasoning is seldom correct. Misbehaviors must be dealt with when they appear. Please do not believe that time alone solves the problem; rather, it feeds narcissism and hedonism.

Other parents reason that if their progeny are in trouble teachers are at fault. Time after time students place blame on teachers (and other authority figures) for their own shortcomings. Mom and Dad must assume that the teachers are right until absolutely proven wrong. No matter the tales of sons and daughters, the teacher is to be supported–and this must not be forgotten as the youth pleads his or her case.

Also, a youth may have been subjected to some terrible event or injury. Because of this, parents may very well ease discipline since they feel sorry for the youth, a grave error. Wise parents will move quickly to deal with the bad behavior. Also, behavior at home may be exemplary. How could teachers consider the child guilty of inappropriate behavior? The answer is simple: because the youth is guilty. Almost always, the teachers are right. Parents should support them, punish their progeny, and shun lawyers hungering to sue.

If parents feel dissatisfaction, they should visit with the principal, superintendent, or teacher in question. If that does not satisfy, they should go to the school board. Parents should not complain about homework and should monitor their child's doing it. They should endeavor to support the schools whenever they can.

When the School Must Be Contested

Parents have a sure responsibility to know exactly what is transpiring in the schools their sons and daughters attend. This must be ascertained by discussions with their children, by maintaining a friendly and close dialogue with the teachers and administrators of the school, and by extended visits to the institution. If both parents work, some vacations days should be so used. They must be seen in the schools.

But there is a time for parents, in love, to question the school when the *Commandments* or *Creed* are disrespected, or when humanism is illegally taught, as, say, in instruction of the New Age. If, in such situations, the school does not give satisfaction, the courts should be utilized. Every logical and effective step must be used to slow the relentless march of the humanistic religion in the schools of the land.

In such disagreements with the schools, parents should consider explaining kindly to their children that there are two views about many things, that the schools often take a humanistic view and the family a Christian one. The youths must be told that the family takes a differing view because of its commitment to the *Commandments*, the truth of the *Scriptures*, Christian precepts, and the *American Creed*. They must assert that the family view is, in this case, more important than the school's. All of this is to be conducted with respect for the schools. At the very least, the sons and daughters will have two views on which to base their decisions. In this the home will have done well in parrying the school's humanistic thrust, and the youth will know precisely where their parents stand.

Peer Group

It is no secret to parents that the peer group looms as one of the greatest potential dangers for their progeny. Perhaps nothing is fraught with more danger to the youth, for, all too often, the group itself demonstrates behavior which is often far worse and more damaging than parents would fear. It is absolutely critical that a youth be a part of a peer group less destructive, evil, and prone to trouble than are those courting disaster.

But what can a parent do? Most important, the church should be the place the son or daughter meets most of his/her friends. This, of course, means that Mom and Dad, along with their children, should be in church whenever the doors open. Certainly, the children should attend everything where people of their own age are involved. Parents should invite these youth into the homes to socialize with their offspring. The bonds of friendship should result in the peer group being comprised of sons and daughters of fellow Christians. Certainly, such groups may behave badly, too; however, there is a better chance for right action than if the friends were nonChristians. Students should not date unchaperoned until late in high school, no matter the pressures they bring on their parents; and strict evening hours should be maintained. If there is a believing church school and if the price is affordable, the students should attend. From the very beginning, the youth should be assigned work at home. He or she should never be loitering around town with his peers without a satisfactory reason. When a youth leaves the house, Mom and Dad must know where he or she is at all times. Even these actions guarantee nothing. Sometimes the finest people have corrupt progeny, and it occurs in church-oriented peer groups, as well. Nonetheless, there is an edge in providing the social environment for the children to become friends with fellow church attendees.

Television

During the childhood days, and extending even into junior and senior high schools, television-viewing must be carefully monitored by parents. Children should talk to their parents about the *few* programs that they will watch, and the parents should approve all of them. MTV is out of bounds, and the Mom and Dad should spell out precisely why, that it evangelizes narcissism and hedonism. Certainly, they should explain (as the book does earlier) about the humanistic focus of the medium and why it must not be watched at will. If, however, any of the humanistic material is viewed, the parents should sit down with the youth and explain the Christian position concerning the matter and also how it fails to meet demands of the *American Creed and the Bible*. The one and only television set would be in a central location, and all family members would use it. Consider allowing children to view one hour of television or computer games (non-violent) for each two hours of reading.

Films

Parents would do well to follow carefully the film ratings. Whenever possible, they should view films that may appear questionable. No youth at any age should attend an R-rated film. Even the very fine films may be loaded with humanistic doctrine, and the parent needs to explain how the varying themes are at odds with the *Ten Commandments* and the *Creed*. They must also be quick to discuss with the youth the tragedy inherent in breaking the *Creed* or *Commandments*. This is also an apt time to teach that sin may be great fun--but only for a season, and it bears bitter fruit in the end.

The parents may not be able to control what television programs their progeny see away from home, but they can surely direct what is watched at home. They should maintain their authority in this matter, no matter the emotional pressure brought by their offspring.

Pornography and Sex Education

Bawdy films and explicit magazines like *Hustler*, *Playboy*, and *Penthouse* will not be allowed in the house, and father and mother will have no pornography between the beds. Parents will explain why pornography is not acceptable because it is in direct contradiction to both the *Commandments* and the *Creed*. At the same time, the youth must be told that it presents a horrible and perverted view of women, who, the filth asserts, live just to give sex to a man, groups, or animals. Regardless of what the purveyors of evil assert, there is more to life than sex, and humans have dignity. They are more than animals in the field, and this the youth must learn.

Part of the answer to why pornography is sinful should be treated in the parents' sex education instruction, and such teaching is, in fact, the job of the parents. Mom and Dad should first deal with what the *Bible* teaches about sex, and they should know well what the *Creed* instructs. Central to these lessons is that sex is a wonderful gift for married people but only inside the bonds of marriage; outside, it is sin. The sex drive, different in men and women, should be discussed and understood--and, at some point, the youth should comprehend that many good people, King David being an example, yield to sexual temptation. Everyone sins, and that is precisely why the Savior chose to come to this planet and die for all of us. If, as Christ indicated, intention is sin, then, in matters of sex, all men and most women are sinners. The youth must be well taught that God pardons such behavior in believers if they have accepted Him and if they ask for forgiveness. They must also reflect the gravity of their sin for which Jesus Christ died to pay the price. The first lesson of sex education is that they must give their lives to Jesus Christ. Then they must set their sights on the difficult task of remaining celibate until the time of their weddings and of praying much to meet the goal.

Certainly, the young people should be taught that, in matters of sex, all that they have learned in the psychology of the self is quite incorrect and horribly wrong. In fact in all matters of love, including sex, they should be taught their mate should be considered first, themselves second. In marriage, it is their responsibility to make sex pleasant and loving for their mate, and that then-- because of their devotion--it is even more meaningful to them. Always, the partner's feelings come first.

There are other crucial issues. They must be instructed that, according to the *Scriptures*, God abhors homosexuality. It is not just another lifestyle to consider; it is surely sin and odious to God. They should also be taught that condoms do not provide safe sex; their failure rate is far too high. The parents must make sure the youth comprehend that abortion is murder, that, at the moment of conception, there is life. Perhaps, more that anything else, Mom and Dad must be exemplars for their progeny. They must hug and kiss; they must show their love. The children must surely note that marriage is really something special for husbands and wives--who are far different from each other in countless ways, yet the two of them together are far better than either would have been alone. The youth must hunger for a similar relationship when they become adults.

And Mom and Dad absolutely must promote a complete and honest dialogue with their children about sex. Nothing should be withheld, nor should parents be ashamed or embarrassed; for they are the first choice to teach their progeny about all matters of sex, particularly the claims of the *Bible* and the *Creed*. Parents absolutely must not shirk this crucial instruction.

Computers and Cyberspace

It goes without saying that computer knowledge and skills are demanded of young people as they prepare for the job world. To deny them this preparation is too often to relegate them to second class vocations. Schools are rapidly endeavoring to meet this need by supplying computer education. But parents should, when money is available, invest in a home computer for their children and for the entire family.

The youth, however, should not be turned loose in *cyberspace* on the *Internet* or *World Wide Web*. Parents must surely speak frankly with the computer salesman who sold them the machines. They must learn the dangers and police use of the computer. At the same time, they should secure parental control software and learn how to utilize it. Use of the computer must be strictly controlled.

Unless father or mother require a second computer for business, there should be just one in the home, and it should be in a central location and shared by the entire family. Youth should be monitored when they use the computer.

Moreover, parents must make sure that too much time is not spent on the computer, neither on the *Net* nor on games. The youth should be playing football with neighbors or friends, contemplating life, sharing dreams and concerns with others, and reading the *Bible*. Years ago the word *bookworm* had negative connotations. Well-rounded young people today must not be allowed to become *cyberworms*.

Adolescent Music

This problem is of major importance. For the past three decades and more, music has assumed the rarified level of both religion and philosophy to multiplied millions of the youth. The results have been and remain disastrous. Parents should surely know this music thoroughly; they must comprehend the recurrent themes and ideas. In this they will be debased and shocked, for the worst is a clear danger to both their children and the social order, as well.

Even the best of it is worrisome, and all of it represents a social problem of the first order. Most of it romanticizes narcissism and hedonism.

This adolescent music must not be acceptable in the home, unless parents and progeny are listening together and discussing it. Out would come the *Commandments* and the *Creed*. The words, the ideas, the insane bellowing, the violence, would all be measured by these two great listings, and there would be dialogue between all family members. The adolescents may scoff at the discussions, but that is to be expected. The conversations may bear fruit later, when the youth escape the hormonal adolescent years.

As indicated earlier, MTV should never be allowed in the home; it desecrates nearly everything recommended in the *Commandments* and the *Creed*. Vile *gangsta rap* should never be allowed in the home. Instead, Christian melodies, not all contemporary, should be the music of the home. Non-Christian music of high purpose and nobility should be part of the choices in the home, too. About this parents must be firm.

College

Parents should cooperate with their churches in presenting Christian institutions of higher education as the places of choice to attend. Visits should be arranged, preferably through the church. If the parent has been successful in locating his son or daughter with a church peer group, it is well for parents to take them to visit the college. Subtle but effective salesmanship should be used to sell the institutions to the youth. The Christian college is absolutely critical for the progeny of believers.

If the son or daughter does attend a secular university or college, the parents should carefully explain the dangers to the faith. Then four actions should be instigated: First, find a Christian housing unit in which the students will reside. Second, advise them to make their closest friends from among those living in the house. Third, ask there and in the church attended who the believing professors are; take their classes and spend time getting to know them. Fourth, find a believing church and join campus Christian groups. All of these together will act as a hedge against the humanistic religion being presented to the students, but disaster still lurks.

Openness

In most cases, schools are enthusiastic about teaching the concept of openness, an ideal central to the bankrupt and embarrassing anti-value of *political correctness* and pivotal to the religion of humanism. At the family alter, in family forums and discussions, Mom and Dad might very well consider again producing a list of the values included in both the *Commandments* and the *Creed*. The huge question would be: Should we, as Christians, be open-minded to all things? Then the following topics might be discussed: Should we remain open to murder, adultery, cruelty, homosexuality, and other debasements of the *Commandments* and *Creed*? If we remain open-minded about such topics are we, in fact, closed-minded about the *Commandments* and the *Creed*? The youth must be educated that the Christian faith and the *Creed* demand closed-mindedness on much that is *politically correct*.

Moral Relativism

Parents must battle the cancer of moral relativism and situation ethics that are taught, more or less, in most public schools in the nation. Quite like the recommendations made for openness, parental discussions should focus on the problem, again considering the *Commandments* and the *Creed*. It is critical that the home take a firm stand on this matter. The youth must not believe that there is any credibility to the perverse philosophy; they absolutely must understand that moral relativism is a grave error and an abiding danger to Christianity and the *American Creed*. The *Commandments* and *Creed*, they must comprehend, are absolutes. There is a right, and there is a wrong, no matter what the schools teach.

Recall that when Abraham Lincoln was a lad, his mother, soon to be in Glory, took him daily on her lap and read the *Bible* to him, holding up the *Ten Commandments* as right and true. In all the days before his conversion to Christ, he recalled what she had taught him, and it affected his behavior profoundly. So too, should Moms and Dads today hold up the *Commandments* and *Creed* as their children learn what right and wrong are.

Responsibility

Sons and daughters must be taught responsibility. Parents would do well, in love, to demand that the youth keep their rooms clean, get their own clothes ready for school when they are old enough to do so, work to earn spending money, do homework on time, and have no car unless they buy it and its insurance from money earned by hard work. Yes, it is easier to let kids have their way, to yield to the demand that *everyone does it*. Though giving in makes momentary peace, it is a serious error. It is impossible to overestimate the critical import of teaching responsibility, the lack of which is a sure omen of a nation in grave crisis. Responsibility is utterly crucial.

Gender and Feminism

In discussions and at the family alter, the biblical view of men, women, and marriage should be studied and understood by the entire family. The views of character and marriage indicated in the *Creed* should also be analyzed and discussed. This is, of course, important because, precisely in this area, humanistic liberalism will probably be taught in the schools--and this to the destruction of the family. Mom and Dad must model the historic sex roles and demonstrate to the youth that men and women are far different from each other, and that this very difference is desirable, the sum result being something far better than each of them would have been separately. Boys should be brought up to be boys, and girls should be raised to be girls--and both to have pride in their gender.

Other Choices

The parents would be wise to follow the news concerning the social order at large and the schools in particular. The local newspaper, a big city newspaper, and television news should be carefully monitored. The actions of the state and national legislators should be studied, as should Supreme Court decisions. At the same time, the parents would do well to attend every school board meeting. Running for the school board would be excellent.

They must become active (the liberal humanist would likely say, pro-active). Perhaps they should write letters to the editor of the local newspaper when the *Commandments* and/or the *Creed* are debased. They may phone call-in programs or write to legislators; they could also organize parents and write to advertisers when the media negates the *Creed* or *Commandments*.

And So?

Children of the baby boom, youth of the pernicious and disastrous late 1960's and early 1970's, now adults and parents or grandparents, may throw up their arms in angry frustration and announce, "I don't have time for anything else; neither my wife nor I have time for all of this."

Oh, yes, they do! If they have time for nothing else, they do for this. Their children and the nation stand at risk. Put away the fetters of hedonism, narcissism, selfishness, and the trauma of the baby boom. Stand firm. The children come first, and the proper raising of them is beyond a doubt the parents' greatest triumph and obligation.

Oh, yes, they do have time. They must, for the home is sinking in the terrible quicksand of humanism. And remember, you, the family reading this, are responsible, when you send a child to school for the following personal preparation: a Christian background; knowledge of the *American Creed,* the *Ten Commandments,* and *the Beatitudes*; a biblical background; discipline; responsibility; respect; a sense of right and wrong; and good work habits. It is these goals to which parents should and must utterly dedicate themselves.

CHAPTER NINE

WHAT THE CHURCH MUST DO

In the village of Wentworth, New Hampshire, sitting quietly on a hillside, nestled among white birch and maple trees, there is a little white church that is called "home." It is a place where memories abound, where truth is proclaimed, where life is made to stand still and where people are able to "taste and see that the LORD is good." Years ago, that little white church began the annual tradition of a "Homecoming Day" when friends and family could return, reminisce, and spend time talking about the good old days. A familiar song was penned to the tune of "The Church in the Wildwood," and its words are as follows:

>There's a church on a hillside in Wentworth,
>And to us it grows dearer each year.
>With the memories of those now departed
>And the friends who each Sunday are here.
>
>There's a welcome to those who live near us,
>And to those who are far, far away;
>And with pleasure we see there are many
>Who return for our Homecoming Day.
>
>Think of the years of your childhood,
>When you came to this old Sunday School;
>Where we learned precious verses of Scripture
>And to live by the old Golden Rule.
>
>(Chorus) O Come, Come, Come, Come...
>Come to the church on the hillside,
>Return to the faith of your youth
>Where God's Word is proclaimed from the pulpit;
>With *the Bible*, our *Textbook of Truth*

(Words by Wilfred Tatham)

The church, the song, the quiet New England setting is nostalgic, reverent. It is a place to regain focus, to fan the flames of faith and stoke the embers of righteousness once more.

Unfortunately, the "Little White Church on the Hillside" is the exception rather than the rule.

What Happened to "The Church in the Wildwood?"

It has already been clearly shown in this tome that our society has fallen helpless to the vices of narcissism and hedonism and humanism. To be sure, these enemies of society are also the enemies of the Church–the body of Christ–those individuals who have placed their faith in Jesus Christ alone for salvation from sin for all eternity. The *Old Testament* book of *Judges* shares a principle for destruction from its place in history that has taken root today: "Every man did what was right in his own eyes." Sadly, the "Judges Principle" has invaded the church. The era of relativism, pluralism, and attitude of tolerance has sounded the battle cry for the death of authority and the destruction of any absolute standards.

The Worship of Self

The church has been infected by the world–the kosmos–that world system of evil under the direct influence and control of the enemy of God, Satan the great deceiver himself. No longer does the church appear to be "in the world yet not of the world."Instead, she is seen as being "in love with the world, and proud of it."

If Rodney King Were a Theologian

Many will remember the infamous question posed by Rodney King, a victim of the savage Los Angeles riots some years ago, when, before a barrage of media, Mr. King asked, "Can't we all just get along?" Certainly this was a valid request given what King and others endured at the hands of rioting looters. Unfortunately that mind set has grown in prevalence to the extent that society has gone to the bargaining table in its quest for peace at any cost, and we have settled for peace without sacrifice, which results in peace by manipulation. We have agreed to a cessation of hostilities without any change of heart. And the result has been a direct banishment of God Almighty from society, from the home, from schools, and in many places, from His Bride, the Church.

What the Church Must Do

The New Social Order

The United States of America, Land of the Free and Home of the Brave, finds itself living life behind the liberal curtain where instead of "In God We Trust" the new phrase to a few is "Tolerance For All." Absolute truth is mocked by the naysayers as relativism is seated upon the throne of human reasoning. Our pluralistic social order is actually a society in chaos. The future is unclear because individuals, trapped in the time reduction warp, fail to cease from all their activities long enough to plan goals, form objectives, and dream of the future. Solomon reminds us that "without a vision the people perish."

Who actually takes the time to consider what it is that our narcissistic, hedonistic society is promoting to this and the future generations? Presently we are living life for today because today, right now, it "works" for us. The truth, however, is that while we live life for the here and now we are merely "painting the roses red" in a vain effort to appeal to the senses and to partake of the instant gratification binge in our land. We are an advanced world, having at our disposal more information each day. Yet we are as the apostle Paul wrote, "Ever learning yet never coming to the knowledge of the Truth."

THE CHURCH IN CRISIS

Technological Advances (vs.) Crumbling Foundations

Gone are the days of quill and ink, studying the *Bible* by flickering hearth and oil lamps. Ours is a day of technology. Computers and word processors have eased the burden of time constraints with the latest high-tech Bible study software available. The Internet provides access for pastors and teachers to a multitude of biblical research sites as well as seminary libraries around the world. And that's just the beginning. We have multimedia presentations that wow the masses in today's world who, thanks to our advanced society, are now visual learners with an attention span of less than ten minutes, albeit seconds for some. Surround sound, cell phones, video teleconferencing, high resolution desktop presentations to enhance our worship–all of these things, to be sure, have their place. Yet they create for today's pastors a new world order that, until recent years, Bible colleges and seminaries have not equipped nor prepared future church leaders to utilize. The trend in many churches has been a quest for more, bigger, better high tech presentations that relate to the senses instead of the heart. To mingle with other members of the clergy and speak of a literal study of the Word of God as the sole basis for proper Bible interpretation gains looks from others as if one had recently been exhumed from the grave. In many churches a post mortem has been conducted on Doctrine. The Church of Jesus Christ is in a crisis like never before because, in an effort to better communicate with the unsaved in a manner consistent with their intellectual and social station in life, she has forsaken the basics of the *Bible* and a true preaching of fundamental doctrine.

Preaching Cold Oatmeal

Ask any person in the average fundamental/evangelical Bible believing church today if he would enjoy a seminar on Situational Bioethics and Genetic Research from a Christian Perspective or a seminar on how we got our *Bible* and why it can be trusted, and the majority choice will be for Bioethics. Why do people respond to the teaching of Bible doctrine as if they were being forced to eat cold oatmeal? We propose the answer lies in the individualistic world around us where people who comprise the body of Christ, the Church, have become so involved in what the world has to offer by way of convenient, instantaneous gratification of self, that too few care. Individualism is bringing about the demise of society as we have known it. It used to be in the decades of the boomers and busters that society fostered a sense of belonging and identity. Why is it that charitable contributions to churches and social organizations is at an all time low? It is because our society has changed from one that socially interacts to one that seldom interacts. We don't have to rub shoulders with others. From the convenience of our bedrooms, we can file our job reports and speak with potential customers around the world by means of the Internet and teleconferencing. We have little need of learning how to interact with others in a socially acceptable manner. No longer is there a need to be polite, to be sensitive to not so much what we are saying as much as to how we are saying it. We have little need of looking socially acceptable, no business suits, dress codes. We are players in a nation that is evolving from a society that is social to one of single entities. Our individualism is turning us into isolationists. Individualism and isolationism begets our laissez-faire attitude which is symptomatic of our selfish mind set. We live for ourselves, provide for ourselves, plan for ourselves, and we could care less about the world around us. The reason so few care is that we have acted like Pinnocchio, sailing away to the Land of Toys, living in a fantasy world that grows thick scales of delusion over our spiritual eyes and fosters a false view of reality.

And what are pastors and church leaders to do? They wrestle with knowing what to teach–the fundamentals of the faith as found only in the *Word of God*–yet doing so in such a manner that it will "stick" in the minds of those warming the pews on Sunday morning, and that hopefully will last

What the Church Must Do

longer in their memory than the average television commercial. It is an honest struggle that leaves many men in ministry frustrated on two fronts: first, because they know what people need to hear, and, second, because they have for the most part little or no understanding of taking what are the fundamentals of Truth and utilizing modern methods of communication (i.e., the Internet, Web pages, Multimedia Presentations, etc.) effectively to teach that truth to people who need to hear, yet listen by means of new technological ways of communicating. It is little wonder that many pastors are leaving their churches upset, frustrated, burned out and broken, feeling like failures in their calling and unable to compete with the humanists and cults surrounding them.

THE CHURCH PROVIDING ANSWERS

A Return to the Fundamentals of Church Life

There are a number of facts the church must face if she is to be used as an instrument of grace, to return America to the golden dream of its heritage found in the *Creed, Commandments,* and *Beatitudes.* The following facts must be addressed before the church can be used as God's tool for change:

1) Prayer must be a significant force in church life.

In the book of *Acts* we find the fundamentals of the early church which included the teaching of the apostles, the breaking of bread, the fellowship of the saints and prayer. The traditional prayer meeting of the church is turning into a thing of the past. No doubt it is the least attended function of the church. Manipulating the day, time, and place of its occurrence is as effective as placing a band-aid on a gaping wound. The true problem is a spiritual malaise of the heart. The following "obituary" lends support to our example:

> Mrs. Prayer Meeting died recently at the First neglected Church on Worldly Avenue. Born many years ago in the midst of great revivals she was a strong healthy child, fed largely on testimony and Bible study, soon grew into world wide prominence and was one of the most influential members of the famous church family. For the past several years Mrs. Prayer Meeting had been failing in health, gradually wasting away until rendered helpless by stiffness of knees, coldness of heart inactivity, and weakness of purpose and will power. At the last she was but a shadow of her former happy self. Her last whispered words were inquiries concerning the strange absence of her loved ones, now busy in the markets of trade and places of worldly amusements. Experts including Dr. Works, Dr.

Reform and Dr. Joinher disagreed as to the cause of her fatal illness. They had administered large doses of organizations, socials, contests and drives but to no avail. A postmortem showed that a deficiency of spiritual food, coupled with the lack of faith, heartfelt religion and general support were contributing factors. Only a few were present at her death, sobbing over memories of her past beauty and power. In honor of her home going, the church doors will be closed on Wednesday nights, except the third Wednesday night of each month when the ladies Pink Lemonade Society serves refreshments to the men's Handball Team.

People have become so enamored with self that there is little time devoted to prayer. Individualism breeds a contempt for even the suggestion that man is dependent upon God. Our independence is proudly exalted each time we solve our own problems and profit from our own innovative strategies. Yet all it takes is for life to place a speed bump in our path too big for us to handle, and where do we turn? In desperation and panic we run to the place of prayer, blow off the cobwebs and beg God to make the hurt go away so we can return to life as we know it on Easy Street. In *Ephesians 6* the apostle Paul writes about the spiritual warfare children of God are in the midst of, listing for us the various elements of the Christian tools of spiritual warfare. The interesting thing is that Paul lists prayer, if we may be so bold, as the oil that keeps the armor in working condition. Without prayer, our battle is pointless. Jesus said, "Ask, that it may be given to you; seek and you shall find; knock and it shall be opened to you. For to him who asks it shall be given, and to him who seeks he shall find and to the one who knocks it shall be opened." (Matthew 7:7,8) There is an element of force in that passage, a command from our Lord to keep on asking, seeking, knocking. Prayer must be persistent.

Dr. David Jeremiah, Senior Pastor of Shadow Mountain Community Church in California, writes the following about prayer in his book *Prayer: The Great Adventure*:

> ...Serious prayer is almost driven by necessity. We don't pray because we *ought*, we pray because we are without any other recourse.... Prayer...has to be born out of a whole environment of felt need....Could it be that one reason we have great problems is that God wants to show us great solutions?...Prayer is my Declaration of Dependence....We tend to use prayer as a last resort, but Jesus wants it to be our first line of defense. We pray when there's nothing else we can do, but Jesus wants us to pray before we do anything at all. (Copyright ©1977 by David Jeremiah, Multinomah Publishers, Sisters, Oregon.)

And yet, there are still smoldering embers of the fires of prayer from days not so far gone by seen scattered in various areas and activities. Each year in September students, parents, area clergy and others make a pilgrimage to an event known as "See You At The Pole" to pray for their schools, surrounding the school flagpole prior to the beginning of the school day. There are "Concerts of Prayer" groups and prayer group chapters in various places. Interestingly enough, even the most recent attack on Christianity and the children of God that happened Wednesday, September 15, 1999, in Texas. A deranged gunman invaded a local church where a teen youth group was holding a prayer rally following the annual "See You At The Pole" event, and opened fire, killing himself and seven others, and wounding still others. Even some of the school shootings that took place during the decade of the '90s were preceded by students engaging in prayer or Bible study. Could it be that the enemy of God, Satan, sees the value of prayer, and takes the prayers of Christians far more seriously than we do? Is this part of the answer to the malaise in churches today, and could it provide answers to the senseless carnage left behind shooting rampages where times of prayer have been a factor? If churches are to be involved in turning the tide of America's spiritual demise, the people of God must stop laying down the weapons of prayer. They must take up the shield of faith and the sword of the Spirit which is the Word of God, and with all prayer as Paul writes in Ephesians 6, must enter the fray with all confidence, remembering "greater is He that is in you than he that is in the world." (1 John 4:4)

2) Worship Does Not Equal Entertainment

The following statement is true: the message (that salvation is gained by faith in Christ alone apart from any works of sinful humanity) must never change; yet the method must change with each new generation. The danger, however, is to be so focused on perfecting our method of reaching the lost and feeding the flock that we tend to forget the message. To be sure, we live in the entertainment era of church life. How are local church pastors able to "wow" their people when they have just been "wowed" by some of the greatest pastors and teachers in the nation whom they tuned to earlier on television? Often people attend a local church for a while until something else comes along with more "bells and whistles" to capture the attention of the crowd, and they move on because "the church just isn't meeting our needs." Unfortunately "needs" are often defined as modern tools of convenience and creature comforts, having nothing to do with a clear exposition of the *Word of God* and how that biblical truth can impact life here, now, today. Yes, we must be modern in our approaches in sharing the message, but not to the extent that the message is shrouded by the methods of delivery. Worship teams, overheads, video projectors, surround sound, praise bands, lapel Mic., seeker services...all of these can and should be utilized to the extent that they are tools to more effectively to deliver the message. They must never, under any circumstance, take the focus away from the message.

3) Our Audience Has Changed

In the 1020's modernism surfaced as the enemy of fundamentalism. Many churches left mainline denominations and formed independent fellowships in an effort to maintain the pure doctrines of the faith. Modernism has had many relatives over the years, including humanism, liberalism, relativism, pluralism, tolerance, just to name a few. As a result of these social philosophies, our audience has changed from Boomers to Busters, to Gen-Xers and now Gen-Yers. In the social rebellion of the 1960's-1970's, the search for a deeper meaning began. Now, after three decades of aimless wandering in various philosophical quagmires, the present generation is fed up with the smoke and mirrors of New Age gurus who promise the world and deliver emptiness and lies. Today's generation of seekers is on an unprecedented quest for absolute truth that is pure and undefiled. They have seen the results of the past generations of seekers who chased after faux rainbows and found nothing at the other side with which to answer their innate questions about the meaning of life. Today's generation has experienced the tragedy of broken homes, immorality, and the pursuit of materialism at all costs. This generation of seekers wants solid answers and is not willing to take "no" for an answer! Indeed, the Church has a line outside its doors waiting to get inside...if she would only look away from her own internal distractions. Church research experts have written that the top ten people groups that would be considered "open" to church solicitations and on a search for Truth includes the following:

Second time visitors. The old adage is true; "You never have a second chance to make a first impression." If your first impression is polished, professional and personal, your visitor will most likely return. Second timers are those who are definitely seeking for something the church has that caught their attention the first time they came.

Close friends and relatives of newly saved individuals. People who have come to experience a personal relationship with Jesus Christ have gained answers to their quest. Missing pieces to lives are made complete. When one is newly saved it is a tremendous event! New believers usually come and sit closer to the front (at times even on the front row) acting like spiritual sponges, soaking in everything they hear from God's pulpit. They have a desire to share that incredible personal experience with others who are close to them. And often family and friends will attend to see what is so life changing as to have been able to change my friend or loved one. Again the seeds of righteousness are sown in hearts that are heavy and looking for answers.

People going through divorce. Divorce is an epidemic in America. It is too convenient, too available. Young couples come to the altar and recite vows of love "'till death us do part," all the while in the back of their minds saying to themselves, "If it doesn't work, I can get a divorce." Experts have determined, and we believe, that individuals who have experienced divorce will agree that the deliberate ending of marital union by means of divorce has untold negative repercussions. Psychological and physiological stresses and manifestations of depression, fatigue, even the shortening of life, as well as a complete change in friendship circles, being viewed differently by society and family, not to mention the strain of being a single parent many times...- these factors and others drive people to look for answers. The church must be ready to reach out to those who have ridden the white waters of painful divorce. To say we don't believe in divorce is not enough. The fact is divorce still happens. To bury our heads in the sand is cowardly at best. The church must promote a Truth that is trustworthy to this group of seekers who have thought they could never trust again.

Those in need of a recovery program. Addictions, be they from alcohol, drugs, gambling, sex, pornography, food, force people to look for truth that is foundational. The allusion of their addiction has lowered self-esteem, destroyed discipline, and created a vacuum where love once existed. Churches must be ready to share Truth with those in need of help, sharing that Jesus is able and willing to love them just as they are in order to make them just like He is, so that His righteousness may be seen in their lives by means of experiencing a personal relationship with the King of kings and Lord of lords.

First time parents. Now here is a fun group! Two young people darken the doors of a church carrying the wonderful manifestation of their love, dressed in bright colors, smelling that baby smell. In their eyes you can see the enormous weight they are already contemplating with regards to the future they hold in their arms. What do we teach our child? Where do we look for answers? Is there anyone who can relate to the immediate life changes we are now experiencing? For so long we have just been two, living for ourselves.

Now those things we have been putting off can be avoided no longer. We must gain spiritual insight in molding this precious life in our charge. What better place to seek for answers and "how to" insights than a local church where families are the fabric of life.

The terminally ill and their families. Without any doubt, this is the group with the most questions and also without the most answers. If God is good, loving, just, then WHY...? Ministering to this group involves a tenderness that must come from the very heart of God. Too often when death comes and grief washes over the lives of those left to carry on alone, well-meaning folks quoting cliches and best wishes fade away. Grief is faced alone. Few of those who came to mourn are comfortable enough to call, to care, to reach out. Many neither know how to help nor what to say because nothing is comforting. The people of God in the churches across our land need to learn that death is a part of life that one day every one of us will face personally. All the more reason to begin now in preparation, by means of reaching out to those who are victimized by the cold fingers of death that have taken their loved one. Practical ministries of helps in the home by means of meals, helping with daily chores, even visiting with the one who is ill, are classic examples of our extending a cup of cold water to those in dire need. Grieving people come to the church to face God and to find answers. Oh that we be sensitive to such needs, not having to experience personally ourselves such loss in order to arrive at the compassion such grief requires.

Couples with marital problems. Counseling two people in marital crisis is without a doubt one of the most draining spiritual challenges. Infidelity in the church is at an all time high. Unfair expectations, a lack of clear understanding of biblical roles of husbands and wives, as well as other issues stemming from past failures contribute to the breakdown of the marriage bond. The basic root problem is a failure to communicate in such a way that differences are understood and challenges worked through. Yet the results of true mutual repentance and heart changes far exceed the weight of the challenge. *God's Word, the Bible* has relevant answers for struggling couples awash in the current of marital conflict. Church leaders are wise to equip their people to befriend struggling couples, sharing by means of *the Word of God* and personal insight and example of what God has done and can do for all who will reach out to Him.

Parents with children problems. When all else has been tried, the appointment is made by the parents with the local clergy to discuss what is wrong with one of the children. Often these folks are incredibly open, because they have tried everything else and still nothing has worked. They will ask the question, "Where did we go wrong?" Again, the church has a golden opportunity to share biblical principles of parenting, relationships, and the key to success being found in a personal walk with Jesus Christ. Great care must be taken to avoid non-judgmental attitudes. A solid outreach to parents and their children will serve as a catalyst to drawing them into the body of Christ, but only when they see in the church a group of people who truly care about their need.

<u>The unemployed and financially challenged</u>. Individuals who are out of luck and have no ready recourse will turn to the church when things get desperate. Often not on Sundays, but perhaps quietly during the week when the embarrassment of asking for assistance is at a minimum, will they enter the church. Great care should be taken to discern and help a true need, as well as not only to meet the physical need, but to use the somewhat captive audience format as a tool of witnessing, sharing what Jesus Christ can do in their lives and how a personal relationship with Him can provide incredible resources for their needs they never knew were possible.

<u>New residents</u>. Folks moving into a community are looking for friendships, acceptance, a sense of belonging, a place to put down roots. Welcome ministries should be a vital and vigilant force in each local church to make those outreach impressions. If churches don't make themselves known, one can be sure that cult groups will do the job! Welcome baskets, brochures, and invitations to different events at the church as well as in the town are wonderful gestures to a group of seekers looking for a place to belong.

Interestingly enough, of these ten groups, the two most receptive groups are those in transition and those under tension. Unfortunately we are by nature creatures of avoidance when it comes to the problems of another, often because we have problems aplenty of our own. Yet hearts are tender and spirits are soft when crisis strikes without warning. Jesus never said ministry was an option created with comfort and convenience. His own example of reaching out when it was at times most inconvenient serves to challenge the church and its people to get involved in the lives of those around us who are searching for answers in the midst of turmoil.

4) Our Mission Must Change

The *Great Commission* passage from *Matthew's* gospel must be read more than once a year at the annual Missions Conference. The church will not survive if she fails to reproduce herself in the lives of present day seekers. Instead of churches exploding with the fruits of gospel outreach toward the lost, seeking world around us, we are experiencing spiritual implosion as we find ourselves members of the only army in the history of the world that shoots its own wounded. Due to the infection in the church of immorality, divorce, teen sexuality and greed, we are in a constant fight for survival trying to avoid being a victim of friendly fire. We have forgotten our status as a hospital for sinners and have redesigned our programs to provide a hot house for Son-Flowers. Someone has well asked the all too familiar and yet still applicable question: "If you were on trial for being a Christian, would there be enough evidence to convict you?"

5) We Must Repair Our Crumbling Foundation

The key for the church's involvement in returning America to its golden dream is found in a return to the fundamentals of our faith found only in the *Word of God, the Bible*. This alone is the truth today's seekers need. This alone is the fulfillment to their quest for answers and absolutes. The search for truth has begun to turn the tide of tolerance to one of being intolerant of those who are selling tolerance. People are tired of investing false hope in false gods that leave them emptier than before. Now is the time to rid the church of those religious hucksters who seemingly sell spiritual placebos and conscience salves. Church liturgy and creeds of the past are no substitute for the absolute trustworthy truth of *the Word of God, the Bible*. Pastors must return to the fundamentals of the faith in order to teach today's generation Who God is and how He desires to love and care for them in a unique and personal way. We must show them beyond a doubt that *the Bible* is *God's Word*, fully authoritative for life and practice, the supreme authority. We must demonstrate that it is totally trustworthy and true. We must exert ourselves toward a presentation for biblical evidences that will present *the Bible* as it truly is–far superior to any other religious teaching. We are challenged to show that it works for life today, not just two thousand years ago. Its reliability and relevance are key in winning the lost to Christ. Answering the question as to Who God is creates a channel of communication whereby the lost can see God's love for them as well as His holiness and justice and righteousness and mercy and grace. God has a divine plan for mankind generally and for them specifically, and there is a vast treasure awaiting all who will trust in His Son Jesus. An understanding of the Person and work of Jesus Christ, the eternal Son of God, is the evidence needed, for even Jesus said, "He who has seen Me has seen the Father." We must present Jesus as He is, fully God and fully man, able to be sympathetic with the needs of those who seek Him, all the while without sin and fully able to meet any and every need. The greatest need to be shown is man's need of a Savior from sin. Salvation must be taught so that it is more than just easy believism, a fire insurance for eternity. If salvation is relevant for eternity only, so what? Careful time must be spent in showing seekers how salvation from sin is necessary for victorious living today, not just for facing death tomorrow.

Today's people are seeking in desperation for the bottom line. And if the church fails to provide the answers to their quest, the world will go elsewhere to the cults, their minds blinded by the cunning deceptions of the evil one.

What the Church Must Do

WHERE DO WE GO FROM HERE?

The Church–All Natural

Historic Christianity stands on the threshold of a new millennia, ripe with the expectant and imminent return of Jesus Christ for His Church. We are surrounded with multitudes who are presently carrying the death sentence of a Christless eternity in hell. As a result, we dare not shy away nor apologize for our efforts to return to the fundamentals of our faith found only in the *Word of God*. Pure doctrine, properly and lovingly communicated in a fashion that makes it not only palatable but applicable and profitable for living a victorious life in Christ today, is free from efforts to add to or water down the truth. Many churches are afraid to offend anyone, so many church leaders fail to address the issue of sin, instead making references to mistakes, telling us that God understands, and that He really doesn't expect us to be perfect. Groups promote love (which is really tolerance dressed to go to church) in an effort to sugar coat just about anything that might rub someone the wrong way, especially if it puts a finger on some sin issue that might offend.

The Church–Her Internal Resources

Any wise project developer takes the time to assess the resources at his disposal. The church is wise to do the same in each local congregation. Such resources can be categorized into three areas:

1) Spiritual Gifts

Wise is the church that periodically preaches on the spiritual gifts of the believer in an effort to assist the flock in determining their various places of service within the local church body and in the world around them. Every born again child of God is spiritually gifted in at least one area, some in more than one. Church leaders do well to share with congregations how they can assess their spiritual giftedness by means of direct *Bible* teaching as well as by a variety of spiritual gift inventories that are on the market and are quite accurate in their questionnaires. Interestingly enough, all the spiritual gifts left for the church after the apostolic age are needed in the church and in the world around us today.

Following is a summary of such wonderful enablements given to the body of Christ, which include:

Gifted Leaders *(Ephesians 4:11,12)*

Evangelists. We hear little about local evangelists in church circles today. What we do hear pertains to certain geographical regions where in the Bible Belt of the South churches have evangelistic meetings, revivals, and even a few staff evangelists. Larger churches have a minister of evangelism as part of the pastoral team. Although "times have changed," the need for church evangelists has not changed; to be sure, it is a greater need than ever before. Are there those in our churches with a heart for reaching the lost with the message of salvation? Equip them!

Pastors/teachers. There is no greater calling in life than to be called of God as a minister of the Gospel of Jesus Christ to a local body of believers. Pastors are to be teachers of the Word of God, able to apply doctrine as well as working to protect, nurture, comfort and feed the flock under his care. More churches are losing pastors today than there are men finishing theological training to replace the exodus. This must change. The church must assist young men who sense God's calling on their lives to pursue the ministry.

Teachers. Teachers are not always pastors, but simply teachers. Perhaps they are not gifted in evangelism or pulpit skills or comfortable with pastoral care, but they can teach. They study the *Word of God*, write books, teach seminars, and work in making the foundation of true *Bible* doctrine the core of a church body. Who are the intellectual scholars in our churches? Who are those with whom study and academics seems to just "click"? Encourage them to pursue teaching.

Prophecy. *(1 Corinthians 12:10)* Today's gift of prophecy has to do with the proclamation of the *Word of God*. Church history is full of stories of great proclaimers of Jesus Christ, and we are blessed with many of the same "prophets" today.

Knowledge. *(1 Corinthians 12:8)* Individuals who are able to look at the *Scriptures* and make observations based on the facts before them and make sound conclusions from those observable facts are those with the gift of knowledge.

Wisdom. *(1 Corinthians 12:8)* Wisdom differs from knowledge in that knowledge allows one to gather information from observable facts, while wisdom enables one to take the facts and make skillful application for daily life. Pastors, teachers, counselors, laity, anyone who is able to take the *Word of God* and draw applicable conclusions for life here and now, all share the gift of wisdom.

Prophecy, knowledge, wisdom–these gifts are still in use today. They have not ceased when the Canon of Scripture was closed after John wrote

Revelation. Prophecy still exists because there are still many who proclaim the Word of God. Knowledge exists because there are still many who are biblical scholars in seminaries and Bible colleges across the world. Wisdom still exists because we are still in contact with many who take the truth and apply it to daily life.

Gifts of Men

Leadership/Administration. Individuals who are able to see needs and organize goals and objectives as well as being able to mobilize and organize a group of people to reach those goals, objectives, and needs have the gift of leadership/administration. The literal term means "to steer a ship." People in the church with this gift are able to make determined decisions for the good of the whole church body. We would suggest that pastors normally have this gift, and that elders should be gifted in this area according to *1 Timothy 5:17*. Yet we dare not limit leadership to those who hold biblical offices. Leadership must exist at all levels of the laity in the church properly to organize and mobilize the body of believers to carry out the work of the ministry in their midst and in their communities and around the world.

Serving. *1 Corinthians 12:28* translates the word for serving as "helps." It is a little word, but a powerful one, for it implies the gift of being a support, a helper. In *Romans 12:7* it is translated "ministry." Literally it implies being able to take a burden off someone else and place it on yourself. This is the complimentary gift of leadership. We would suggest this includes a sort of inner church "middle management" role. The leadership gifted individuals lead and the servers help carry out the plan alongside the leaders. People with the gift of serving carry out their ministry in a variety of conceivable ways. It has been said by many scholars that serving or helping is the most needed and thus the most common gift. We need helpers and servers for without these gifted members of the church we cannot accomplish anything! Not all are called to teach or preach or sing but there are many who can take meals to those who are sick or shut in, or help clean the church and grounds, or take occupational skills such as in the medical, financial, mechanical fields and be of assistance to others all around them. Demonstrating hospitality toward others is a wonderful means of sharing the gift of serving. Helpers and servers are those who can use their incredible gift most anywhere.

Giving. There is a clear distinction between the obligation of believers and the spiritual gift of giving. It is thus: every individual who claims the Name of Jesus Christ as Savior is obligated by virtue of that relationship and motivated by loving obedience regularly to support the financial needs of the local church. We believe this must take place on a regular basis according to *1 Corinthians 16:2*. It is unfair, albeit unbiblical, for some in the body of

Christ to think that, because there may be others having occupations with larger incomes, that those individuals should be burdened with the responsibility of regular giving to the church and her ministries. Every child of God must give. The motive should be out of gratitude for God giving us so much by the sacrificial death of His Son, the Lord Jesus; we are expected to obey and to give. The amount of giving is not so important as the pattern of giving which must be regular, cheerful, and proportionate as God has prospered each of His children. The spiritual gift of giving implies from the text found in *Romans 12:8* that those who have this gift exercise it with liberality. The Greek construction means to "super give." It means that there are some whom God chooses to bless with a sort of "Midas touch" who are to go beyond the normal when it comes to their financial giving, because they are gifted in this way. Motivation plays a part in this spiritual gift. The term "liberality" in the above Romans verse indicates a simplistic giving, one with a single motive, sacrificial giving. If there is a need we are to give. Most give with a motive to meet the need as well as to be sure there is enough left over for themselves. Those who are to be "super givers" give with only one single motive–the need. Nothing else enters their thinking. Not once is the issue of gratitude or pride found in the motivation of a "super giver." Often they are to give secretly, so that the left hand has no idea what the right is doing.

Old Testamental biblical tradition tells of an area within the temple in Jerusalem known as "the Chamber of the Secret." This area was visited twice daily by two different groups of people. Earlier in the day, worshipers at the temple could enter the "chamber" by means of a single door leading from within the temple yard. Inside the "chamber" was a closed door which led outside the temple walls. Worshipers could leave various articles of food, clothing, and money to be used for those who were destitute, impoverished, widows and orphans. Later in the day, the inner door from within the temple yard was sealed, and the outer door leading from outside the temple walls was opened, allowing only those needy individuals to enter and take what articles they could use. Neither group, the givers nor the receivers, saw what one group gave or another group took. Thus the name, "the Chamber of the Secret."

"Super givers" are to give secretly, not for public exhibition which is hypocritical and, biblically speaking, merits no heavenly reward for its hypocrisy. And to be honest, the gift of giving may not relate to the amount an individual has to give, although one must have something to give. Some who have little give away all they have. Some who have much don't have the gift, while others who have much do have the gift. The bottom line of being a "super giver" is in having a desire to give when a need arises.

Mercy. There is little difference between what this spiritual gift is and how it operates in the body of Christ, the church. In *Romans 12:8*, literally mercy translates "pity" or "compassion." Mercy applies toward those who are in misery due to their situation. There is an emphasis toward heart compassion for those who suffer, enabling one to be sympathetic toward others, and thus to come alongside those who are poor, sick, orphaned, widowed, destitute. Often "super givers" are also gifted with mercy, yet even by itself, mercy is used without giving anything except our hearts. It is characteristic of God Himself; about this David wrote of God:

> The Lord is merciful and gracious, slow to anger and plenteous in mercy....So great is His mercy toward them that fear Him....As a father pities his children so the Lord pities them that fear Him. *(Psalm 103:8,11,13)*

Faith. The gift of faith is the ability to see what is beyond the visible, to view obstacles as challenges. *1 Corinthians 12:9* lists the gift of faith for us, implying it is an intense ability to trust God in unusual circumstances. People with the gift of faith are prayer warriors in the church. When we have a need, we desire these warriors are made aware because they have faith that seemingly activates the power of God on our behalf. People with faith give us assurance, support, and encouragement that God is still God.

Discernment. The literal translation means "to see something thoroughly, to judge clearly, to see through to the truth."*1 Corinthians 12:10* translates this the "distinguishing of spirits." Christians with this gift serve as the "watch dogs" of the local church, being spiritually enabled to point the finger at false teaching and heresy and error invading the body of Christ.

Exhortation. Exhortation as found in *Romans 12:8* comes from the Greek term for "comforter," meaning one who comforts, advises, strengthens another. It is the ability to come along side someone who had deep spiritual need and strengthen/encourage them. When we attempt to aid someone with a problem, a burden, and build them up by means of encouragement and strengthening and comforting we help bear the load and fulfill the law of Jesus Christ.

2) A Solid Foundation

The author of the following traditional hymn knew about the importance of solid foundations, and penned the following familiar lines:

> How firm a foundation ye saints of the Lord,
> Is laid for your faith, in His excellent Word!

The foundation of *the Word of God, the Bible, the Scriptures* is essentially our greatest resource in the church's effort to assist homes and schools in returning America to her moral underpinnings. As mentioned before, this generation is tired of serving and searching for false gods. Our society is fed up with religious placebos and conscience salves. People desire truth, something that can be taken as an absolute for living life today. The only absolute truth is that which is contained in the Bible. There we find the truth about the One Who alone is the Way, the Truth and the Life, apart from Whom (Jesus) no one comes to the Father in heaven. *(John 14:6)*

What must churches and church leaders do to utilize this incredible resource?

Local churches and church leaders who are committed to a return to our godly heritage must, in a united effort of both clergy and laity, return the church to "spiritual boot camp." Each generation in the local church must see the importance of understanding *the Bible* and what it says about God–Who He is, how He loves us, what His will is for our lives. This process involves a total commitment of each individual believer in growing toward a daily personal relationship with Jesus Christ. It means living in obedience to *God's Word* in precept as well as in principle, and doing so out of loving desire to please God, not for fear of what consequences disobedience will bring.

In any given congregation there is a group we will call the "core" who do ninety percent of the work, and usually make up about ten percent of the congregation. This core group must be increased in order for a return to the basics to be successful. Strength is found in numbers, as well as excitement, encouragement, and a sharing of the load of ministry inside and outside the church.

A process must be designed whereby there is a determined "separating of the men from the boys." Such was the case in the days of Gideon, when God chose only three hundred men to defeat the enemies of Israel under Gideon's leadership. *(Joshua 7:1-22)* Who are those individuals–men, women, young people–who desire to follow after the things of Jesus Christ? A process must be in place to assist church leadership in growing the core group. It can begin in the following areas:

Church Membership

Some scholar has written,"The meaninglessness of church membership is a widespread and disheartening reality....At the core of the problem was the customary procedure of adding new members without the slightest bit of real challenge to commitment."

Another has rightfully argued that,
The refusal to grapple with the issue of entrance into the Christian church is not toleration; it is betrayal of the gospel which we preach....A surrender to Christ is a surrender to His people--total involvement in the life of the church. Candidates must explore their faith seriously. The church's

What the Church Must Do

determination to make membership genuine--even difficult--rather than nominal, is shocking and even resented by Christians of a softer inclination. Commitment in a community environment means participants can no longer commit themselves to the Lord in the abstract. Nor can they commit themselves to one another on a superficial plane. Community always tests the integrity of commitment.

It is God's will that every believer be a meaningfully related, faithful, serving and accountable part of a visible body of believers under the pastoral oversight of elders. Take a moment carefully to examine the following *Scriptural* passages:

1 Peter 5:2-4 Shepherd the flock of God among you, exercising oversight not under compulsion, but voluntarily, according to *the will of* God; and not for sordid gain, but with eagerness; nor yet as lording it over those allotted to your charge, but proving to be examples to the flock. And when the Chief Shepherd appears, you will receive the unfading crown of glory.

Hebrews 13:17 Obey your leaders, and submit *to them*; for they keep watch over your souls, as those who will give an account. Let them do this with joy and not with grief, for this would be unprofitable for you.

Membership is a means for defining one's commitment.

Ephesians 4:1-16 I therefore, the prisoner of the Lord, entreat you to walk in a manner worthy of the calling with which you have been called, with all humility and gentleness, with patience, showing forbearance to one another in love, being diligent to preserve the unity of the Spirit in the bond of peace. There is one body and one Spirit, just as also you were called in one hope of your calling; one Lord, one faith, one baptism, one God and Father of all who is over all and through all and in all. But to each one of us grace was given according to the measure of Christ's gift. Therefore it says,
"WHEN HE ASCENDED ON HIGH,
HE LED CAPTIVE A HOST OF CAPTIVES,
AND HE GAVE GIFTS TO MEN."
(Now this *expression,* "He ascended," what does it mean except that He also had descended into the lower parts of the earth? He who descended is Himself also He who ascended far above all the heavens, that He might fill all things.) And He gave some *as* apostles, and some *as* prophets, and some *as* evangelists, and some *as* pastors and teachers, for the equipping of the saints for the work of service, to the building up of the body of Christ; until we all attain to the unity of the faith, and of the knowledge of the Son of God, to a mature man, to the measure of the stature which belongs to the fulness of Christ. As a result, we are no longer to be children, tossed here and there by waves, and carried about by every wind of doctrine, by the trickery of men, by craftiness

in deceitful scheming; but speaking the truth in love, we are to grow up in all *aspects* into Him, who is the head, *even* Christ, from whom the whole body, being fitted and held together by that which every joint supplies, according to the proper working of each individual part, causes the growth of the body for the building up of itself in love.

Hebrews 10:23-25. Let us hold fast the confession of our hope without wavering, for He who promised is faithful; and let us consider how to stimulate one another to love and good deeds, not forsaking our own assembling together, as is the habit of some, but encouraging *one another*; and all the more, as you see the day drawing near.

1 Peter 4:10-11. As each one has received a *special* gift, employ it in serving one another, as good stewards of the manifold grace of God. Whoever speaks, *let him speak*, as it were, the utterances of God; whoever serves, *let him do so* as by the strength which God supplies; so that in all things God may be glorified through Jesus Christ, to whom belongs the glory and dominion forever and ever. Amen.

In our understanding of salvation, we must be careful not to separate justification from sanctification. By the same token, in our understanding of Christian growth, we must be careful not to separate sanctification from the ministry of the local church. Distinguished author Charles Colson has written,

> There is today a widespread belief that one can be a Christian or develop one's own faith system apart from the church. The proposition is ludicrous. For everyone regenerated by God is by definition a part of the universal church. It's not a matter of choice or membership. And following the pattern made normative in the book of *Acts*, each believer is to make his or her confession, be baptized, and become part of a local congregation with all of the accountability that implies. So membership in a church particular is no more optional than membership in the church universal.
>
> From the beginning it was clearly God's plan that the body would be made manifest to the world by gathering into confession communities to fulfill His mission--that is, to administer the ordinances, preach the *Word*, and make disciples. Thus, immediately after Pentecost, He established the pattern: Individual believers were to gather into particular communities."... "...Membership in a confessing body is fundamental to the faithful Christian life. Failure to do so defies the explicit warning not to forsake the assembling together."... "...When someone is converted and thereby comes into the church universal,

the first step of discipleship is membership in the church particular. It is the duty of those who are involved with new converts to guide them not just into a *Bible* study or fellowship group but into a local church where the *Word* is taught....(*The Body*, Chuck Colson; Copyright ©1992, Word Publications, Waco, TX.)

And pastors must teach biblical truths in a truly relevant manner. The message being given from the sacred desk each Lord's Day must of course originate from the Bible; however, it must also be practical, speaking to the needs of society. Certainly the need of a Savior is crucial. Every opportunity should be taken to share an invitation for others to enter into a personal relationship with Jesus Christ. Yet the messages from the pulpit must penetrate real life issues. Church leaders should not feign away from teaching about sexuality as God designed it to be enjoyed. Sermon series on the family, evolution and creation, the New Age Movement and other cultic groups, worldliness invading the home and the church, how to guard your heart from the poisons of humanism, narcissism, hedonism should be planned and carefully delivered. Young people should be taught how to defend their faith as well as how to present their faith from a logical standpoint in an effort to impact their peer groups. Efforts should be made to promote positive peer pressure from Christian youth as they rub shoulders with other young people their age who are outside of church life. What does *the Bible* teach about marriage and divorce? What about the plethora of ethical issues such as euthanasia, biogenetic research, cloning, war, capital punishment? The needs are endless and the opportunities abound to make *the Word of God* truth for today.

Church Doctrine

The local church must have a doctrinal statement in its constitution for the following reasons:
> *Because the writers of the New Testament themselves gave the example of simple doctrinal summaries.*

An example would be found in *Acts 2:2:*
> And suddenly there came from heaven a noise like a violent, rushing wind, and it filled the whole house where they were sitting.

And again in *Acts 8:32-38:*

> Now the passage of Scripture which he was reading was this:
>
> HE WAS LED AS A SHEEP TO SLAUGHTER;
> AND AS A LAMB BEFORE ITS SHEARER IS SILENT,
> SO HE DOES NOT OPEN HIS MOUTH.
> IN HUMILIATION HIS JUDGMENT WAS TAKEN AWAY;

WHO SHALL RELATE HIS GENERATION?
FOR HIS LIFE IS REMOVED FROM THE EARTH.
And the eunuch answered Philip and said, "Please *tell me*, of whom does the prophet say this? Of himself, or of someone else?" And Philip opened his mouth, and beginning from this Scripture he preached Jesus to him. And as they went along the road they came to some water; and the eunuch said, "Look! Water! What prevents me from being baptized?" And Philip said, "If you believe with all your heart, you may." And he answered and said, "I believe that Jesus Christ is the Son of God." And he ordered the chariot to stop; and they both went down into the water, Philip as well as the eunuch; and he baptized him.

Examples are continued in the following passages:

1 Corinthians 2:1-2. And when I came to you, brethren, I did not come with superiority of speech or of wisdom, proclaiming to you the testimony of God. For I determined to know nothing among you except Jesus Christ, and Him crucified.

1 Corinthians 15:1-5. Now I make known to you, brethren, the gospel which I preached to you, which also you received, in which also you stand, by which also you are saved, if you hold fast the word which I preached to you, unless you believed in vain. For I delivered to you as of first importance what I also received, that Christ died for our sins according to the Scriptures, and that He was buried, and that He was raised on the third day according to the Scriptures, and that He appeared to Cephas, then to the twelve.

Philippians 2:6-11 ...Who, although He existed in the form of God, did not regard equality with God a thing to be grasped, but emptied Himself, taking the form of a bond-servant, *and* being made in the likeness of men. And being found in appearance as a man, He humbled Himself by becoming obedient to the point of death, even death on a cross. Therefore also God highly exalted Him, and bestowed on Him the name which is above every name, that at the name of Jesus EVERY KNEE SHOULD BOW, of those who are in heaven, and on earth, and under the earth, and that every tongue should confess that Jesus Christ is Lord, to the glory of God the Father.

1 Timothy 3:15-17. But in case I am delayed, *I write* so that you may know how one ought to conduct himself in the household of God, which is the church of the living God, the pillar and support of the truth. And by common confession great is the mystery of godliness:

> He who was revealed in the flesh,
> Was vindicated in the Spirit,
> Beheld by angels,

Proclaimed among the nations,
Believed on in the world,
Taken up in glory.

Hebrews 5:11-6:2. Concerning him we have much to say, and *it is* hard to explain, since you have become dull of hearing. For though by this time you ought to be teachers, you have need again for someone to teach you the elementary principles of the oracles of God, and you have come to need milk and not solid food. For everyone who partakes *only* of milk is not accustomed to the word of righteousness, for he is a babe. But solid food is for the mature, who because of practice have their senses trained to discern good and evil. Therefore, leaving the elementary teaching about the Christ, let us press on to maturity, not laying again a foundation of repentance from dead works and of faith toward God, of instruction about washings and laying on of hands and the resurrection of the dead, and eternal judgment.

1 Peter 2:2. Like newborn babes, long for the pure milk of the word, that by it you may grow in respect to salvation.

1 John 2:13. I am writing to you, fathers, because you know Him who has been from the beginning. I am writing to you, young men, because you have overcome the evil one. I have written to you, children, because you know the Father.

1 John 4:2. By this you know the Spirit of God: every spirit that confesses that Jesus Christ has come in the flesh is from God.

Because the apostles referred to a "Body of Truth" that could be identified, believed, retained and defended.

The examples from Scripture continue:

2 Thessalonians 2:15. So then, brethren, stand firm and hold to the traditions which you were taught, whether by word *of mouth* or by letter from us.

Romans 6:17. But thanks be to God that though you were slaves of sin, you became obedient from the heart to that form of teaching to which you were committed.

2 Timothy 1:13-14. Retain the standard of sound words which you have heard from me, in the faith and love which are in Christ Jesus. Guard, through the Holy Spirit who dwells in us, the treasure which has been entrusted to *you*.

Every local church needs people who are committed toward carrying out its mission to the world locally and globally. Membership is nothing less than a Christian's public commitment to growth and service in a local fellowship of believers. The Scriptures are very clear that wherever a Christian lives, he is to be involved in the Lord's work, including active participation in a local church ministry. (He.10:23-25)

It is worth taking a moment to think through the biblical basis for local church membership and the requirements candidates for membership should fulfill. By clearly defining this membership process, the core group will be more likely to increase its numbers and ability to serve one another.

The Biblical Basis for Membership Rolls

The Scriptures neither explicitly require nor preclude a membership list. In fact, the New Testament does not teach any more about the need for this than it does about Sunday School, instruments to use in worship services or how to take the offering. However, biblical precedents and analogies for the local church form a sound basis for the legitimacy and usefulness of a membership roll. Note the following passages and their implications:

Acts 2:4. It indicates the Lord added to the Church those who were saved. The Jerusalem church leadership must have had some form of record keeping since definite numbers of new believers were registered.

1 Timothy 5:9. This verse gives reference to a list of widows to be financially assisted by the church. If there was a list of widows, we may deduce there were also lists of members in good standing.

1 Corinthians 5:2. Here it mentions excommunication is required for a disobedient professing believer who refused to respond to correction after church discipline had been lovingly applied. Without a membership roll it may have been difficult to implement this process. Membership crystallizes a believer's spiritual accountability to a local body of believers.

1 Corinthians 14:33,40. Here emphasis is found for the need for peace, order and propriety in the life of the church, not confusion. A membership list helps maintain order and clarity.

Suggested Requirements for Membership in a local church

Public profession of salvation before the church family.

It is essential that membership rolls be comprised of truly born-again people, as explained in *the Word of God*. Those seeking membership should be strongly encouraged to follow the Lord's example of obedience in the ordinance of believer's water baptism. In most cases, baptism should follow the literal interpretation of the term indicating baptism by immersion.

Commitment to spiritual growth according to the Scriptures.

Members desire to cultivate their relationship with their Lord and with other believers through *Bible* study, prayer, participation in the church's worship services and obedience to *God's Word* through the empowerment of the indwelling Holy Spirit.

Willingness to serve in the local church.

Members understand their biblical responsibility joyfully to serve one another. The church leadership is committed to helping every member find avenues of service in which he may use his God-given gifts.

Support of the church's doctrinal position.

Candidates for membership receive orientation designed to familiarize them with the Church Statement of Faith. Every member should understand the church's doctrinal position and be in agreement with its general principles. If differences of conviction based on *Scripture* develop after membership is formalized, members are expected to work with the church leadership toward agreement in harmony with the *Scriptures* and the church constitution.

Membership orientation

On some sort of regular basis a seminar should be offered for those wishing to become members. The class may cover a variety of topics, some of which are as follows:

1) Who is the church? (Definition)

2) Why are we here ? (Purpose)

3) How does membership benefit me?

4) Are there requirements for membership?

5) Are there responsibilities of membership?

6) Where does this church intend to go?

7) What is the structure of the church?

8) Where can members be involved in ministry?

As a requirement for membership, individuals should attend a membership seminar. People unwilling to commit to this process most likely will not fulfill those membership responsibilities after joining and should not be allowed to join.

Suggested Outline for a Membership Class

I. Our Salvation

  A. How to know for sure you are a Christian

  B. The symbols of salvation

    1. Baptism

    2. Communion

II. Our Passion as a Church

  A. The reason we exist

  B. The intention of our ministries

  C. What we believe–our doctrinal statement

  D. The values we practice

III. Our Methodology

  A. History of (name of the local church)

  B. Outreach

  C. Development of the Christian Growth

  D. How it is accomplished

IV. Our Structure

  A. How we will grow

  B. Our affiliation

  C. The importance of church membership

V. The Quiz

Responsibilities and Privileges of Members

Members have the opportunity to participate in decisions affecting the life of the church by voting at all congregational meetings. In addition, church leadership positions are open to members expressing an interest and who meet the qualifications for those positions, as well as demonstrating a spiritual commitment to fulfill those ministries. The pastor and church officers will

What the Church Must Do

seek consistently to encourage and train members for spiritual leadership in as many areas of church life as possible.

Suggested Membership Covenant

"Having received Christ as my Lord and Savior and been baptized, and being in agreement with (Name of) Church's statements, strategy, and structure, I now feel led by the Holy Spirit to unite with the church family. In doing so, I commit myself to God and to the other members to do the following:

1) I will protect the unity of my church

...by acting in love toward other members

...by refusing to gossip

...by following the leaders

Romans 14:19; 1 Peter 1:22; Ephesians 4:29; Hebrews 13:17

2) I will share the responsibility of my church

...by praying for its growth

...by inviting the unchurched to attend

...by warmly welcoming those who visit

1 Thessalonians 1:1-2; Luke 14:23; Romans 15:7

3) I will serve the ministry of my church
...by discovering my gifts and talents

..by being equipped to serve by my pastor

...by developing a servant's heart

1 Peter 4:10; Ephesians 4:11-12; Philippians 2:3-4,7

4) I will support the testimony of my church

...by attending faithfully

...by living a godly life

...by giving regularly of my finances

Hebrews 10:25; Philippians 1:27; 1 Corinthians 16:2

Signed:_____ Date:_____"

(taken from the book, *"The Purpose Driven Church"* by Pastor Rick Warren, Copyright ©1995 Zondervan Publishing House, Grand Rapids, Michigan; p.321. Used by permission)

Church Discipline

Church discipline is as much the function of a local church as the preaching of the pure doctrine of the Gospel. Discipline in the church is not optional but mandatory--it is an absolute necessity if we are to be obedient to *the Scriptures. Matthew 18:15-20* and *1 Corinthians 5:1-5* clearly proclaim this necessity. We are told in *1 Thessalonians 5:14* that the church is required to warn those who are disobedient. *2 Thessalonians 3:6-15* suggests warning and if necessary, withdrawing from a brother. *Titus 3:10* commands the members of the church to withdraw from one who causes division. *1 Timothy 5:20* advises the public rebuke of those who persistently sin. Given these commands it is unequivocal that church discipline is not an option.

The Purpose of Church Discipline.

The New Testament gives three purposes for church discipline: to restore and reconcile the sinner (Mt.18:15; 2 Co.2:5-8); to maintain purity(1 Co.5:6,7); and to serve as a deterrent from sin (1 Tim.5:20). Reconciliation with the local assembly is not warranted until there is a turning of the heart of the one disciplined. (2 Thes.3:14) This discipline is not to humiliate or shame the offender but to encourage the individual to repent and be reconciled. Paul warned the Corinthians that the "leaven" in their midst would permeate the entire "lump" unless they "remove the wicked man" (First Corinthians 5:6,7,13). Church discipline is to maintain purity in the local church. Paul instructed the elders in Ephesus to rebuke in the presence of all those who continued in sin so that the rest may be fearful (1Tim.5:20). Deterrence from sin is another purpose for church discipline. In summary, the Bible does not advocate that only the sinless can be members of the Christian church, rather the Bible addresses those who persist in the very sinful activities from which they have been freed through the sacrifice of Christ on the cross. Given the general and specific causes of church discipline, *the Scriptures* teach that church discipline is up to the local church. The local church is apparently given latitude to decide when discipline is necessary based on the Scriptures.

Individuals involved in the process of church discipline who refuse to terminate their membership should be subject to open rebuke before the congregation as long as they remain a member. Upon open rebuke before the congregation, if individuals still refuse to repent of their sin, their membership should be terminated by the church board and they will be excommunicated from the fellowship. If it becomes necessary for the church to break fellowship with the member under discipline certain principles should be kept in mind. Breaking fellowship does *not* involve alienation of the affection and relationship of those within the immediate family of the disciplined member. The spouse and children should not be encouraged to break all association with a spouse or parent under discipline. Any contractual obligations between the disciplined member and other members of the church must be honored. Individuals under discipline should not be forced to stay away from the regular meetings of the church. Since *Scripture* teaches that they should be treated as an unsaved person, certainly they should be invited to sit under the teaching of *the Word of God* as any unsaved guest or visitor would be welcome to do. Unrepentant members under discipline should be treated as unbelievers because they are not walking as believers. It means to keep loving as Jesus loved publicans and sinners. It means to reach out to them in witness but not to relate to them as a member of the body of Christ.

The attitude of the church membership is crucial in carrying out this most serious step in discipline. Excommunication must be motivated by love and exercised in such a way as to encourage the possibility of genuine repentance and restoration. Members of the church should be encouraged to make contact with the sinning member and plead lovingly for them to repent and be restored to the fellowship.

When church discipline leads to genuine repentance, often the tendency is to keep the repentant offender at a distance. Full restoration to joyful fellowship is often denied. The Apostle Paul wrote in *2 Corinthians 2:7,8* that a believer's responsibility toward a repentant sinning brother is three fold: forgive, comfort, and reaffirm love. To help assure that spiritual healing results from church discipline, the offender should be told of the church's forgiveness, encouraged in his or her Christian life and growth, and shown tangible evidence of God's love. To neglect this step after repentance is to create an opportunity for Satan to create bitterness discord and dissension in the church.

Church discipline has certain risks. Yet Christ did not give the church authority to ignore sin. Buy following biblical procedures and administering discipline out of love and with a view toward restoration, the church can have a clear conscience before God and continue to receive His blessing. If we truly mean business about building up the core, the committed, we must not shy away from the biblical mandate of church discipline.

3) Evaluating our Geographical Resources

The final resource at the disposal of the local church includes the collection of individuals, items, places and opportunities that are close at hand in the communities where we live and the people with whom we inteact. What individuals make up the local congregation? What talents, skills, hobbies and abilities as well as interests are to be found within the church body? Efforts must be made to channel that information toward fitting members of the body of Christ with opportunities for serving one another. Another consideration includes the geographical, cultural, industrial and professional scenario of the immediate community. Local churches must network their area resources in an effort to more efficiently bring the church into the playing field of society where people live and move and have their being. Churches should investigate what careers and vocations are found in their towns, cities and municipalities. Are there local groups to become involved with in a greater effort to impact the immediate community for the cause of Christ? What about the local Lions club or school board or PTO? Are there uncompromising opportunities to be involved in local clubs and seasonal celebrations? People gifted in these areas should be focused toward impacting their surrounding neighborhoods. More and more there is a focus within youth groups to vacate the comfort zone of the church *Bible* lesson and monthly fun time in order to impact the world outside the church; however this is not yet the norm in fundamental evangelical circles. Why not get youth involved in community projects? How about organizing a family impact event such as whole families being involved in serving holiday meals at the homeless shelter? The opportunities are endless for offering, as it were, a cup of cold water to someone in need.

Support groups should be investigated and formed for various people groups: parents of infants and toddlers, those raising adolescents, those experiencing empty nest syndrome. Groups are needed to help with divorce recovery, sudden death of a spouse or child, and for those dealing with terminal illness. If these groups are established, and in doing so, the church maintains its primary message: teaching the *Bible* and Salvation through Jesus Christ, the impact may well spread like wildfire. People will see the church striving to meet real genuine needs. Many will come and bring their children. Over time membership will increase and the impact will be felt for generations.

Church leaders must encourage their people to interact with those outside of the church if we are ever to encourage their coming inside the church. How else will the world around us see what we are about, unless we leave our "hot house for Son-followers" and return to our original purpose of being a "hospital for sinners"? Wise church leaders have always said, "People will not care how much you know until they know how much you care." Our care toward others is demonstrated by getting personally involved in their lives, entering into their own worlds, living as salt and light in a decadent, dark society in search of answers, looking for hope for life today and eternity tomorrow.

What Can We Expect?

We have shared three resources the church has at its disposal which, if fully utilized, investigated, and carried out, can equip the church as a partner with the forces of the home and the schools to return our nation to its moral foundations. Spiritual giftedness, once it is understood and once believers are equipped in a thorough knowledge of their own gifts, will transform the church body from a group of observers to a troop ready for spiritual ministry. The pure and unashamed teaching of Bible doctrine will provide fresh soil so the roots of our faith can grow deep and remain secure. Taking opportunity to inventory our surroundings will expose delightful and challenging avenues for service and outreach into the lives of the unchurched who are hurting and needing the love of Jesus Christ.

Yet what we can immediately count on is a period within the church of escalation before de-escalation. In other words, change is not something the church likes very much. Often we repeat tongue-in-cheek what has been labeled as the seven last words of the church" which are, "We've never done it this way before." Changes made to assist folks in the body of Christ toward spiritual maturity are quite similar to growing pains in the physical body. And with the nature of people being what it is, change is not an easy thing, often a very resisted event in the life of a local congregation.

We should not fear change, for it can be good. Change is imperative if the church is to survive as salt and light in the world today. Church life must be lived differently than it was ten, even twenty years ago. Experts tell us that our social culture changes every four to five years. Should not the church be willing to modify its approach to doing ministry in such a manner as more effectively to impact its intended audience?

As stated before, the message never changes. It cannot, for it is Jesus Christ, the same, yesterday, today and forever! Yet the method must change with each new generation as we attempt to be used of God to reach others for Christ in this era entering the next millennium. We dare not change to the point of compromise. That would defeat the purpose. We assert that if the church utilizes the three resources of spiritual giftedness, Bible doctrine and local resources, doing so in a manner that impacts the very life blood of the church body individual by individual, the dangers of compromise may be altogether eliminated. The focus will be on others rather than self.

We must add this final note of warning. It is nothing new to the reader, yet a fitting reminder for all who claim the Name of Jesus Christ. It is this: Behold, He comes quickly! The return of Jesus Christ for His church is still an imminent event. Time's hour glass is running out, and countless millions are still without the Savior. The church must regather herself, counting the cost, and press forward toward the mark of the high calling of God in Christ Jesus. We must echo the voice of missionary martyr Jim Elliot when he wrote,

"He is no fool who give up what he cannot keep to gain what he cannot lose."

The simple, humble truth remains the same for each of God's children. We agree with the principles and practices of outreach being perfected into new bolder better opportunities to maintain the message of hope in Christ. Yet the church leadership cannot effect this task. Nor can the person who sits next to us each Lord's day morning. The truth is that revival begins with each individual first. It must begin with "me" before it can ever penetrate the life of another. If individuals fail to catch the vision and see the need and count the costs of discipleship for the sake of America's soul, we are, as the apostle Paul said in his letter to the Corinthians, "of all men most to be pitied."

Let us then with a renewed sense of purpose and vision surrender to the leading of God's Holy Spirit. May we submit to the Master's plan as clay in the hands of the potter. And as our lives are transformed individually, may we join together collectively as the renewed army of Jesus Christ, ready to be salt and light in the world around us lost, dying, without hope, and needing a Savior.

A PERSONAL NOTE TO THE READER

It has been our purpose in this literary effort to demonstrate that there is hope for America. We firmly believe that, should the principles shared in these pages be taken to heart by each individual reader, the fires of revival will spread in our land. By the cooperative efforts of home, schools and church, America's sunset can become a sunrise of renewal and hope for today and for eternity.

You, the reader, may not fully agree with what we have presented in these pages as viable opportunities for change and renewal in our country. You are entirely right to holding your own opinion. Quite frankly, you may think we are wrong entirely.

Yet, what if we are entirely right? Where does this leave you, the reader?

Perhaps you have seen yourself portrayed in the various scenarios of the book. Perhaps that portrayal has made you uncomfortable. It may have even left you with a bitter taste, wanting to challenge various statements, yet realizing in all honesty that we are correct in our presentation. Now you are confronted with a choice: agree with what we have shared and explore how you can be involved in the renewal process, or turn away from our efforts while you continue to cling to false hopes and dreams that drift like clouds without rain.

We would ask you to consider one very crucial message which we have tried carefully to weave throughout this book. It is the message of love. What the world needs is true love, a love that is sacrificial and not self-serving. Our world needs a love that looks beyond self-preservation toward the needs of others all around us. We need a love that bears the message of hope, eternal hope.

That message is found in *the Bible, the Word of God*, where we are told about a wonderful place called Heaven. It is the place where God dwells, and from where love, real love, originates.

The following fable portrays how we might feel if we could see into heaven for an instant: A boy had a sister who was dying. He heard that if he could secure a leaf from the tree of life in heaven, she would be healed. So he approached the gate of glory and made his desire known to an angel. The celestial being suggested to the boy that even if his sister would be healed he could not guarantee she would never again be sick, suffer disappointment, or go through trials. Just then the angel deliberately opened the gate a little wider so the youngster could see inside. He could scarcely believe his eyes! Everything was wonderful and beautiful beyond description. After thinking for a moment, he exclaimed, "Forget the leaf! May I come in with her?"

If you are a child of God--meaning if you have trusted in Christ alone for your salvation the Bible promises that the moment you leave this life you will go to Heaven. To be absent from the body is to be present with the Lord. Everything Scripture says about the death of believers indicates that they are immediately ushered consciously into the Lord's presence. Heaven is where God's people will dwell together with Him eternally, utterly free from all the effects of sin and evil. God personally wipes away all tears from the eyes of His children. In Heaven death is finally conquered. There is no sickness, nor hunger, no trouble, no tragedy, just absolute joy and eternal blessings. It is hard to imagine because we have known nothing but this life with its sin and calamities. In Heaven we will be perfect. Here we know only imperfection. In heaven we lose all traces of human fallenness. We will have souls that are perfectly free from evil forever. We'll never utter a selfish word or have an evil thought. We'll finally be able to do that which is totally righteous and holy and perfect. Can you imagine yourself behaving in such an incredible way? In Heaven there will be no temptation because the world and the flesh and the devil are absent. There will be no persecution or disunity or hatred or disagreements or disappointments. There will be no need to pray or fast or confess sin or repent because there will be nothing to pray for or confess. No weeping there because there's nothing to make us sad. We will experience perfect pleasure, perfect comfort, perfect knowledge, and perfect love.

But Heaven isn't just a state of mind. It is a real place. I would like to have you imagine eternity. It is a dawn that never fades! How thankful we can be to have hope beyond the grave and into the Father's waiting arms. It is a simple message to understand for young and old alike. It is the message of love. If you by faith have received Jesus Christ as your personal Savior from sin you are eternally saved. If you don't know Him personally, you are eternally lost. Salvation is a gift that can be yours free for the taking. The decision to receive God's gift of everlasting life is the most important one you will ever make. Today that is still true.

A personal walk with Christ can be yours if you agree with the fact that you are a sinner, you need a Savior, you cannot save yourself, and you need what Jesus Christ alone offers freely as a gift to you. If that is true, we invite you to pray the following prayer as your own personal prayer to receive the salvation God desires to give to you:

A Personal Note to the Reader

Dear God, I need You, not just for today or for when things get out of my own control, but every moment of my life I realize something is missing. I've tried other things, and the emptiness and unsettled feeling remains. I know I am a sinner. I admit I can do nothing to rid myself of sin. And I by faith believe that You loved not only the world, but me individually so much that You gave the very best You had–Your own Son Jesus to be the solution to my sin. I by faith believe that His death on the cross paid the price for my sin. Right now I receive that payment as my own, and I ask Christ to be my own personal Savior. Please God, come into my life, and make me Your own child. I pray these things in the Name of Your only Son, Jesus Christ, Amen.

If this is your heart's desire, and you have prayed this prayer, it would give us tremendous joy to know about your decision to trust Christ as Savior. We encourage you to contact us below, in order that we may share your joy, pray for you, and if you are interested in knowing more about the Christian life as a child of God, we would be glad to send you helpful information to explain the walk of faith.

Dr. Alfred Lindsey

Rev. Mike Deblois

5135 N. 1250 Road

Colchester, Illinois 62326

E-mail: argylemd@netins.net

EPILOGUE

THE DAWN CAN COME AGAIN

It is dark in Key West. In the black, black night after the sun has set, the seekers wait, nervously scanning the somber ebony sky waiting for tomorrow, for yet a new day, for hope. There on the lonely beach, facing east, they wait. No song of birds is heard, no joyful singing voices. Not a sound is heard, save the wind's rustling. It is cold there this January night. Lonely, confused, they huddle together, waiting, and looking--staring into the eastern sky. They are restless, nervous, perplexed. Will tomorrow come? Is there yet hope? Is the dark, dark night to end?

So they group together in the chill of the long night recalling the splendor of the sunset, the magnificent yearning for utter beauty enjoyed just a few hours earlier. But soon it was night, and now they yearn for dawn, for light and hope. It is colder now, and the seekers wait in loneliness and sorrow, even in fear. Will the light come again?

And then:"Look!," shouts the child, "Look! Morning comes!" Jumping to their feet, the seekers sprint toward the ocean, excited, thrilled. There, on the horizon, is the first gleam of sunrise. It is tomorrow. Birds sing; gulls soar toward the light. Pelicans grumpily awake, preen their feathers, and glide out to sea, skimming the water. Excited little sandpipers scurry toward the water, then, as quickly, away. A fishing boat embarks. Now there is a glowing ball on the horizon, rising slowly, then faster. It is bigger and climbing. There is light! On the beach, the seekers cheer. Day has come again. Hope is reborn; there is yet another day.

And the majestic morn, reborn in Key West, can occur in the rest of the dear land. It can transpire if the nation's foundation is repaired, the very foundation cemented by *God's Word* and the *American Creed*. It is not too late.

Abraham Lincoln warned:

It is the duty of nations, as well as men, to confess their sins and transgressions in humble sorrow, yet with assured hope that genuine repentance leads to mercy and pardon, and to recognize the sublime truth announced in the *Holy Scriptures* and proven by all history that these nations only are blessed whose God is the Lord.

And never forget God's promise in *2 Chronicles 7:13-14:*

If I shut up the heavens so that there is no rain, or if I send the locust to devour the land, or if I send pestilence among my people, and my people who are called by My Name humble themselves and pray and seek My face and turn from their wicked ways, then I will hear from heaven will forgive their sin and will heal their land.

Church, home, school, and the reader of this book have the grave responsibility to prepare a godly people to experience this amazing healing, else there is little hope to save this precious land where, for a season, man's spirit soared, where, for a season, the sky was lit bright with hope and freedom. It was the morning of a holy dream. But now it is sunset, and the dark, dark night approaches. The dawn can be called back. It must be, for the dark age of godless humanism, the terrible black, black night, will destroy the beloved land. And all will be dark, darker than the dark dreams of Lucifer.

INDEX

Abortion, 33, 86, 118

American Civil Liberty Union, 110

American Creed Questionnaire, 148, 152, 154, 156, 169, 174, 178, 179

American Creed, the, 76, 79, 194, 214

American Dream, 7, 8, 13, 14, 33, 34, 57, 123

American Tradition, 27

androgyny, 113, 118, 174

Apostle's Creed, 204

baby boomers, 73, 94, 120

Beatitudes, 188-190, 192-194, 198, 214, 219

Bible, the, 8, 16, 231, 247

Bilingual-Bicultural Act, 44

blacks, 44, 48-52, 95, 100, 163

boomers, 73, 94, 120, 218, 222

busters, 218, 222

censorship, 122, 123, 178, 179

Christian faith, 10, 38, 71, 75, 80, 112, 179, 185, 212

Christian schools, 87, 111, 135-137, 184, 185, 202-205

Christianity, 9, 11, 16-18, 20, 35-36, 40-41, 52, 57, 59-63, 66, 70-71, 73, 82, 98, 101, 108, 111-112, 114, 118, 122-123, 127, 147, 160, 189, 197, 203, 243

Church discipline, 242

Church doctrine, 235

Church membership, 232, 238

Civil Rights Movement, 17, 18, 44, 67, 99, 113

communism, 14, 37, 38, 44, 54, 92, 140

Elementary and Secondary Education Act, 67

Environmental Education Act, 65

Headstart, 68

Title I, 67

Title II, 68

Constitution, 25, 31, 41, 60-62, 65, 67, 71, 81, 94, 96, 110, 119, 141, 150, 165, 235, 239

court cases, 66

Abingdon School District v. Schempp, 64

Edwards v. Aquillard, 64

Engel v. Vitale, 64

McCollum v. Board of Education, 64

Pierce v. Society of Sisters, 67

Stone v. Graham, 63

Tinker v. Des Moines, 63

decision-making process, 16, 19, 41, 47, 66, 157, 158, 161, 162, 166, 170, 181, 184

discipline, 19, 61-63, 168, 169, 199, 206, 214, 223, 238, 242, 243

divorce, 13, 23, 81, 120, 199, 201, 223, 225, 235, 244

Doctrine, 17, 18, 41, 66, 119, 131, 136, 173, 208, 218, 227, 228, 233, 235, 242, 245

Drug Abuse Education Act, 68

elite power educators, 187

elites, 14, 26, 28, 46, 59, 60, 83, 85, 103, 107, 109, 113, 116, 117, 119-121, 123, 124, 129, 138, 145, 146, 168,

184

equal opportunity, 49, 50, 97, 100, 139, 152, 172-174

ethnicity, 13, 46, 49-51, 55, 95, 142

evolution, 41, 42, 130, 131, 143, 179, 180, 235

existentialism, 39, 79, 101, 102, 156, 165

experimentalism, 157, 159

feminism, 113, 114, 117, 120, 213

First Amendment, 41, 62, 64-66, 110, 113, 119, 131, 180, 185, 202

Four Cardinal Principles of Hope, 145

Decision-making Process, 157-162

Knowledge of the American Creed, 148-152

Melting Pot, 162-163

Societal Skills, 163-166

gender, 45, 49, 113-117, 174, 213

genes, 96, 98, 100, 104, 181

gifts of men, 229

giving, 18, 128, 212, 229-231, 241

Headstart, 68

Heaven, 232, 235, 236, 247, 248, 252

Hebrews, 233, 234, 237, 241

hedonism, 17, 34, 77, 82, 175, 187-189, 198, 206, 208, 211, 213, 216, 235

heroes, 9, 27, 42, 57, 77, 91-93, 104, 111, 134, 163, 177, 178, 202

higher education, 34, 39, 40, 43, 47, 95, 98, 127, 128, 166, 173, 211

Hispanics, 44, 49-52, 95, 99

humanism, 8, 16, 17, 22, 30, 31, 35-43, 59, 60, 65, 66, 72, 74-76, 78-80, 103-105, 107, 108, 116, 117, 119, 121, 123-125, 130, 137, 141, 143, 146, 147, 156, 157, 165, 206, 211, 213, 216, 222, 235, 252

humanistic psychology, 18, 64, 89, 127

Jesus Christ, 8, 9, 19, 27, 29, 37, 40, 41, 54, 60, 65, 83, 102-104, 108, 109, 111, 112, 114, 117, 124, 125, 136, 139, 140, 142, 145, 179, 184, 185, 203-205, 209, 216, 218, 222, 225-229, 231, 232, 234-237, 244-246, 248, 249

Klein, Jerry, 76

knowledge, 14, 16, 24, 28, 34, 39, 43, 83, 89, 90, 98, 108, 119, 124, 125, 130, 135, 145, 146, 157, 173, 176, 181, 184, 188, 203, 210, 214, 217, 228, 229, 233, 245, 248

love, 5, 10, 11, 48, 55, 75, 76, 79, 81, 110, 113, 115, 118, 120, 121, 128, 139, 141, 166, 170, 187, 191-197, 199, 200, 206, 209, 212, 216, 223, 226, 227, 233, 234, 237, 241, 243, 245, 247, 248

Make Yourself Creed, 201

mass media, 7, 18, 20, 38, 43, 52, 59, 63, 71, 75, 91, 92, 113, 117, 132, 134, 137, 142, 171

melting pot, 53-55, 58, 147, 156, 162, 163, 171

mercy, 194, 226, 230, 231, 252

moral relativism, 109-111, 143, 156, 157, 212

Mosaic Law, 88, 188, 192, 194,

INDEX

198, 200

MTV, 73, 122, 171, 208, 211

music, 11, 51, 73, 75-78, 82, 120, 122, 132, 163, 210, 211

myth, 93, 163, 177-178

narcissism, 17, 34, 77, 82, 187-189, 198-200, 206, 208, 211, 213, 216, 235

National Education Association, 85-88, 109, 183

nihilism, 39, 79, 101, 102, 156, 165

openness, 111-113, 143, 165, 175, 211, 212

parents, 5, 22, 37, 42, 51, 52, 63, 65, 75-77, 79, 80, 83, 86, 87, 89-91, 93, 94, 111, 112, 117, 118, 120-123, 126, 128, 130-137, 143, 153, 172, 175, 177, 180, 182, 184, 187, 190, 192-214, 221, 223-225, 244

Peer group, 18, 20, 38, 52, 53, 71, 89-91, 104, 117, 120, 132-134, 137, 192, 207, 211

philosophy, 8, 17, 18, 20, 37-39, 41-43, 47, 49, 57, 63, 64, 70, 75, 77, 82, 101, 103, 104, 108, 109, 113, 119, 120, 140, 146, 165, 173, 175, 180, 210, 212

Planned Parenthood, 88, 175

pluralism, 18, 29, 45-47, 139, 147, 216, 222

Politically correct, 43, 57, 96, 112, 114, 115, 121, 212

pornography, 81, 82, 120, 178, 208, 209, 223

poverty, 13, 21, 26, 52, 67, 77, 97, 98, 100, 103, 137-139, 143

practical judgment, 157-158, 160,

161

prayer, 9, 11, 64, 65, 219-221, 231, 239, 248, 249

psychology, 18, 20, 41, 47, 48, 64, 81, 89, 98, 101, 102, 104, 120, 126, 127, 165, 170, 175, 209

race, 13, 34, 48, 49, 51, 52, 55, 60, 63, 79, 95, 97, 142, 163

Red Flag Misbehaviors, 189-190

relativism, 109, 119, 123, 124, 143, 156, 157, 165, 212, 216, 217, 222

schools, 7, 8, 10, 15, 17, 19-28, 30, 36-38, 40-47, 49, 51-58, 61-70, 74, 79, 81-84, 86-88, 90-92, 94-104, 108-153, 156, 158, 159, 161-177, 179, 180, 182-185, 187, 202-208, 210-213, 216, 221, 231, 245, 247

self-concept, 45, 125, 127, 136, 138, 143, 168

sensate order, 188

sex, 19, 21, 42, 56, 72, 73, 75-79, 81, 82, 86, 88, 91, 95, 113-123, 143, 174, 175, 202, 208-210, 213, 223

sex education, 72, 79, 82, 86, 113, 117-119, 121, 143, 174, 175, 208, 209

situation ethics, 109, 110, 212

social problems, 16, 21-23, 45, 67, 100, 137, 146, 159, 184

social psychology, 48, 89, 98, 170

socialism, 42, 43, 54, 60, 70, 74, 85, 140

socialization, 83, 121, 199, 202, 205

societal skills, 163, 164

socioeconomic class, 24, 51, 56, 96

spiritual gifts, 227

teachers, 5, 22-24, 26, 34, 36, 42,
43, 47, 48, 63, 65, 77, 79,
80, 85-87, 91, 99, 109-111,
119, 123, 129, 143, 144,
156, 166, 168, 170,
172-174, 178, 184, 199,
202, 203, 205, 206, 217,
221, 228, 233, 237

television, 71-75, 78, 103, 122, 128,
131, 132, 136, 153, 171,
199-201, 208, 213, 219,
221

terminally ill, 224

tough love, 192

universities, 24, 29, 34, 40, 43, 47,
48, 67, 92, 98, 102,
113-115, 127, 140, 166,
173, 174

values, 8, 14-20, 27-34, 38, 41, 42,
45-48, 53, 55, 59, 66,
70-72, 74, 75, 79, 80, 90,
92, 93, 101, 103, 109-112,
117, 118, 120, 123,
135-137, 141-143,
145-148, 152, 153,
155-158, 160, 162, 165,
169, 171, 174, 175, 177,
178, 187-190, 192-199,
201, 202, 212, 240

village concept of child rearing,
120

violence, 13, 19, 21, 58, 73, 75,
77-79, 95, 102, 120, 122,
126, 139, 141-143, 168,
170, 182, 191, 194, 211

vouchers, 86, 180, 184, 185

wisdom, 31, 51, 80, 102, 150, 162,
176, 193, 195, 196, 228,
229, 236

women, 47, 49, 61, 81, 83, 86, 92,
113-118, 120, 137, 171,
174, 196, 209, 213, 232

work ethic, 11, 32, 53, 91, 126, 130,
138, 139, 150